ANNAPURNA CIRCUIT

❖

HIMALAYAN JOURNEY

Andrew Stevenson

CONSTABLE · LONDON

First published in Great Britain 1997
by Constable and Company Limited
3 The Lanchesters, 162 Fulham Palace Road
London W6 9ER
Copyright © Andrew Stevenson 1997
The right of Andrew Stevenson to be identified as the author of this work has been
asserted by him in accordance with the Copyright, Designs and Patents Act 1988
Reprinted 1997
Paperback edition 1998
Reprinted 1999
ISBN 0 09 478980 0
Set in Monophoto Sabon 11pt by
Servis Filmsetting Ltd, Manchester
Printed in Great Britain by
St Edmundsbury Press Ltd
Bury St Edmunds, Suffolk

A CIP catalogue record for this book
is available from the British Library

ANNAPURNA CIRCUIT

DEDICATED TO THE PEOPLE OF THE ANNAPURNAS

CONTENTS

❖

ACKNOWLEDGEMENTS

❖

Thanks are due to Kirsten for encouraging me to undertake the journey in the first place, for her support during much of the gestation period while I was writing this book, and for her editorial suggestions. To my mother and father, Jackie and Jay, Kevin and Tina, Sally and Dale, Scott and Louise, Elsa and Tor, for being there. To Chloe and Oliver, Cooper and Katie, Alexandra, Endre, Emilia and Bendict, Laura and Christopher for keeping it all in perspective. To Agnes for sharing her own spirituality, putting the pieces together and back on the wall again, and for her observations on the typescript. To Annita and Mark for their special contributions. Thanks to Rosemary Jones for her detailed editorial comments on two early versions of the typescript, and to Audette Excel for her succinct remarks. A special thanks to Sally for logistical support in printing out discs sent from different corners of the world. To Shree Ram Shrestha for his support in Nepal. To my agent Bruce Hunter, and to Carol O'Brien at Constable Publishers, for their enthusiasm and for making it all come true. And finally, to all those who have worked on producing this book.

'A journey of a thousand miles
begins with the first step.'

Tao 64

'The only Zen you find
on the tops of mountains is the
Zen you bring up there.'

Robert M. Pirsig

PROLOGUE

————————— ❖ —————————

Her meticulous handwriting materialises out of the fax machine beside my desk: 'Thomas's mother's funeral is at 3.00 this afternoon. We can meet in the parking lot of the crematorium at 2.55. Love, Kirsten.' A hand-drawn map indicates the quickest route to get there.

Early, I sit cosseted inside the protective cocoon of the idling car, heated seats and Automatic Climate Control shielding me from the miserable February chill of a pallid winter day. Anaemic sunlight filters ineffectively through the hanging fog.

Kirsten's BMW pulls into the parking-lot. She is already crying although I know her grief has little to do with the funeral. Together we slip discreetly into the back row of the chapel of the crematorium. Curious, I sit next to the aisle. The centre of our attention is a shiny white casket, dominated by a bouquet of flowers.

With Western precision, at three o'clock exactly, the minister steps out of a hidden entrance. He reads aloud from notes placed on the podium in front of him. Piped-in music accompanies the minister's artificially amplified voice as we half-heartedly sing a hymn none of us seems to know. The pre-recorded music stops, and on cue, four pillars supporting the immaculate casket are electronically activated so the coffin slides discreetly backwards, disappearing conveniently from sight. Like flushing a toilet. There is no connection with death, we are avoiding the issue. I wonder if her body is even in the casket.

It does not seem possible that this is all there is at the worldly farewell of someone who lived in this community some sixty years. Her life fizzled away in a few forgettable sentences and a large inheritance to her only son. Fur-coated friends and relatives file out of the chapel, shake hands formally, enter their cars, and drive into monochromatic oblivion.

I thought the funeral service would clarify my muddied mind, make me realise that, whatever the problems, I am at least alive. Unsure whether any of us stepping out of that chapel today could really say we are living, least of all myself, Kirsten and I return to our cars and drive off to our respective offices, where once again I am confronted by the demands of running a business.

Unable to concentrate on the pressing issues at hand, I daydream of getting off this whirling financial merry-go-round, of taking a break somewhere where life is more vivid and intense.

SHAY AND EASY

❖

DUMRE–TUTURE

'*Namaste!*' The leper presses his fingerless fists together in greeting.

'*Namaste*,' I reply, 'I salute the god within you.' I peel off a fifty rupee note, the equivalent of a dollar. He squeezes his palms on either side of the crisp bill. In this land of karma, the beggar has rendered me a favour, and it is I who should be grateful.

For the next couple of months, my worldly possessions are stuffed on my back, as if I were a turtle waddling under its protective carapace. Apart from the vague notion of walking around the Himalayas, I have set no targets, no schedule, nowhere to be. My only plan is to be home in Norway, in two-and-a-half months, in time for Christmas.

The sun pokes its way through the layers of cloud and it becomes hot and humid. With each kilometre my pace is reduced until I reach Tuture, which provides a fortunate shelter against turbulent skies, just as it gets dark. A *bhaati* owner's daughter welcomes me into their tea-house by lighting incense and candles beneath cartoon-like posters of three of the Hindu gods: Ganesh, easily recognisable with his elephant's head, the god of prosperity and wisdom; Shiva, the creator and destroyer, who controls the beginning and end of time cycles, recognisable with his trident; and Parvati, also known as Annapurna in her benign form, the consort of Shiva and mother of Ganesh.

Satiated with *dal bhaat*, heaping plates of rice, lentils and spinach-like greens, I haul myself up a ladder into an open dormitory and lie on the tiny bed-frame, distended stomach uppermost, perspiring although clad in only a cotton T-shirt and nylon running-shorts. Eight meagre Nepalese room-mates study me intently. I try to converse with them, but they don't speak English. Physically exhausted, unleashed spectres of neglected responsibilities haunt my dreams.

TUTURE–BHOTE WODÅR

Harnessed waters trickle tamely through glittering irrigation channels and iridescent green paddy. I rest by the roadside and a red dragonfly diverts my attention as it flits onto my knee, rainbow-wings quivering. Sweat stings my eyes as I tilt my head to empty a raised flask of water. It is another three-hundred-and-fifty kilometres round the Annapurnas to Pokhara, crudely measuring the distances and excluding ascents and descents. The route to this point is flat, and I am exhausted. Studying the 'Around Annapurna' tourist map I see I have not even reached its southernmost edge.

'One pen,' a child asks cutely, hand outstretched.

'No pen.'

'Give me pen,' another chimes in.

'No pen.'

The brigade of children give up asking and play hopscotch. I drop my pack against a tree and join them, after watching them long enough to grasp the rules. They laugh as I hop with them.

Outside the open *bhaati* dormitory that night, someone persistently blows what sounds like a sea-shell, accompanied by *puja* prayers, chanted way off-key. The conch-blasts punctuate my restless sleep as I illuminate my watch to calculate the time back home.

BHOTE WODOR–SIMBACHAUR

Mynahs produce an incredible racket, then with the suddenness of a blast of shotgun pellets, they are gone. The rutted trail of a lesser-used 'alternative route' winds its way into horizontal terraces carved out of the mountainsides, delineating heights as precisely as the contours of a map. Rice fields pour down craggy slopes like molten green lava.

I walk for hours, oblivious of time, lost in my own thoughts, plodding instinctively along the myriad network of raised paths skirting the paddy fields. The creaking of the back-pack, the pad of my footsteps, my breathing, become familiar sounds. As the sun sets, I stumble, both from fatigue and lack of light. My shoulders hurt where the back-pack has hung as if loaded with rocks; my heels are taut; my body aches everywhere. I continue walking in the dark before reaching an unlit hamlet. Physically spent, I stop to lean the pack against a wall, and bend my knees to relieve the burden from my shoulders.

A male American voice calls from the shadows: 'Come on in!'

Two Americans. 'Shay,' an attractive girl with long blonde hair and a ready smile, extends her hand in greeting.

'Easy. From California.' Dark and also fit. Without the formality of asking whether I agree, they include me in their negotiations for an overnight stay in the mud and stick home of a Gurung family. Any previous and vague philosophical desire on my part to be alone has dissipated after fourteen hours walking in solitude.

The owner clears his family's room of clutter and three beds appear from under the debris. I sit on the edge of one, leaning forward, dripping perspiration on the mud floor. Adults and children crowd into the adjoining room to watch us. A black puppy bites and fights with my fingers as I undo my bootlaces. Shay watches Easy, meticulously bandaging his toes.

'Mind if I ask how old you are?' Shay asks me.

I answer, puzzled by her question. Easy studiously cares for his feet, ignoring her. She turns to me, 'Easy's been bummed out because he thinks he's too old for all this. Wants to quit and head back. We've been walking for only two days.'

Easy remains fixated by his blood-stained toes.

'I'm going on,' Shay says. This is not an angry statement. 'Easy did the Annapurna Circuit ten years ago in seventeen days, including a diversion up Dhampus Pass. He used to do triathlons, including the Iron Man.' She looks over at him. He is still preoccupied with the blisters on his feet. 'Now he can't handle a couple of days walking on relatively flat ground.'

Easy retorts, 'I'm bummed out because I have diarrhoea, and blisters, and because I was stupid enough not to bring my good hiking-
boots.' He attends to his feet with the concentration of a professional.
'And,' he admits, 'because I think I am too old for this. I'm bummed
out just getting here.'

'Physicians?'

'Nurses.' She ignores her irritated companion. 'So, why are *you*
doing this trip?'

The question is direct and I'm dangerously close to replying more
candidly than I want. 'You know, needed a break,' I shrug off the question and make light of its answer.

Neither of them says anything, expecting me to continue with my
explanation.

'Too target-oriented.' They remain silent. 'Wasn't enjoying what I
was doing, wasn't sure what it was I was striving for.'

Thoughtful silence as we examine our feet.

'Been here before?' Easy asks.

'First time as a tourist.' I extract dry clothes from the pack. 'What
about you?' I ask stiffly, avoiding the possibility of summarising myself
in a neatly packaged résumé. Let these potential friends form their own
impression of who I am rather than the personality I contrive to present.

'Disillusioned with the materialistic life back in California,' Easy
offers. 'Taken leave for six months, figure things out. Move to the
Midwest. Montana, Idaho. Maybe Canada.'

Dal bhaat is served mercifully quickly, and eaten without ceremony.
We blow out candles and our captive audience melts into the darkness
of the night. I lie back, totally debilitated. Refugees of Western affluence, we fall asleep, comforted by the exoticism of a chosen, fleeting
poverty.

SIMBACHAUR–BAHUNDANDA

The temperature is cool, the skies monsoon dark. Thick fog blankets
the path. At a well-stocked shop, I tell the owl-like shopkeeper perched
on the counter I wish to buy a pair of flip-flops, just like Easy's.

[18]

'No flip-flops.'

A stack of flip-flops is piled high on a shelf. I point at them. He shakes his head wisely, negative.

I nod my head. 'Those are exactly what I want,' I tell him emphatically. 'Flip-flops.' I reach over the counter and take a pair. He pulls them away from me with surprising determination. 'How much?' I ask, grabbing them back. Easy is there to help negotiate, which he likes to do, especially in Nepali.

The shopkeeper retorts 'No! No good,' and reaches out to retrieve them. I pull them away, out of reach. Why does he have them if he does not expect to sell them? 'Yes, yes, good, very good. How much?' The shopkeeper gives in and sells them to me, reluctantly. Without bothering to try them, I wedge them, still wrapped in their clear plastic packaging, between the roll-over bar at the top of my knapsack and an attached Therma-rest mattress. Easy buys candles, without any reticence from the storekeeper.

Shay and Easy outpace me on the well-trodden path as I struggle under my heavier load. I had weighed each item on the kitchen scales at home. Every item brought along was deemed indispensable. Nevertheless, in Kathmandu I unloaded two heavy pairs of woollen socks, a woollen shirt and a pair of jeans. I regret not taking more out of my movable wardrobe and mentally cast out several more items. My choice of a Norwegian-army external-frame pack was a good one, I realise, as it is far more comfortable than any internal-frame pack I have owned. Extending over my head is an optional U-shaped aluminium extension. The decision to equip the pack with the protective addition proves to be luckier than I could have imagined.

Stopping at a stone *chautara* resting-place under a banyan tree, I watch three young Nepalese girls and two older women ascend the path, carrying loads of fodder that overwhelm them in size. They stop at the same *chautara*, placing their loads on the waist-high stone ledge. One young girl is a physical beauty. 'Fourteen years old,' she proudly tells me in response to my question. They suggest we switch loads. Putting her load of fodder behind me, I place the tump-line over my forehead, Nepalese fashion. Straining, I labour in a small circle before putting the load down again, amazed that this slender girl can carry such a heavy weight. They laugh at my exertions.

We continue up the path together, but their pace is even slower than mine, and I pass them by, feeling sorry for the girl, her head bent down against the load, perspiration dripping off her pretty face. I am doing this out of choice, as a holiday, and for fun. She faces a lifetime of this daily drudgery, yet she can still laugh about it.

A blast of cold wind down the valley stirs my expectations and drives me forward; but strangely there is no immediate objective, just a vague sense of going higher, into the Himalayas.

'Hey, Andrew!' Easy's smiling face sticks out of a window on the upper floor of a tidy *bhaati*. 'We've got a bed for you. You're sleeping with Shay and me.'

I drop my pack on the rough-hewn wooden floor of the *bhaati* room, and strip. The shower, a large barrel suspended in the branches of a tree, is located beside the drop toilet. As a sanitary measure, I try to slip my feet into the newly acquired flip-flops, but they are both left-footed. Belatedly I understand the judicious shop owner's reluctance to sell them. He was too polite to lean over the counter to see if I was equipped with two left feet. Perhaps a shipment of left-footed flip-flops was in stock, the right-footed ones still coming up the trail?

Over dinner, Easy the entertainer reads lines from his outdated Nepalese–English dictionary bought in a second-hand bookshop in Kathmandu. 'Wash the dirty diapers in this pan and do not throw the water into the river.' He searches for more appropriate sentences. 'Here's one for you Andrew. "*Ek haptaa ko kulli chaahinchha.*"'

'What's that mean?' I ask, ever the straight-man to Easy's quick wit.

'I need porters for one week,' he replies, laughing at his own joke and slapping me good-naturedly on my tender shoulders.

The electrical grid extends only as far as Bhulebhule. A pressure lantern hanging over the communal dining-table exposes half-a-dozen smiling Western faces. We sit eating as much food as we want, drinking beer or soft drinks from bottles carried up here on a porter's back. Outside the little enclave cast by the light of the *bhaati* lantern, we have little knowledge of the life of the people who live within a stone's throw. The remote medieval-like village hugs a mountainside high in the foothills of the Himalayas. I wonder how the villagers regard this annual invasion of tourists? Are we all welcomed as a source of needed income, or are our opulent lifestyles an unfortunate reminder of their own poverty?

Easy disappears into the *bhaati* and rushes back out. 'Hey Andrew!'

he yells, interrupting my contemplations. 'There's a long-distance phone call for you. Quick!'

I am off the wooden bench before I realise the absurdity of my reaction in this primitive environment.

'Just joking,' Easy chuckles, straddling the bench at the table to join us.

In our room, in the dark, Easy tries to light one of the candles he bought in Bhulebhule. It splutters, but will not catch. 'Trick candles. Guaranteed to last for ever. Need a blow torch to get 'em going,' Easy concludes as we change in the dark, and he thankfully leaves the phone off the hook.

BAHUNDANDA–SHYANGE

Easy strolls ahead, making friends with two Nepalese boys, improving his language skills. Shay tells me about her previous marriage to a surgeon.

'He was a workaholic. Worked twelve, even fourteen-hour days. We became wealthy; bought a beautiful house, two fancy cars. But we hardly ever saw each other. He was always working, and I became lonely and unhappy. I decided to leave him. It was awful. There was no bad feeling between us. He hadn't done anything to hurt me deliberately. We just lived separate lives, his world of work superseding our life at home. We had no children to hold us together. Leaving him was the most difficult thing I ever did.'

Although she tells me this in a matter-of-fact manner, her voice betrays her lingering emotions. 'Later, I met Easy at the hospital, where he was working temporarily. He was the opposite of my ex-husband: fun-loving, spontaneous, affectionate, spiritual, non-materialistic, loyal. I've been living with him for three years now, and would like to have children.' She watches him talking with the two boys. They are all laughing at something Easy has said. 'I'm disappointed marriage hasn't come up, at least not to the extent that he has actually proposed to me.' We all stop to peer into the gorge. She is silent, contemplating. Easy moves ahead again, conversing with the youngsters. 'I've given myself a deadline. If Easy does not propose by the first of January, I'll blow him off.' She thinks about this for a while, then laughs. 'I've already had a proposal from a guy we met in Thailand, from Oregon. He asked me to let him know if it does not work out with Easy, because he would like to marry me. Oregon . . . sounds kind'a attractive you know . . .'

She asks me about Kirsten and I tell her.

'Sounds like quite a woman.'

'She is,' I reply, bewildered at my own confusion.

We follow behind a grey-haired porter who plods methodically up the trail, carrying a stack of five wooden crates full of Coca-Cola on his back. Each crate holds twenty-four full bottles. Dominating his tiny, fragile-looking ankles and knobbly knees, his calf muscles swell like inflated balloons, pulsating veins criss-crossing the bulging calves with each step ascended. Shoeless, not much more than five foot tall, almost bent double with the weight of his burden, he leans on a thick bamboo pole with each step. He is one of the legions of porters who have carried salt, rice and other basic trading goods up and down these valleys for centuries, crossing borders, oblivious to the boundaries relatively recently defined by Western powers. I follow him for hours, which gives me plenty of time to wonder about the absurdity of this man struggling to carry liquid up these monsoon-soaked mountains to cater to the tastes of Westerners seduced by the far-reaching marketing stratagems of Coca-Cola.

There is a pattern, an ebb and flow, to the tourist traffic. An early-morning rush hour of Get There People: typically, trekkers who have signed up with a European, American or Kathmandu-based trekking outfit. Up at six and gone by seven, they leave a retinue of porters and camp crew in pursuit carrying tents, tables, chairs, food and whatever other accessories are needed to make them comfortable. Permitting the tide of Get There People to flow past first, the remaining trekkers (like myself), staying at local *bhaatis* along the way, are relatively alone for the rest of the day, as we all circulate anti-clockwise around the Annapurnas.

At midday the sun comes out and it becomes uncomfortably hot. Shay, Easy and I swim in a stream, washing off dried blood from our legs, gory evidence of leech bites. 'Have you figured out why it is that we all go anti-clockwise around these mountains?' I ask, soaking up to my neck in the cool water, watching trekkers filing over a rickety wooden footbridge, all moving in the same direction.

'Because the climb up through the Thorong La, the pass between Manang and Mustang, is more gradual approached from this side, and there's a *bhaati* halfway up. Coming up the other way, it's steeper and further to climb from the *bhaatis* at Muktinath.' Easy sinks into the water and surfaces spouting water. 'Any other questions for the living oracle?'

We dress in clean and dry clothes. I hang my wet laundry to dry over the roll-over bar at the top of my pack. Easy tries the pack on for size. He is surprised to find it comfortable, despite its heaviness. His day-pack feels so ridiculously light by contrast that I have an overwhelming urge to run with it, and I do so, as fast as my legs will carry me, laughing aloud joyfully, much to the bewilderment of porters resting by the path, apparently eating their own weight in *dal bhaat*.

'Do you have enough warm clothes with you in those tiny packs?' I ask when they catch up.

'Easy's planning on moving so fast he won't feel the cold.'

We reach Shyange, a splatter of whitewashed buildings flung against a cliff face like vultures' droppings. Easy arranges rooms for us in the upper dormitory of a lodge. Beds are jammed tightly next to each other with no space in between. Trekkers' perspiration-drenched clothes hang from ropes stretched across the rafters, adding to the already claustrophobic atmosphere of the attic room. As it gets dark, it starts raining. Over dinner, a torrential monsoon rainfall hammers the slate roof.

It is cosy in the *bhaati*, protected from the rain, served hot food and drink. We tell funny stories, laughing hardest at the misadventures Easy narrates. He tells us about his early medical training. 'Once, we nursing students were in the lab studying our urine samples under microscopes, labelling everything we could identify. One of the girls in the class couldn't identify something in her own urine sample. She asked each of us to help, but none of us knew what it was either. Eventually the lab assistant came over. He peered through her microscope, looked up at her, and told us deadpan, "No doubt about it, that there is genuine sperm!"'

A Nepalese approaches the table and asks us, 'Why you is laughing?'

'We are seeing who can tell the funniest story,' Easy explains.

'The owner of the *bhaati*, he has died,' the porter retorts, as if delivering his own punch line.

'Died? Or dying?' Easy asks seriously.

'Dead. Maybe dying,' the porter replies cryptically.

Easy follows him into the kitchen. A few minutes later he is back. 'He's right. Almost dead. Hardly read his pulse, barely breathing. Wrists thin as fingers. He's been wasting for months.'

A few feet away, the owner of the *bhaati* has been dying; oblivious to the drama, we have been enjoying ourselves. Conversation dwindles. What was fun now seems obscene. Half-an-hour later one of the lodge owner's family beckons to Easy, 'Please, come.'

Easy returns once again to the table. 'He's dead.'

'What'd you do?' Shay asks.

'Felt his pulse. Nothing. Listened to his breath, checked his eyes. He's dead. I knelt beside him, put my palms together and said "*Namaste*", then pulled the sheet over his head. He's lying in the middle of the room, with about fifteen family members around.'

Wails from the kitchen. Collectively we retreat to the dormitory upstairs. The weeping of the grief-stricken family continues throughout the night. But we are all so tired that we, too, sleep the sleep of the dead.

SHYANGE–TAL

Ascending the path together, Easy confides to me, 'I'm going to propose to Shay when we get to the top of Thorong La. Been planning it since we agreed to the trip, months ago. But don't tell her.' He looks sideways at me as we walk, to make sure I have registered the confidentiality of the conversation. I have heard both sides. Shay, in love with Easy but fed up he has not proposed, is planning to 'blow him off' on the first of January if he does not cough up. Easy, meanwhile, is romantically and secretly planning his marriage proposal months in advance. I hope I am still with them when they cross Thorong La.

The overnight rain has taken some of the moisture out of the air although candy-floss mist sticks to the paddy fields. I climb up the steep path, in places built into rock walls, at other times carved under rock overhangs. The valley becomes tighter, a narrow gorge with little direct sunlight. We drink directly from sources, without using water-purification tablets, for there are no longer villages or fields above us. A screen of mist lends a perpetual dream-like ambience to the trek.

Once again the old man carrying the five crates of full Coca-Cola bottles leads the way. His calf muscles inflate and deflate. I am thankful for a second day with this silent companion moving slowly in front of me. He sucks in air and blows it out forcefully with each step, like a steam engine. I imitate him. With each step he straightens the leg, and pauses, for a fraction of a second, allowing a brief but deliberate respite. The technique, learnt over a lifetime of bearing heavy loads on his back, functions well, as I discover while adapting the way in which I walk. I imitate his methodical style, his rhythmic breathing, and soon I become him. But his bare feet are thick with calluses patterned with deep cracks like an elephant's foot. My feet are encased in Italian leather and cushioned with Vibram soles.

The landscape changes. Scarcer villagers, fewer rice paddy fields. Terraces are planted with maize and barley. Increasing numbers of Tibetan refugee settlements are apparent as they colonise the Himalayan foothills. The gentle slopes of hillsides give way to steep-sided mountains. Strangely, there seem to be fewer foreigners. The tops of the mountains loom high on either side of the hand-carved pathways and staircases creeping along this historic route, which traders from Manang and Tibet have followed for centuries, efficiently expediting cargoes through apparently impenetrable mountains.

At a wayside *bhaati*, Easy spreads out the 'Around Annapurna' map and imitates a mad cartographer. 'Mmm. Let's see,' he says maniacally as he scratches his dishevelled head. 'Put a couple of contours here.' He draws imaginary contour lines on the map. 'And a few more there, and several here, there a few dozen, and hey, let's be totally crazy and throw in a couple hundred there just for good measure.' He draws a confusion of imaginary contour lines over the route we have just come up. 'There! That should slow those suckers down.'

Dal bhaat is served. No utensils are provided, we use our fingers to eat. Easy eats with his left hand. 'Definitely not cool eating with your left hand, Easy. Bad etiquette. And you know why as well as I do,' Shay teases him.

'I'm a southpaw.'

'Easy,' Shay continues, 'it is bad manners to eat with your left hand. "When in Rome, do as the Romans do." We are in Nepal and the Nepalese eat with their right hands.'

Easy switches, struggling to maintain the same dexterity. His elbow sticks out awkwardly at right angles as he fumbles to get food into his mouth, daubing his face and emerging beard in rice and lentils.

Insignificant, we weave our way through the cloud-congealed Himalayas, Easy and Shay once again leaving me behind as I struggle under my heavier burden. A rock outcrop rises vertically a thousand metres, like a giant monolith, on either side of which lie deep gorges. I could gently cast a pebble and have it land in the valley bottom. But instead of standing stupidly on the edge to lob stones into the crack, I cringe and hug the inner walls of the path. When it starts to drizzle I shelter lonely under a rock overhang, fearful of slipping on the out-wardly sloping wet rocks into the fissure looming below.

Further up, the gorge unexpectedly peters out into a wide valley. Without the rumbling of the river or the rushing of waterfalls, there is a pervasive silence. I have entered a peaceful dale, enclosed by verti-cal mountains which are covered in lush vegetation of bamboo, pines and, where the mountain is too steep, a vibrant green moss. Shangri La.

A stream in the valley runs so calmly on the flat valley bottom, it forms a slow-flowing lake. It feels unnatural to shuffle one's feet on unimpeded horizontal ground. A breeze wafts gently, neither hot nor cold, swirling the mist in no particular direction. Horses graze peace-fully on thick grass. I walk through a Buddhist commemorative monument straddling the path, a *chorten*, and spin the cylindrical drums of prayer wheels on the inner walls in a clockwise direction as I pass by.

'Welcome to Manang District,' a sign greets at the entrance to the village of Tal. The architecture differs from anything we have seen so far. Stone buildings, low and flat, with large riven wood shingles on horizontal roofs held down by boulders. Yak skulls adorn the entranceways. At the far end of the village I ask three hippie-clad trekkers, two long-haired boys and a girl sitting on a bench in a court-yard, 'Have you seen an American couple pass by?'

'How should we know?' Their accents and attitude exude hostility.

Easy's voice proclaims, before I take umbrage, 'We're up here. There is one big bed for Shay, you and myself.'

I strip and wash myself under the freezing waters from a tap in the garden, then stroll around the village. A waterfall tumbles a hundred metres over the cliff face onto the angled wooden blades directly powering a grinding millstone. Beside a nearby *chorten* at the edge of a shallow depression at the foot of the falls, three ghostly yak, their thick, shaggy coats silvery with the spray from the falls, feed silently on beaded grass.

Evening. We sit around the dining-table lit by pressure lanterns. The family live in this one room, centred around a fire in the middle of the floor. Against the far wall are beds, covered in Tibetan carpets, doubling as sofas. Another wall is dominated by a cabinet hewn from heavy planks riven and smoothed with a hand adze. Cats and dogs, including a huge Tibetan mastiff, relax in the room with us.

The *bhaati* owner's daughter asks me, 'Pen?'

'No pen,' I reply.

'Sweetie?' she persists.

'No.'

The youngster methodically interrogates each one of us for pens, sweeties, rupees. Giving up on us, the little girl hangs a clear plastic bag on a nail of a supporting beam. We can see inside the bag a collection of some thirty pens. Taking our lead from Easy, imitating her pleading voice, we stretch out our hands and demand, 'One pen, one pen.' She coyly grabs the bag and hides them behind her back and retreats to her bed on the other side of the room to continue her homework, the bag discreetly placed behind her. Easy joins her and asks her plaintively, 'Pen?' She shakes her outstretched palm vigorously in his face and continues to write in her book, ignoring his pleas, 'Pen, pen?'

Finally she says, without looking up, 'One pen six rupees.' She leaves the offer open, take it or leave it.

'No, six rupees, one pen,' Easy counters. 'Twenty rupees, three pens.' Her younger brother sitting on the end of the bed, who has been studiously ignoring us, looks up sharply: a business deal in the making. He sidles up to his sister. She has automatically supposed that Easy has made an unacceptable counter-offer. Without bothering to do the calculation, she shakes her head vigorously, waving her hand negative.

[27]

She keeps her nose buried in her notebook with a cultivated air of indifference, waiting for Easy to accept her original offer.

Her little brother is no slouch. He multiplies, adds and subtracts, rupees signs jingling in his eyes. He mentally checks his computation, and desperately pokes his sister in her side with his elbow and whispers vehemently to her, undoubtedly explaining that Easy's offer of twenty rupees for three pens is more than six rupees per pen. Before she has fully grasped the situation Easy says, 'OK, no pen.'

Her eyes widen when she realises the almost unforgivable mistake she has made. A Manangbhot trader-in-training outwitted by a foreigner. 'Yes,' she says, belatedly, 'three pens twenty rupees.'

'No,' Easy replies rascally, enjoying this, 'no pen.'

'Yes pen.' She nods her head vigorously, and her brother pulls out three of the most chewed pens she has. 'Three pens twenty rupees possible,' she offers generously.

Easy shakes his extended hand in front of her face, and walks back to the dining-table. 'No pen.' She follows him with her little brother, trying to close the deal. Eventually she gives up. It is not easy to get the better of a Manangbhot, even if only seven and eleven years old.

The three unfriendly trekkers enter the room. We occupy the only table. They ignore us and sit huddled on a bench looking at a map. Easy asks them to join us. They decline. Easy, never one to give up an opportunity to make new friends, offers them his chair, saying, 'Where're you guys heading tomorrow?'

Without looking up, they reply, 'We don't know.'

'Hey, what kind of Germans are you?' Easy asks in feigned surprise.

Fortunately, dessert arrives. 'Here, have some pie,' he proffers. He holds out the apple pie enticingly to them. 'Try it. It's good. You'll like it.' They cannot resist and each takes a large bite, decimating the dessert.

We are all quite giddy and light-hearted when we go upstairs to our dormitory. Stuffed in the room with two English girls and Yanzeh, an American from Hawaii, we are like children at a summer camp, with about the same mentality. In turn we tell the scariest stories we know until there is a pounding on the wooden planks separating our dormitory from the Germans' room. The German girl's heavily accented voice filters between the planks dividing our sleeping-quarters,

'Please, can you stop telling stories? Zere are nine so far, and I am translating each one. I cannot sleep if I am translating stories.'

Easy whispers, 'Anyone know any scary stories in German?'

We giggle ourselves to sleep.

TAL–BAGARCHAP

Shay meditates beside the *chorten*, umbrella above her for protection from the spray of the falls. The three silver-beaded yak lie ghost-like in the wet grass. Yanzeh is stewing a pot of marijuana tea while executing yoga contortions on his mat. Easy is either meditating or sleeping upright on the end of our bed. With Easy, you never know. The two English girls have gone. The Germans are still translating our stories or catching up on their lost sleep.

Our secret valley appears locked in at both ends. Where we entered, a white tuft sneaks over the lip into our secluded hollow. The gorge we ascended yesterday must be dense with clouds. At the other end of the valley, it is impossible to see where we will exit, the walls on either side are sealed tight.

As we prepare to leave, the *bhaati* girl hovers around our rooms like a magpie, waiting for us to depart, so she can check the floors and beds for pens, sweeties, rupees and priceless diaries. I carefully count my notebooks before putting them in my pack. I follow behind Shay and Easy, and tell them, 'The view reminds me of the Canadian Rockies; high mountains devoid of human habitation, pine trees, puffy-white clouds in a blue sky.'

They look at the sky-high mountains as they walk, then Shay turns around, stopping, blocking the path. 'Andrew, do you feel like a Canadian?'

'Sometimes. Memories of Canada when I lived there for a year as a ten-year-old seem so different from the Canada I left a couple of years ago. That's one reason why Norway seems so attractive. The changes don't seem so overwhelming. There's more a sense of continuity. On the other hand, it's so homogeneous a country it isn't so easy to assimilate into, as it is for immigrants to North America.' We continue walking, admiring the lofty heights.

We pass the last of the bamboo and palm trees at a waterfall. The closed-off valley marks the transition of one climatic zone and the beginning of another. We are moving into the rain-shadow of the Himalayas. Despite the fresher temperatures, Easy still wears only flip-flops on his blistered feet.

By the time I reach Bagarchap, Easy has already found a lodge where we have our own bedroom cubicles. I strip out of my sweat-drenched clothes and take a cold shower. As I towel myself dry in the privacy of my coop with a view over the terraced fields, I watch *zopkios*, a cross-breed between cows and yak, feeding in the brown fields below the *bhaati*. They are bigger than cows, their coats thicker, horns longer, and the easiest give-away, they have shaggy tails. Some almost look like massive yak, others more like scrawny cows. Their munching is audible from the room, as they chew dry maize stalks.

A man, his wife and daughter, collect the dry stalks and heap them onto a blazing bonfire, the rising heat-waves plainly visible. Blue-brown smoke billows over the fields. The child stands still, her hands outstretched like a scarecrow. Smoke gyrates around her, as if she were creating a disturbance, although she is not moving. She remains motionless, the smoke enveloping her, whirling and twisting and turning about her form, as if she were the source. It is a strange apparition, almost supernatural.

Waiting for dinner, Easy pulls out the defaced 'Around Annapurna' map and lays it out on the table to examine, providing us with comforting representation on a smaller scale of what we have walked. Easy assumes his familiar manic look. 'We should have a First Fold Celebration. We've crossed the first horizontal fold on the map. We can have celebrations every time we cross a vertical or horizontal fold, and a really big one when we hit the centrefold.'

In the privacy of my own room, I lie down and think about why I have come on this pilgrimage. Like the fumes enveloping the sorceress girl in the midst of the churning smoke-filled field, unharnessed thoughts gyrate around me wildly. Kirsten has written several notes sealed in envelopes to be opened during the trip. I open one, chosen at random.

'Remember, the way is more important than the goal.'

It is almost as if she had been there to remind me.

BAGARCHAP–BHRATANG

A cock crows as I doze, and I am reminded that I am not only in the countryside but in the Third World, where cocks wander free and crow with the dawn. Opening my eyes, but still ensconced in the warmth of my sleeping-bag, I see the mountains framed through the window, tinged by the sunrise for the first time. They seem so close and yet so high and rise so steeply they block from sight the loftier, snow-covered Himals which must be somewhere all around us too. The light is intense. The clouds have gone and the sky is clear in the crisp morning light. The freshness of the day is all-pervasive, as if we have been reborn. Even my thought processes seem to have cleared overnight.

In the kitchen the owner of the lodge, a mere boy, has started a fire in the oven. I sit in front of it, alternately drinking from a hot cup of milk tea and holding my palms out to the open flames to warm them. Large chunks of firewood are thrown in and soon there is a glow of burning embers, but the kitchen remains cold.

I ask the owner, 'What are the names of the mountains around us?'

'Just hills,' he replies and shrugs off my question.

Just hills. We are now almost at two-thousand metres. The 'Just Hills' must be well over three-thousand metres high. Each jagged peak would have its own name back in North America or Europe. Here they are Just Hills, dusted with a frosting of fresh snow, a reminder that winter is around the corner.

Shay and Easy sleep in, taking advantage of the privacy of their own room. I leave them a note saying I have already gone, knowing they will easily catch me up.

Years ago, a Swiss girlfriend told me, using a French expression, 'Andrew, you are always walking beside your shoes'. Figuratively speaking, my thoughts were always somewhere else, where I wasn't. Leaving Bagarchap, I deliberately listen to the sounds of the river, and the pad of my footsteps on the ground echoing my heartbeat. During the days my inner and outer beings are gradually falling into a rhythm; the dichotomy between spirit and body disappear. For the time being, there are no external schedules constraining me; no phones, no fax machines, no pagers, no memos, no mobile telephones to distract me from what I am doing. My own inner rhythm dictates my life.

A snow-covered Himal sprawls over the V-cut of the valley, its sheer face of brilliant white snow rising vertically upwards. After a week of walking towards and through the Himalayas under cover of clouds and mist, blocked by surrounding Just Hills, at last a sight of one of the Annapurna Himals, Annapurna II, just under eight-thousand metres high.

In an adjacent field two women and a boy bend double to harvest golden-brown barley. The wind catches the tops of the ripened barley in waves, swirling eddied patterns. Behind, a cliff face soars several hundred metres, divided in two by narrow valleys. I try to take a photograph of the scene to take back home and show others, but the automated camera will not work and I am forced to experience in the present, rather than photograph the view for posterity.

'Hearty welcome to Chame.' The banner's message smacks of Nepalese officialdom which must rank in the same league as the notoriously inefficient Indian bureaucracy. The village of Chame, despite its isolated location high in the mountains, is a distant outpost of the Kathmandu-centred government. A cement *chorten* topped by a corrugated-tin roof straddles the path. The original copper prayer wheels have been stolen, replaced by empty tins inscribed not with prayers but with instructions in Nepali on how to prepare instant powdered milk. I am determined to pass through this government outpost quickly. Yet according to descriptions of early Western explorers, the village once must have been very attractive. It is sad to witness the changes in this isolated mountain hamlet, exposed to the foibles of its new population of civil servants and the swarms of trekkers buzzing through.

Indo-Aryan offspring of Nepalese officials with Hindu tikas marking their foreheads ask me for pens. Tibetan women making carpets smile at me benignly as I labour around slabs of Tibetan rock-salt stacked against a wall. Despite the Chinese occupation of Tibet and virtual closure of its borders since the 1950s, the traditional rock-salt still threads its way down through the valleys.

'Chame Shopping Centre', a wooden shack the size of an outhouse, is presided over by a Hindu who sits cross-legged inside the cramped quarters selling combs, razors, soap, packaged soup, woollen socks, hats, gloves, sweaters, and no doubt, cheap pairs of right-footed flip-flops.

The village's inevitable dog pack singles me out for attention. I nervously wave my bamboo ski-pole at them, an effective anti-rabies device, but this seems only to confirm their suspicions that I am an intruder, and they bark and snap at me more viciously. One of the dogs has an inflamed swelling the size of a tennis ball protruding from its anus. The scraggly pack resolves my desire to keep moving.

Getting tired, I also feel the beginning of a headache, the type caused by altitude, which is hard to believe, for I am well under three-thousand metres. Walking to 'the next lodge' unexpectedly takes more than an hour, but the walk through the peaceful pine-needle-strewn path compensates for the fatigue I feel.

The village of Bhratang is simply a cluster of a few buildings, preceded by a long *mani* prayer wall containing stone tablets with Tibetan inscriptions and a *chorten* built over the path. Before the Annapurna Circuit was opened up to foreign trekkers, Bhratang was inhabited by 'Khampa' refugees.

Long known as unruly rebels and bandits from the Kham province of Tibet, the Khampas were to become Tibet's last hope for freedom, as the tall and powerfully built warriors waged a rearguard action for many years against the occupying forces of the Chinese Communists. Eventually forced to retreat to bases in Manang and Mustang, internationally recognised as lying within the borders of Nepal, they were protected against retaliation by the Chinese invaders. From these bases, with American support, they continued to strike at the Chinese army. But America's covert support was not so much for Tibet's freedom as it was part of American strategy to destabilise Communist governments all over the world. And so the Khampas long ago became expendable in America's dealings with China, when the United States recognised the Chinese Government in the early 1970s. With no support from the USA the Khampa bases in Manang and Mustang became redundant as staging-points for guerrilla raids into Tibet. Huddled in villages like Bhratang, paranoid of possible Chinese reprisals, the Khampas melted further south, away from the border.

Snuggled on the valley floor of the Marsyangdi Khola, dominated by towering mountain peaks on all sides, the quiet loneliness and desolation of Bhratang lends a certain atmosphere worthy of its colourful background as a guerrilla stronghold. Sadly, the hamlet now has the appearance of a ghost town; just another footnote to Tibet's final death throes against their Chinese invaders.

Only one empty lodge is open and the owner beckons me inside and talks to me at length. Like many Manangbhot, he has travelled extensively, to Hong Kong, Singapore, Thailand, India. He served in the famous British Gurkha army, in effect as a mercenary, but the pay was not enough for this ambitious man. 'If I stay in Gurkha army, now I have salary of only one-thousand-and-sixty rupees,' he says derisively.

Manang was a self-contained kingdom until the eighteenth century when King Shah of Gorkha united the warring kingdoms of 'Nepal' into one. In tribute to their allegiance, Manang was given special privileges including the right to trade freely without paying duty. Originally intended for traditional Manangbhot traders bringing up rice and taking down salt to and from India and Tibet, the privilege entitles the modern Manangbhot to import goods from overseas without paying duty, further encouraging their trading instincts.

June, he was born in that month, goes to bed, leaving me with the candles flickering over my notes, and the ink-black, star-filled sky above. I stroll through the ghostly village, almost empty of its previous occupants, and circle the long *mani* wall, spinning inscribed prayer wheels. Easy and Shay are nowhere around.

BHRATANG–UPPER PISANG

I stumble half-asleep into a typical Tibetan interior, an open hearth and fire blazing in the middle of the room, three scruffy children sitting hunched in front of the flames, hands outstretched, palms absorbing the heat like miniature solar panels. The glow of the flickering flames illuminates faces in the dark room as they stare sleepily into the fire, clothes dirt-brown, hair standing on end, coated in dust.

A gargantuan figure fills the doorway, blotting out the early morning light: a giant of a man, wearing a Tibetan *chupa*, or robe, hung on enormous shoulders over which his long, partially braided grey hair hangs loosely. He is not only tall, but powerfully built. He is a Khampa and his apparition is not a disappointment. After reading so much about the Khampa warriors, I would not have expected anything less.

I timidly greet 'Nameste' but he laughs awkwardly and hooks his thumb at himself and bellows, 'Tibetan.' His teeth are dominated by one gold-capped stump. Perceiving he has my full attention, he proudly unsheathes a silver knife with chopsticks attached, from under the folds of his dirty cloak. A silver amulet box decorated with turquoise, pink coral and garnets set in silver gilt is partially revealed hanging in the folds of his robes like a Scottish sporran. He reveals the contents: clay images, rolled papers with Tibetan text, all with protective powers against . . .? He hardly looks as if he needs protection. The presence of this man fills the room, he seems larger than life; a Khampa, a little long in the tooth, and short of several too, but impressive nevertheless. He asks for, and gets served immediately, a thermos of tea and a bowl of rice.

The Brahmin teacher assigned to the local school joins us for a cup of tea. Despite his priestly caste's proclivity to arrogance and superiority, the spindly Brahmin is timid in the presence of Gargantua.

'There are only thirteen children at the school,' he tells me, warily, as if I might inform the Ministry of Education in Kathmandu it is not worthwhile keeping him posted there. I have the presence of mind not to ask him if he likes working in this desolate outpost surrounded by untouchable bhotia.

Brown pine needles carpet the ground underfoot, silencing my progress up a wide valley, dramatically different from the claustrophobic gullies of the last days. To the right a solid sheet of massive rock rises a thousand metres or more, curving smoothly into a right angle, like a giant skateboard wall turned on its side. The smooth escarpment is so steep that its slopes are devoid of vegetation. It is difficult to comprehend the vastness of this stratum of rock or the earth's forces that formed it.

The washed clothes hanging on my back-pack dry in no time in the arid climate. Other than the green fir and pine trees, everything else is brown, as I enter the rain-shadow of the Himalayas and a spectacular view of Annapurna II unfolds, lying south as I now approach the Tibetan border and plateau. I have wound my way through the Himalayas and entered into another world. In the distance the village

[35]

of Upper Pisang strategically straddles the ridge of a hill, overlooking the desert-like valley.

My head begins to hurt so much I can no longer ignore the pain. I sit down to rest on a spur overlooking the glacier-fed Marsyangdi Khola; my heartbeat seems to throb correspondingly in my head and waves of nausea overwhelm me. I try lying on my back, perfectly still. I have never experienced altitude sickness at a height of only three-thousand metres before. I search for excuses, as if reluctant to admit recognising the insidious symptoms.

Before the final steep climb up to Upper Pisang, I unexpectedly come across Shay by herself, squatting underneath her black umbrella, beside a heap of used toilet paper and sanitary napkins which she burns. She is staring intently at the flickering, almost invisible flames in the bright sunlight, crying. 'It's just my period. I'm always like this.'

I stand with her, idly watching the papers burn.

'Andrew?'

'Yes?' I have learnt, when Shay says my name before she embarks on a subject, that she is about to ask or say something serious. This time she pauses longer than usual before saying anything. I look at her. 'Yes?'

'Are you still married?' She is not being inquisitive or cruel. I sense more than anything she is concerned.

'Yes.'

'But you're thinking about it?'

'Yes.' I turn my gaze back to the mound of ashes.

'For the same reasons?' Her question is not obvious, but I know she refers to her explanation for her own marital break-up.

'Yes.' Perhaps it is triggered by her tears. Perhaps it is the altitude. More than likely it is because I have been bottling up this disheartening aspect of my life. My face scrunches up as I try to block out the surge of emotions. I feel as vulnerable as a child. Shay holds me. 'I'm so lonely,' the words barely come out in gasps for air.

'I know,' she says.

Eventually, having vented my emotions, I laugh at myself, at us. 'Wish I could say it was just my period. But it's not going to disappear in just a couple of days.'

'No, but at least you won't have it every month for the rest of your reproductive life either.'

Purged, we climb together in silence towards Upper Pisang, past yak grazing on rocky slopes. I drop further behind, barely able to keep my headache under control. If it gets much worse, I will start vomiting. Shay moves on ahead after asking me if I am all right, not moving far away, but giving me space to lick my wounds. Each step, with the heavy pack, has a corresponding effect on my headache. I stagger a couple of times, not so much from the weight of the pack, or fatigue, but because I am losing my sense of balance. I am still about one-hundred metres below the village when Easy comes skipping down, still in his flip-flops. He takes my back-pack. While this slows him down a bit, it gives me renewed life. A Tibetan-looking woman finds the three of us, the only person we encounter in the apparently deserted village, and she enthusiastically beckons us to follow her.

'This better be good,' Shay mutters, at the limit of her endurance and taking the words out of my own mouth.

We are shown into a bunker-like stone building and another woman appears, almost beside herself with excitement. The dwelling is three storeys high, with notches carved into tree trunks serving as stairways from one level to another. The ground floor is an enclosed courtyard for animals; the second floor is living quarters and kitchen. The upper level, a sunny open area, is used to winnow and store grain. During daylight, the upper level serves as the general work area, the fuel-wood stored on the perimeter of the roof serving as protective walls to form a sun-trap.

Easy wants to explore the village. I follow Shay as she climbs up the notched tree-trunks to the upper floor. She lies in the sun on a mat which is spread out for her, under the protection of her umbrella. I lie spread-eagled on my stomach on a bench. I do not want to move, ever. Keeping still, I can reduce the pounding in my head below nausea level. Shay starts giggling; I don't have the energy to ask why.

When the nausea subsides, I slowly raise myself into a sitting position. I must use sunglasses to gaze across the open desert-like valley, at the Annapurnas, their sides blindingly silver-white. Snow blows off the crest of Annapurna II like smoke against the cobalt-blue sky. Massive clumps of snow and ice cling to the almost vertical north face, leaving ugly overhangs suspended dangerously. The peaks and ridges, fluted columns of ice and snow, are another world, totally removed from this one. I remove sweat-soaked boots and cardboard-stiff socks and let them dry in the sun beside my purple, puckered feet.

Hundreds of prayer flags reach up from bamboo poles on rooftops, fluttering their printed entreaties in the breeze. Semi-terraced, and apparently barren stony potato fields descend down the slopes into the valley. The mercurial river snakes far below, its roar now only a dull rumble. Alpine choughs drop out of the heavens, wings folded as if in prayer, as they plunge downwards.

Easy returns. There is a good feeling about the place and we decide to spend the night here. Our Tibetan-looking hostess is beside herself with joy when this decision is conveyed to her. A young girl hides in her robes, clearly terrified of us as our hostess proudly reveals our bedroom. She is desperately excited and nervous, and I wonder if she has ever had guests before. I gently lie down on one of the beds which is small and narrow, adorned with spotless Chinese embroidered bed-sheets and pillow-cases, the pillows and mattresses stuffed roughly with straw. I drape a T-shirt over my head and try to ignore the waves of nausea.

When the others leave the room, I take the T-shirt off my face and find myself staring at the opposite wall, decorated with a single poster: 'Nothing can bring you peace but yourself.' I place the T-shirt over my face again, and think about it. Where did the poster come from? Why is the poster in such an outlandish place as this? Who put it there? Is it just conicidence? I think about the posted advice for a while before going down to the kitchen where a less profound certificate hangs conspicuously on the sooty wall.

King Mahendra Trust for Nature Conservation
Annapurna Conservation Area Project
and
Hotel Management and Tourism Training Centre
HMG Ministry of Tourism
present this
Certificate of Participation
to Saishama Gurung
for having participated in the Training Programme
'Lodge Management Course for Owners/Operators'
held at Manang July 19 to July 25 1989

Four years ago I had taken a week off a busy work schedule super-vising Canadian-funded rural development projects in Nepal, to walk with Kirsten a tiny portion of the Annapurna Circuit, from the town of Pokhara in a circle to Hille, Ghorepani, Ghandrung and back. I remember it was pitiful to see the cut-throat competition among the lodges. One lodge in particular stands out in my memory, in the village of Hille, where the young boy running the tiny *bhaati* told me we could stay at his lodge for free, if we just ate there. The situation is improv-ing. Even here in this remote village, the cooking-fire is no longer the traditional open hearth. A clay/mud oven conserves heat, burning less fuel-wood. A pipe made of tin-cans conducts the smoke out of the oven and the house, through the roof. Previously I had found staying within some of the *bhaatis* unbearable because of the smoke-filled rooms.

The fixed menu is cleverly formulated too. A number of Western-style meals can be concocted with little effort: 'spaghetti' is boiled Chinese noodle soup (without any herbal or packaged mix) with tomato ketchup. After a day's trekking, this tastes surprisingly good. Pizza is Tibetan bread with vegetables and tomato sauce on top. The prices for meals, like the bed rates, are fixed, cutting price competition, but adding pressure on the provision of quality. Standards of sanita-tion are improved too. Toilets of some kind are provided in almost every *bhaati*, although some are only basic drop toilets with a hole cut in the floorboards. Sanitation in the preparation of food is better now. I have not been sick, at least not so far.

Had she not taken the training course, Saishama would not have had the faintest idea of what kind of sleeping or eating arrangements Westerners required. In isolated Upper Pisang, off the direct trade route, these villagers would not have had a tradition of hospitable *bhaatis* for passing travellers. Far from it. Traditionally they would have locked themselves up in their mini-fortresses at the sight of a for-eigner.

Despite the pain of my thumping head, I want to explore the village of Upper Pisang. I descend the notched tree-trunks and start by walking the length of a long *mani* wall, methodically spinning the prayer wheels, and chanting quietly to myself the Buddhist mantra '*Om Mani Padme Hum*'. Climbing higher, I stop, out of breath, with my head still throbbing persistently.

A woman walks alongside the prayer wall below, diligently spinning the wheels. She is the first person I have seen in the village besides Saishama and her friend. As she returns on the other side of the *mani* wall, a *zopkio* bellows. To my amazement, without breaking her stride, the woman bellows back. Another *zopkio* answers, and she bellows again, perfectly imitating the different sound of the second beast. She moves from the *mani* wall to touch one *zopkio* reverently on the forehead.

I climb to a larger building, the village *gompa*, a Tibetan Buddhist monastery, decorated with ornately carved wooden window-frames painted bright colours. The rooftop is festooned with vertically aligned Buddhist prayer flags flapping gently in the breeze. Passing along the side of the building partially built into the dry stone earth, I enter a half-closed doorway and hear faint music.

There is no one in there, and what I hear is not a radio, but voices singing. An inner door leads into a perfectly dark room. I stumble into the cavity and the voices become clearer and louder. The singing is enchanting, timeless, otherworldly. A bell chimes rhythmically. Unable to see, I drop to my hands and knees, and groping along the dirt and stone ground, crawl deeper into what seems like a pitch-black cave. Are they women or children singing? Are they inside this space, too? I close my eyes to stop them searching vainly, and listen intently. When the music stops, the cave walls absorb the last notes, and absolute silence matches the total darkness. I see the darkness and listen to the silence, no longer with my eyes and ears but with my whole inner being, the shadows and sound of my own life flickering and reverberating about me, and for an instant I have transcended my body and floated away free, perfectly at peace. The headache has gone and I crawl back out of the cellar doorway, into the brightness of the world, wondering if I have trespassed.

At another heavy door I pause, unsure if I should enter, and it is opened for me and I am drawn in. Groups of people, mostly men, stand on the sunny, open mud-roof terrace of the *gompa* levered into the hillside. I hear the singing again, clearer and louder than before. There are tatty little shoes lined up neatly outside the entrance. I take my giant boots off, place them beside the tiny assorted footwear, and enter the shadows, to watch and listen.

Front centre is dominated by a golden Buddha draped in yellow robes with white *kata* scarves in his hands. On either side of the central figure are two other statues, Bodhisattvas. One is probably Avalokiteshvara, reincarnated as the Dalai Lama. In front of the Buddha, fumes from burning incense sticks and yak butter candles flicker beside bowls of rice and cakes laid out in offering.

A lama sits to the left, reading and chanting from rectangular prayer sheets, occasionally ringing a bell. His features are oriental, almost Chinese, with crew-cut hair and wire-rim glasses. Next to him is another, similar in face, but older; and next to him is a heavy-set, tough-looking man, most probably a Khampa, with square shoulders and a face that could be American-Indian. From his left ear hang large chunks of pink coral and turquoise. His braided hair reaches down his back. He yawns often and audibly. Beside him a young boy takes the block of prayer sheets from the lama, bundles them between painted and gilded wooden blocks, wraps them carefully in red and yellow cloth, ties them with crimson ribbon, before placing the prayer block in one of one-hundred-and-eight cubby holes. Periodically, the boy beats a drum hanging from the ceiling, with an S-shaped stick, or crashes two bronze cymbals in a horizontal motion, as the lama unwraps a new block of prayers and reads from them in chanting cadence. Enormous telescopic trumpets made of copper with brass fittings are propped against the wall.

Pillars support the belfry-like roof. Lining the walls of the raised central portion of the roof are one-hundred-and-eight smaller statues of Buddha. I know that for Tibetans the number one-hundred-and-eight is sacred. The number of beads contained in a Tibetan rosary is one-hundred-and-eight and many women in Tibet and Mustang go so far as to plait their hair in one-hundred-and-eight strands. Nailed to the pillars hangs incongruously a banner reading 'Souvenir of Hong Kong Racetrack'. To the right, a snow leopard skin has been nailed to the wall. Above me hang Dakanis, fierce minor goddesses, represented by hideous masks of stylised, sutured skulls with protruding fang-like teeth, big ears, demonic eyes, and decorated with crowns and necklaces of smaller skulls.

With the best will in the world, I cannot relate to the paraphernalia and esoteric rituals accompanying the beautiful chanting. In the blank isolation and darkness of the cellar below, the singing had been an inspirational, almost spiritual experience. Now it is submerged in a

[41]

conglomeration of esoteric images and accessories collected over the centuries, rendering the Buddha's philosophic flair a faint shadow of the original. Buddhism as a philosophy I could appreciate. Becoming entangled in the esoteric religious relics, even a gold or brass statue of Buddha, I find difficult to relate to in a spiritual sense. These symbols, no matter how effective to the villagers as a means of communion with their deeper selves, are alien to me. I am, despite myself, wrapped up in other rituals and relics, meaningless to me in a certain sense but nevertheless part of my Christian identity.

There are aspects of pure Buddhist philosophy I find inspirational, but they would not provide the spiritual answers I seek. As Saishama's poster in our bedroom points out, the answers to life's questions are locked up within ourselves, where we are. Only we can nurture the relevant seed of truth. But to get at that kernel, we have first to crack the hard outer shell.

I had embarked on this trip searching, expecting perhaps to become convinced of the merits of Buddhism, and maybe even become a Buddhist. For many, the appeal of Buddhism lies in the belief that salvation is open to all, depending neither on dogmatic faith nor on divine grace, but only on understanding 'the way things really are': unsatisfactory, impermanent, devoid of essence. But it seems to me that the ultimate Buddhist aim in understanding the world, to reach the state of nirvana and thus escape the cycle of rebirth, is somehow a negation of the splendour of life. When the chips are down, recognising that all life is suffering helps to keep things in perspective, but the meaning of life remains a yawning gap. The dawning realisation that Buddhism is not likely to be the magical panacea to my introspective searchings is in itself a release. Even this conclusion fits in with the Buddha's message: we must each see for ourselves what brings contentment, clarity and peace, and then follow that path.

Women chant and swing their prayer wheels of silver, brass, coral, turquoise and wood. The block-printed prayers contained within the cylinder body are offered to the deities invoked. The momentum of a metal ball on the end of a chain keeps the wheel spinning consistently. The women in front of me, clad in traditional Tibetan clothing, braided pony-tails, prayer wheels in hand, chat to one another, turning curiously to see who has come in. They are all old and yet down in the dark cave cellar of the *gompa* their singing voices sounded like those of children.

Singing also, but almost inaudibly, are half-a-dozen decrepit dusty men. They peer through prescription glasses as thick as the bottoms of Coca-Cola bottles. The lamas are offered tea and biscuits. The men and women intermingle as they go out. They obviously know one another well. One old woman, so bowed over that she hardly reaches my waist, hobbles out, but not before an old man catches her eye and imitates her hobbling gait, much to each other's amusement.

When I entered the *gompa*, I was anxious to do the right thing. I did not want to offend. Now I realise there was no danger of that. Some women gossip; others pray; the young lama chats and laughs with a woman in front. The other lamas drink tea during the recitation of prayers. It is a relaxed, friendly, appealing atmosphere.

Alone, back on the roof terrace of our *bhaati*, in the late afternoon sun, I reflect on the intense experience of the *gompa* cellar as shadows cast by the mountains creep up the sunlit valley. The jet stream blows snow over the top of the Annapurnas. The entire northern mountain face is in shadow, but the windblown snow catches the orange sunset on the opposite side, lighting the ridge-line in an eerie glow, as if the summit of the ice-bound mountain is on fire. The fiery image dies, and curtains of mist swoop as if drawn across a stage. Prayer flags shiver on rooftops, darkness envelops us. Purged, the energy dissipates.

UPPER PISANG–BRAGA

I do not want to leave Upper Pisang. I had toyed with the idea of going to Tibet instead of Nepal. Heinrich Harrer's book *Seven Years in Tibet* had intrigued me, but its sequel, *Return to Tibet*, described a world now shattered. I can hardly contemplate the physical, cultural and spiritual destruction that the Communist Chinese have inflicted on Tibetans and Tibet, yet the record is quite clear.

In the decade 1949–1959 the People's Republic of China invaded Tibet. The Dalai Lama, the living Buddha, the 'god-king' and spiritual leader of Tibet's largely Buddhist population, remained in the country until 31 March 1959, when he fled from Tibet to Nepal and eventually to exile in India. In 1959 the International Commission of Jurists reported that vivisection, disembowelling, dismemberment, beheading, burning, beating to death, burying alive of victims, were punishments used by the Chinese to intimidate the Tibetan population.

Here, only some dozens of kilometres away from the Tibetan border, is a more authentic living 'Tibetan' environment than in Tibet itself. I want to linger, at least a day longer, maybe a week, to learn and experience more of the approach to Buddhist philosophy offered in Upper Pisang. I suggest to Shay and Easy, 'I wouldn't mind staying here. How about you guys?'

'I'm eager to keep moving,' Easy responds, as he packs his diminutive pack.

I feel the first tug of conflict since starting the trip, but say nothing. I could remain here for another week. I do not know what lies ahead, perhaps more villages like this. I do know that ahead of us is Mustang, the 'forbidden kingdom' just over the Thorong La. It is there, in particular, that my imagination had often taken me in preparing for this trip. Over breakfast I stall for time, procrastinating, asking, 'If you could go back in time, when and where would you go back to?'

Shay responds 'I'd be a goddess in Hellenic Greece.'

I could see that.

Easy wants to be the last to give us his choice, so I follow by telling them, 'I would go back to the time of Jesus Christ, and suss out what he really did, and who he really was, and if he really did do all those things the Bible says he did.'

Easy thinks hard. 'Can I bring something back with me?' he asks.

'Sure, I don't see why not,' I answer, making up rules to the game as I go along.

'OK,' he pauses for dramatic effect. He puffs out his cheeks to deliberate. 'Hmm. I'd have to say I'd go back to . . . hmmm . . . nineteen-fifty-one.' He lets the air out of his lungs. He has made a monumental choice, a difficult one.

'Why?' we ask.

'Well, it was a good year for baseball cards. I could pick up a few Nolan Ryans for sure.'

Easy has a collection of thirty-thousand baseball cards worth more than forty-thousand dollars. He keeps the most valuable ones, like those depicting Nolan Ryan, which alone are worth thousands of dollars, in a bank safety-deposit box. Sometimes he goes to the bank to check them out. The cards are interspersed in the pages of books. 'It drives Easy's banker crazy,' Shay tells me, 'when he asks the bankers if he can see his baseball cards.'

Breakfast continues, with Easy daubing his smiling face in lentils and rice.

'Easy has dozens of kids at schools trading, swapping, buying and selling on his behalf.'

'I thought to reach nirvana you were supposed not to covet,' I admonish and press home the attack. 'Do you honestly think your desire to collect baseball cards is exempt from the Buddha's fundamental doctrine of the Four Noble Truths?'

'Yeah.' He looks confused, then he snaps his fingers and points at me to emphasise his insight, a solution to his conundrum. 'But hey, the Buddha didn't know about baseball cards.'

Cleverly, Easy tries to divert us from the topic of his perceived covetousness. 'Did I ever tell you about meeting the Dalai Lama?' I shake my head, Shay nods hers emphatically. 'When I was in India at an ashram to study Buddhism, the Dalai Lama came to visit us . . .'

'Your baseball card collection is what we were talking about Easy,' Shay provokes, cutting him off in mid-sentence. 'It would seem from the evidence, you aren't going to make it to nirvana with that pile of cardboard paper you've carefully stashed away.'

'Heh, you can't get carried away too much with all this stuff. Like, sure, I'm a Buddhist, but, you can only take it so far, you know.' Easy looks at me for moral support. I stare at him stone-faced. 'Well, baseball cards is my limit. Definitely. You know, Buddhism was based on the teachings of the "Enlightened One" who was born mid-sixth century BC, and he wouldn't have even *known* about baseball cards at that time. They didn't even know what *baseball* was. If the Buddha were recycled now, he would covet baseball cards for sure. He'd make baseball cards an exception to the rule.' He looks at Shay, then me, for acceptance of his contrived logic.

'But what about the Four Noble Truths?' I persist sceptically.

'Sure . . . OK . . .' He raises his fingers, grasping them one by one in the fist of his other hand as he counts, 'One: all existence is suffering. Two: suffering is caused by desire. Three: to lessen our attachment to the physical world reduces suffering. And four: that can be attained by following the Eight-fold Path. Something like that anyway.' He looks to Shay for confirmation.

'And . . .,' Shay encourages.

'Attachment brings about rebirth in a lower life, non-attachment to a better birth. The final release from the chain of rebirths is the state of nirvana, which results from total non-attachment and the accumulation of positive karma,' Easy explains by rote. 'Those already on their way to Buddhahood are Bodhisattvas . . .'

'Isn't your baseball card collection sort of jeopardising your next life? I mean, you sound kind of attached to it,' I cross-examine.

'Na. I got the Eight Golden Rules covered pretty well.' Easy counts them off on his fingers. 'Right understanding, right resolve, right action, right livelihood, right effort, right mindfulness and . . . Damn! What's the last one again Shay?'

'Right speech.'

'Oh yeah.'

Our hosts watch us enthralled. Only Saishama's brother can speak Nepali, so he and Easy translate. The brother chops onions on what looks like a chopping-block, but is revealed to be a stool when he sits on it shortly afterwards.

Caught in the momentum of the group, I decide to leave after all. Saishama is heartbroken. She does not want us to go. There has been a strong feeling of friendship. Perhaps it is simply the enthusiasm with which she has hosted us. I delay my departure as long as I can, but eventually I too depart. In the distance, Shay and Easy wind their way along the barren hillside. The distinctive footprints left by Easy's flip-flops are easy to follow in the fine mica-powder on the path.

I recognise a woman hobbling by carrying a *doko*, her conical carrying basket, full of kindling, and she sings as she walks. She is the same woman who was sitting in the *gompa* yesterday looking so incredibly old and who hobbled out to the amusement of the old man. I watch her trudging along the path until her singing fades in the wind.

Below, on the valley bottom, on the other side of the river, the main route wriggles, so wide it seems to be a road. Shepherds above cry high-pitched shrieks at their *zopkios*. Upper Pisang, the buildings, the *gompa* adorned in prayer flags, are revealed through a veil of smoke from cooking-fires. There is almost a physical tugging at my heart leaving this place. One's spirit would be richer if one could be born here, live all one's life here, and die here. Prayer flags tremble loudly as if in confirmation of the insight.

At another long *mani* wall images of Tara with ripe breasts and images of Tantric sex and esoteric *yantras* honouring the deities, tantalise ignorant passers-by like myself. Mummified yak skulls stare sightlessly out from a cavity below the effigies. It is Kirsten's birthday and I scrawl a message on a piece of paper and bury it deep within the stone wall.

The back-pack becomes an almost overwhelming burden as I start another steep climb. The headache returns. I walk slowly, but cannot keep the headache under control. Approaching the village of Ghyaru at three-thousand-seven-hundred metres, my head starts to throb and waves of nausea envelop me. Once again I am only a hundred metres below the village when Easy comes skipping down the path in his flip-flops to meet me, and to take my back-pack. Without it weighing me down, I feel almost afloat, as if giant helium balloons were attached by ropes to the small of my back.

A shepherd gives us directions to the roof of a fortress home where we can get food. An organised Mountain Travel group from California has collected there, having climbed from their tented 'base camp' on the valley floor. Easy is his effervescent, friendly self, but the Mountain Travel guide barely responds, dressed in immaculate safari khaki. He treats us as if we have a contagious disease. Striking out for a day-hike from their sanitised camp on the main trekking route, to explore an advertised 'high-altitude, untouched, authentic Tibetan village', they must have been disappointed to find three foreigners casually ordering *dal bhaat*, with one persistent Californian in flip-flops, T-shirt, running-shorts and baseball cap, who wants to know what the latest baseball scores are back home.

The guide refuses to acknowledge our existence, but Easy is a hard man to put down, and is soon chatting amiably about everything and anything to members of the group. They ask, 'What are you doing here?'

'Hiking.'

'Where do you stay?'

'Places like this.'

They look around sceptically. 'Eating local food?'

'Sure. Tastes great.' Easy makes it sound like such fun, and we seem to be having such a good time. 'Did you see the *gompa* in Upper Pisang?' They shake their heads negative. 'Wow. Bad call. You missed something. Big local shindig there yesterday. Tell them about it, Shay.'

Shay tells them about it as Easy converses with our hostess in Nepali about our lunch order.

One of the doctors asks Easy, 'Are you, like, the tour leader?'

'Nope. We just met on the route, liked each other, and as long as we feel like it, we travel more or less together.'

'How come you speak Nepali?'

'Picked it up on the way.' Easy has got that wicked look in his eyes again. 'Know how much it cost us to have all the freedom in the world to explore the area, and eat and sleep well? Without a guide mind you.' He pauses for the message to sink in as the mono-lingual Mountain Travel guide shifts about uncomfortably. 'About three bucks a day.'

The guide says they have to go and leads the way down the notched ladder. A Californian woman mutters something inaudible under her breath. Easy innocently gives Mountain Travel and their guide a final *coup de grâce*, 'Hey, how much did it cost you guys for your trip?' He asks the question with style, a smile, and a dumb look on his face. They stop on the rooftop before descending the notched tree-trunk and tell him. 'Wow! Bad call again . . .' He shakes his head in commiseration. 'Could've had me as a guide for my expenses only.' He makes a show of calculating, scratching his head. 'Three bucks a day expenses, divided by ten of you guys.' He looks up in mock surprise. 'Hey! Just thirty cents each.'

When they are out of earshot, Shay observes 'You didn't like the guide, did you?' She does not wait for his response. 'I'm not sure that kind of attitude is going to get you to nirvana Easy, or even heaven, for that matter.'

Easy laughs. He is only human. We eat our *dal bhaat* on the roof terrace, Easy smudging rice and lentils with dramatic effect over his increasingly bearded face. Brown, broad leaves collecting in the corners of the kindling windbreaks remind us it is autumn, and winter is coming. We play with a puppy chewing our shoelaces. A prayer flag flutters over us, its top crowned with buckwheat sheaves. A child with severe impetigo smothering his face intimidates us by hovering around unnecessarily close.

We attempt to visit the village *gompa*, but it is locked and we lose each other in the maze of alleyways. I wander around the village, executing pinball bounces off dead-end alleys, before I see Easy and then Shay through a gap in the buildings, rounding a corner of the trail in the distance. I follow them under a sky without the faintest hue of pollution or a single vaporous cloud. It is so quiet. I can hear the creaking of the pack on my back.

I catch up to Shay burning another stash of sanitary napkins at the edge of the trail. She carries her opened umbrella above her head in one hand to shield her from the intense rays of the sun, holds up her ankle-length skirt in the other, as she watches over her little fire. I wait. We are both listless from the high altitude.

Above, a dozen griffins soar, effortlessly, thousands of metres high. There is a spirituality about this valley. Perhaps it is the elevation, the clear blue sky, the silence, the comfortable warmth of the sun on the skin in the crisp air. Perhaps it is because we are so high up we are just that much closer to the gods. Looking at the Himalayan griffins, it is not hard to conceive of being reincarnated as one of them. Two competing yellow-beaked choughs, looking like crows but smaller, ride the crests of air waves, as if tossed about on invisible roller-coasters. They too, are spirits floating, diving, twisting, soaring in the wind.

We are not alone in being affected by the spirituality of this place. *Mani* walls and *chortens* line the path. Large boulders and rock faces are carved with Tibetan mantras. Cairns topped with prayer flags line each hump of every ridge. In this high-altitude environment everything seems to have spiritual connotations, and it does not surprise me that Tibetan historical literature was almost exclusively religious in context.

Although we are more than a kilometre away from the village where we have just had a meal, the whipping of the prayer flags is still faintly audible in the pervasive silence of these lofty mountains. Two vultures soar from below, passing us effortlessly as they ride invisible thermals. If I could choose the next form of reincarnation, it would be one of these birds, high in the Himalayas.

We continue, Shay moving ahead, following Easy's distinctive footprints. At a high point on the path, I see the ruins of an ancient fort a couple of hundred metres below, straddling a strategic spur on a ridge, dominating the valley. I think I recognise Easy sitting on one of the ramparts. A narrow path descends, but Easy's footprints do not seem to lead down it. I gaze down at the ruins, imagining its history.

Who is that sitting on the ramparts, lost in thought? Is he Nepalese? Tibetan? A trekker? Easy? The colour of his clothes blends in with the browns of the stones. Is it a ghost left from the time the fortress was in use? I wave when I think he looks up at me, and I see him wave back. Or is he holding his arms up? The hunched figure lifts gently into the air, hovers still for a second, before soaring over the valley, the sun reflecting off wide, feathery wings.

I take a last look eastwards, the length of the valley, towards Upper Pisang perched on a ridge, the skateboard wall beyond with clouds forming below towards Tal, Manasulu behind that, and Pisang Peak to the north-east. As I watch and study the view, Shay continues on her own, following the winding trail. The immensity of the mountains is humbling. There are no man-made machines or structures to give a sense of self-importance. We are merely ants, crawling on the surface and wrinkles and folds of this earth, itself only a tiny fragment of the universe.

My musings are interrupted by four well-built Tibetan girls sprawled astride the path, their *dokos* empty beside them. Where have they come from? Where are they going? They ask me for a drink of water. I give them my water-flask and they drink. They are all very pretty, and eminently nubile. As I continue on my way, one of them yells after me, in passable English, 'I love you.' I turn around and wave and smile back, flattered. They are being silly. Then they all yell at me, 'I love you,' persistently, loudly and aggressively. I am disconcerted to find that for the first time on the trip I feel intimidated, and I am embarrassed to admit the insecurity imposed on me by the sexual demands of young girls, however imbued with warrior blood they might be.

Wispy clouds dance around the Just Hills on the other side of the valley; the wind blowing desolately is disrupted by a loud thunderclap. Below the summit of Annapurna III, clouds of snow billow vertically upward on the sides and the bottom of the mountain in the aftermath of an avalanche. Although several kilometres away, the sound reaches me against the fierce wind. The avalanche-fuelled snow-cloud blossoms outwards from the valley bottom.

Light. It is everywhere, reflecting off mica in the rocks, the leaves, the river, the snow. It seems to enter my soul, brightening the darkest corners of my heart and mind. I have an overwhelming sense of peace.

Some hours later, time has become meaningless. Passing a severely eroded yellow hillside, I descend alone to the valley bottom. The golden-coloured leaves of poplar trees in the hamlet of Paugba, and stone-walled fields and buildings all catch the sun's soft evening beams in pleasing jigsaw patterns of light. I reach the bottom of the valley, to a peaceful green pasture, and criss-cross a myriad of yak-paths melting into pine forests. The last glimmer of the sun glints off the smooth surfaces of the prayer stones of another *mani* wall, casting into dark relief their carved inscriptions. The orange orb descends behind the Himals, and immediately it gets cold.

The path divides repeatedly. I make arbitrary decisions regarding choice of trails leading through a forest. I am not totally lost. I know I must head west, and I am walking towards the remnants of the sunset. It is peaceful and quiet. I still have not seen anybody on the trail since the last village some hours ago, Easy and Shay being somewhere ahead. My pack begins once again to feel as if it is swollen with boulders and, despite the lower altitude, the headache returns.

Unexpectedly, in a clearing in the trees, I see Shay walking towards me, by herself. Before I can say anything, she asks me, obviously perplexed, 'Where are you going?'

'Where am *I* going? Where are *you* going?'

'I don't know. Aren't I heading towards Manang?' she asks.

'No, you are heading away from Manang. Where's Easy?'

'I don't know. I haven't seen him since we had lunch at Ngawal.' Shay is confused, almost in a state of shock. Realising she is lost, she also realises she is ill-prepared for being alone. Easy has the map and the little food they carry with them. Getting scared as darkness descended, she has already reconciled herself to spending the night out alone.

'What's that you've got in your hand?'

She holds her hand out for me to see. 'A potato I found, to eat if necessary,' she replies.

We have been lucky in crossing paths. If I had taken any of the other innumerable trails heading in roughly the same direction, we would not have met. We continue walking, together. The tops of the mountains turn a cold, steel-blue white, devoid of the direct sunlight. At

[51]

dusk we arrive at Munchi, a collection of abandoned stone houses, with no one around. My throbbing headache is accompanied by waves of nausea. We are an unhappy couple. Shay is not feeling well either, and is distressed about the whole situation. It is almost night when we reach the village of Braga, slumped against a hillside, dominated by its *gompa*. As we walk through a *chorten* and across an empty field, Easy approaches us. In the short remaining distance to the lodge the headache and sickness get worse. As usual Easy takes my pack.

Shay, Easy and I are destined to share a room and the same bed once again. I lie down, on the side nearest the door. Shay, who is also feeling sick, lies beside me. Easy goes into the dining-area to socialise, leaving Shay and me alone in the dark.

'I'm so happy,' she tells me.

I know her well enough to realise she is being perfectly sincere. The intimacy of her breathing so close beside me is lost in waves of nausea engulfing my body. My head feels as if it is on fire and my heartbeat thumps blood into my brain as if my head were too small for my body.

'I know what you mean,' I respond, ignoring my physical discomfort.

After an hour of silence, immobility and heavy doses of aspirin, we both regain our appetites and resurrect ourselves to join Easy in the crowded and warm dining-room. But after dinner of soup, Swiss rösti and rice pudding, I get the chills again and we all turn in, Shay and Easy taking the side of the bed closest to the wall.

I am queasy. My headache returns with a vengeance and, try as I might to ignore the waves of nausea, they eventually overwhelm me. I just have time to extricate myself from the sleeping-bag, fling open the doors of the room, and lean over the rail to puke into the flower garden. During the night I vomit several times, co-ordinating the evacuation of sleeping-bag, room and the insides of my stomach with varying degrees of success. Watery diarrhoea compounds the problem.

As I crawl back into bed with Shay and Easy, Shay asks, 'Andrew, are you all right?'

'No,' I reply truthfully.

'Oh,' she says before falling back to sleep.

It's the thought that counts.

BRAGA–MANANG

The spectacular arrival of dawn is an intense experience, if only because I was not sure I would ever see it. It is obvious I am going nowhere. Easy caters to me, bringing me a constant supply of Cokes because I am so dehydrated. 'Carry on without me,' I tell them, and I mean it.

Easy and Shay move on. The farewell is anticlimactic. I do not feel like getting up or making an effort. We fade out of each other's lives. I spend most of the day sleeping, decidedly unwell. At some point I am woken by a Dutch trekker who is shown into the room. He stands in the doorway, staring blindly into the gloom. 'Is the bed comfortable?' he sniffs, noticing the one large bed he would have to share with me.

'Comfortable enough,' I tell him truthfully, bundled to the eyes in my sleeping-bag.

'I am thinking of perhaps going on to Manang,' he says, allowing himself a graceful exit.

'Yes, I hear the *bhaatis* are good up there.'

'Thank you. I will keep walking.' He leaves the murky room, then returns to poke his head back in. 'I hope you get better.' I have not told him I am sick.

Easy's Buddhist conscience gets the better of him and he returns to wake me some hours later. 'It's nicer in Manang, and I've got you a bed in a room all to yourself. Besides, they have a medical clinic there with doctors specialising in altitude sickness. I've arranged for one of them to see you.' He is persuasive, and I am sick and lonely. He carries my back-pack. It is only a short walk, but I feel so lethargic, and my head pounds so much, I have to stop twice to sit down, then retch.

MANANG

Half-asleep, I hear stomping on the wooden balcony. I cannot imagine what it is. It sounds like a pirate with a peg leg. The room is dark, there are no terms of reference to remind me where this place is. I backtrack my memory until something clicks, then fast forward to figure out where I am.

Still wrapped in my sleeping-bag like a caterpillar in a cocoon, I bravely hop across the room and open the door. A *zopkio* stands on the wooden planking outside, stamping its feet as if for the attention and the company. The temperature is numbingly cold, well below freezing; a crescent moon with Venus at its side, dominates the clear sky. The blue-tinged Himals appear so close, every crevice, wrinkle, overhang and column punches out clearly against the dark royal-blue of the pre-dawn sky. The soft light strangely and misleadingly makes it look as if it is possible to take a casual stroll up to the top of these mountains. Below, the glacier-fed, turquoise Marsyangdi Khola rumbles over the boulder-strewn riverbed.

Sunlight illuminates delicate snow plumes sculpting the summit of Gangapurna. The wind picks up in Manang, the prayer flags on the roofs quiver, smoke curling from rooftops. The village awakens, resembling a Wild West frontier town with its flat-roofed and stone-walled buildings, each one a mini-fortress. This is the district headquarters of Manang, yet it seems untouched by modern civilisation – not a single cement building, no corrugated tin roofs.

Passing the shower stall, I hear Easy's voice from within. 'Fuuuck!'

'What's the matter?' I ask, curious to find out what has got the better of him.

From inside the jerry-built shower shack, Easy's shivering voice tells me, 'The fucking water's come on, I've soaped my hair, and now the fucking water has gone off, and it's fucking freezing in here.' Icicles have formed beneath the shower's wooden floor.

'Easy?'

'What?' he snaps back.

'You've forgotten your, you know, right-mindfulness language.' I laugh silently at my own joke, happy that Easy cannot see my perverse glee. I'm not likely to reach nirvana either at this rate, but what the hell, it's worth for once getting in a few licks of my own brand of wicked humour.

Easy defrosts and together with Shay jointly decide to wait until I have recovered from altitude sickness. I have mixed emotions about this, for I am happy to take my time and stay here alone for some days, perhaps even retrace my steps back to Upper Pisang. I feel the pressure to start trekking again. But I am also happy they are staying with me. I wash my soiled clothes, then walk slowly down to Braga. I want to apologise to the owner there for vomiting so profusely in his garden.

'There are three gods in Nepal,' Tasi the owner lectures me, accepting my apologies. 'Hinduism, Buddhism and Tourism. We here in Braga looked up to tourism as some kind of god. Now I am not sure. I have seen many things with tourists. They bring bad things with them. This hurts me very, very much.' He holds his scarred clenched fist against his heart for emphasis.

Tasi had been a Buddhist monk for thirteen years, originally here in Braga, then at the Swayambhunath Temple in Kathmandu where an American befriended him and promised to help him attain his lifelong wish, to travel to Thailand. The American paid for him to go to Bangkok where he remained for eight years. Instead of going to a Buddhist monastery, however, Tasi realised a secret dream to become a Thai kick-boxer. He earned and spent a lot on women and drinking. On his return to Braga he bought eight yak and went into the mountains to herd them for the summer, to find himself. His first wife left for Kathmandu with his children but he was determined to stay in Braga to help his community. He remarried, and his wife, who had been a Tibetan refugee, helps him run the community-owned *bhaati*.

Braga's *gompa* is open to view, but the five-hundred-year-old artefacts have been locked in a chest and the keys are held by four members of the Braga community, including Tasi. Early explorers, trekkers or climbers have stolen many of the artefacts, and keeping them locked is the only solution, Tasi says.

I buy stamps and postcards. Tasi tells me to put my post in a rusty, unlocked mailbox. 'Don't worry,' he says, detecting my lack of confidence, 'I open box, your mail will go, no problem.' It is hard to imagine how mail could possibly get from here to the outside world. On the other side of the wall of the rusty mailbox, in his provision shop, a snow leopard skin is nailed, and for sale.

'Yak shooted it,' Tasi offers in cryptic response to my question.

'A yak shooted it?' I repeat in incomprehension.

'Yes, leopard want to shooted yak, but yak shooted leopard first,' he clarifies.

Musk deer skulls are laid out for sale too. I suppose they were 'shooted' by the leopard that was later 'shooted' by the yak. There is a mummified yak skull hanging over the doorway. Even the yak got 'shooted' in the end.

I walk back to Manang. Wild-looking characters on ponies canter by. A steady breeze blows. In stony brown fields ponies, mules, yak and *zopkios* feed on either side of the narrow Marsyangdi River sparkling in the sunlight. Choughs play in the wind, folding their wings to descend, spreading them to ascend, ruffling their feathers to fine-tune their flight. A yak is butchered in a field, a man splitting open the exposed muscles of its chest with mighty swings of an axe. Two traders sit by the wayside, more interested in playing a game involving dice, stones and sticks.

At the Himalayan Rescue Association building, the only cement and stone structure in Manang, a daily information session on mountain sickness is given by two British doctors to trekkers about to cross the Thorong La. They pull no punches in their delivery. 'An average of two trekkers each season die from acute mountain sickness here. A German died a week ago in Pisang and another German died ten days ago at Dhampus Pass, both of which are at lower altitudes than Thorong La.' The annual quota of sacrifices to the mountain gods has been attained. I should be safe. 'The lack of concrete knowledge and the randomness with which it affects people makes AMS particularly difficult to predict. Physical fitness does not prevent AMS. Acute mountain sickness can affect people from two-thousand metres and up. Worsening symptoms of AMS include increasing fatigue, severe headache, vomiting and loss of co-ordination. These are signs of high altitude cerebral oedema which can lead to unconsciousness within twelve hours and death soon thereafter.'

I'm not safe.

'If any of you would like a private consultation, you may make an appointment later, for a small fee.'

A sad-looking, orange-haired man with a drooping lower lip asks, 'Hwhat does it mean if you are cold?'

The doctor replies deadpan to Carrot Head's question, 'It means you haven't got enough clothes on.'

I make an appointment. The doctor sits me down and asks me to describe my problems with the altitude. 'Have you had altitude sickness before?'

'Three times on Kilimanjaro. A couple of times in western Nepal.'

'Symptoms worse than you have now?'

'Yes. Totally lost my sense of equilibrium, couldn't stand up.'

'How high was that?'

'Above six-thousand metres.'

'There's no doubt you are susceptible to acute mountain sickness and you have been experiencing high altitude cerebral oedema. Often one of the symptoms of this problem is the lack of clear thinking concerning your condition, and refusal to admit that you have AMS. However, I think the worst is over, and if you feel fit enough, there are no contra-indications to your continuing. However, I would suggest you take Diamox, which acts as a diuretic. You will have to drink copious amounts of water to compensate for the dehydration caused not only by the dry, cold mountain air but by the drug. Take one in the morning, one in the afternoon. You will probably feel a tingly sensation in your fingertips and your toes; ignore it. You should begin taking the Diamox immediately.'

I do not feel ready to begin the climb over Thorong La tomorrow, not if I feel the way I felt today, still listless, without appetite. But the throbbing headache and nausea have subsided. The doctor's diagnosis makes me feel better, if only in releasing me from the pressure of Easy and Shay going up tomorrow. I feel like asking the doctor to give me an official sick-note to present to Easy, requesting him to let me off trekking any further until I feel better. When we meet, I tell them, 'Doctor says I should sit it out another day.'

'We'll wait for you.'

That evening, coming back from one of many trips to the toilet, I pass the open door of the fire-lit *bhaati* kitchen, packed full of porters, guides, *sidhars* and villagers from all over Manang who have come to watch an Indian video. Even curious dogs are sitting at the entrance looking in. The film is about a suave Indian man in love with a delectable young girl who, it seems, cannot stop dancing and singing. The music is catchy, the action and story line easy to follow without understanding Hindi, and soon I too am laughing along with everyone in the room. Electricity has brought video night to this otherwise desolate and quiet mountain village, and with it, the insidious infiltration of Westernised Indian culture, language and values.

MANANG–LETDAR

During the night the Diamox has its effect. I pee copiously and often. The night is cold, below freezing, and to extricate myself from the warm sleeping-bag so frequently is agony. During one of my later runs to the stone wall, when it is almost dawn, I see Easy squatting beside the shower stall, washing his underpants. He asks, 'How are you feeling?'

'Great.' I reply. 'None of the problems of the last three days. How're you feeling?'

He looks at me, 'Pretty shitty.'

'What's wrong?' I ask.

'Must'a been something I ate. Shat myself during the night.' Whimsically he holds up the lathered and clearly soiled underpants as evidence. 'Hey, look, Shay and I are going to split out'a here. I'm getting sick, and kind'a depressed hanging around.'

'OK,' I answer, 'I'm willing.'

Easy looks up from his washing. 'Really? Wow! Let's go!'

Reflecting the familiarity of our budding friendship, I lift a leg and flamboyantly blow out a conspicuously airy fart.

'Show off,' Easy mutters, but adds with a wry smile as he looks up, 'but, nice call anyway.' He resumes lathering his underpants. 'Wish I could give her a good blast too.'

By seven we are already on the outskirts of Manang, and climbing up to Tengi, the last permanent settlement before the pass. Manang lies below, the prayer flags fluttering in the breeze. On the other side of the valley a turquoise, glacier-fed lake is surrounded by steep moraines and towered over by Gangapurna, stark white in the blue sky. Moving slowly, I watch my warm breath forming visible vapour clouds. We are no longer walking along the source of the Marsyangdi Khola. It is quiet, silent, the air pure. I feel fresh and pure myself, far from the daily turmoil of the world.

We have ascended above the tree-line. The last of the dwarf birches are below us on the other side of the river. To the north more Himals emerge over the valley sides, peaks I had not seen before. A yak-herd drives several yak along a shadowed ridge where they are momentarily silhouetted against the mountains, imprinted indelibly like a black-and-white photograph on my mind.

We study the other side of the valley with binoculars, searching for blue sheep. An old man, fingering well-worn prayer beads, mumbles 'Om Mani Padme Hum'; he has only one tooth, prominently displayed like a solitary bowling-pin, just left of centre. He motions to ask Easy if he can look through the binoculars. Easy hands them to him and the old man peers through the lens, then lurches violently backwards as he recoils at the apparent nearness of the mountains. Without removing the binoculars from his eyes, he corrects his stance and leans forward, balancing himself just before he falls on his face, then sways just as far backwards. He pulls the glasses from his eyes to regain equilibrium, laughs selfconsciously, single stained tooth protruding, and sits down cross-legged. He looks through the binoculars again in relative safety, moving backwards and forwards with less alarming effect.

Shay watches in amusement then concludes, 'This is one of those moments in life that you remember years later, and would give anything to be able to relive.'

It does have that quality about it. We continue climbing. Shay is winded, and Easy has the squitters badly, so we stick to our original plan of stopping at a *bhaati* facility at Letdar, at just over four-thousand metres.

Letdar is a simple outpost consisting of a couple of desolate *bhaatis* set up purely for trekkers; we are the only trekkers stopping there, and take a mud room with ceiling and walls covered in blue plastic sheets to keep out the draughts and debris. We name it the 'Blue Suite'. Despite the sheeting, it is uncomfortably cold and draughty, and the blue décor makes it psychologically even colder. So we brave the elements and wait outside for our dinner to be cooked as it begins to snow. Down in the valley a swirling snowstorm congeals around Manang.

Some fifty differently hued yak are poised silently around us: black, black-and-white, brown, brown-and-white. A huge brown specimen without horns resembles a North American bison. Threading the field of yaks, a couple of trekkers arrive and decide to stay at the same *bhaati*. 'Canadian doctors,' they inform us with self-assurance, as if handing out business cards. They shake our hands and proceed to attempt to pigeonhole us too. Easy claims he is a life-guard on California's beaches.

'What do you have to do?' the matriarch of the two asks, not sure whether she should believe him.

Shay answers on Easy's behalf. 'He pumps iron to make himself look good, and chases the girls to make himself feel even better.' The two Canadian doctors are out of their depth. 'He used to be a walking hormone,' Shay adds, then reflects, 'He's cooled down considerably recently.'

The male Canadian doctor takes a roll of toilet paper from his backpack and disappears to the back of the *bhaati*. His better half explains defensively, 'He's got a bit of a headache. Nothing serious. Definitely not altitude sickness.'

With snow swirling around us we go to bed. Our 'Blue Suite' is more like a mausoleum. The Diamox tablets take their effect and I crawl out of my protective cocoon several times during the night to pee in the cold outside. Admiringly I hear Shay urinating into a plastic mineral water bottle in the relative warmth of the room, and I lie awake fantasising how she does it with such accuracy, not being equipped the way I am.

LETDAR–PHEDI

A fresh layer of snow covers the ground. Gossamer clouds against a contrasting deep-blue backdrop float dizzily about. The mountainsides appear less threatening, the heavy snowfall having filled the aggressive columns and crevices and covered the jagged rock outcrops. Fifty sugar-coated yak pose motionless around us.

We are sitting outside on a wooden bench cleared of snow, our backs to the wall of the *bhaati* which acts as a sun-trap, waiting for *dal bhaat* to be served, when the two doctors step sleepily out of their room. The woman casually examines her face in a splintered mirror hanging on an exterior wall. Her half-awake expression soon changes. 'Bob! Bob!' she yells in desperation. 'Come here! Quick!'

Bob scurries awkwardly from the back of the building, hoisting trousers *en route*.

'Look!' She sticks her tongue out. Her tongue is black. He sticks his tongue out. It too is black. 'Let's see your tongues!' she commands us.

One after another the three of us obediently flop out our more-or-less pink tongues.

'Bob, isn't there a fatal rare disease where the first sign is a black tongue?' Their faces are squelched together, vying for visions of their black tongues in the tiny sliver of a broken mirror.

Shay smiles nonchalantly. 'Did you both have upset stomachs last night?' she asks.

'Yes,' the matriarch replies in surprise.

'That's why you've got black tongues,' Shay explains with a logic that escapes the rest of us.

'What . . .?'

'Of course . . . You took some pills for your upset stomach, didn't you?' The two doctors nod. 'They are made out of charcoal and have made your tongues black.'

The two humbled Canadians trundle off, upwards along the barren, snow-laden valley.

On a patch of level ground on the other side of the mountainside, Easy spots a herd of thirty bharal, commonly known as blue sheep. The large male has horns shaped like a 1940s hairstyle, parted in the middle, the horns sweeping upwards and down, and slightly back. His body sports distinct black markings on the underbelly and in front. They look very strange, it is hard to make out if they are deer, goat or sheep, but none of them is blue. Easy tells me they zoologically connect true wild sheep with goats.

The valley, carved by a glacier, sports textbook lateral moraine lines on its sides. An oddly shaped waterfall hangs frozen. Further up the valley, to the north, vertical mountain faces disguise the fact that there is any possibility of climbing out of this apparent dead end.

Much, much later, lost in my solipsistic world of thoughts, alone, walking on automatic pilot, I pass deserted yak-herd huts. I hear a whistle. Someone by the huts signals for me to come back down. I do, and find the 'deserted' yak-herd huts are in fact the infamous bhaati at Phedi, the last stop before crossing the dreaded Thorong La. Without being alerted, I would have continued up to the pass.

Inside the packed bhaati, Carrot Head argues with the woman running the lodge. A protruding lower lip hangs limply from his face, contrasting with a tight upper lip revealing bad teeth. His head is narrow, as if it had been formed by squeezing it in a vice, and is camouflaged in orange freckles matching his hair. 'Hhow can it be so expensive? Fifty-five rupees is too much for one bed, for one night.'

This is the equivalent of one dollar.

She simply shrugs, signifying, 'If you don't like it, leave.'

The three unfriendly Germans we met in Tal have come back down Thorong La suffering headaches and signs of altitude sickness. The two boys and the girl collapse in a heap against a wall.

There is a medieval atmosphere in the dark main room, with its low wooden rafters and stone slab floor. The shadowy images of travellers sitting hunched over tables are revealed by the light coming through a hole in the roof as the trekkers collectively cram over guidebooks outlining their big climb tomorrow.

An ageing leprechaun of an Irishman, wearing a green waterproof oil jacket which reaches down to his mid-thighs, and apparently nothing else, struts into the room. His arms have shrunk sufficiently with the cold that only his fingertips protrude from the sleeves of the jacket. His attention is drawn to the sucking sounds of a water filter. 'What in the dear name of Jesus is that?'

'A water filter,' the more vocal Canadian doctor volunteers on her husband's behalf. 'It cost two-hundred-and-forty dollars, Canadian, at Mountain Co-op. You can buy it for less in the States, probably for about two-hundred, but with the exchange rate difference, it's only about ten bucks cheaper.'

'Why don't you use iodine tablets then? Cheaper. That thing must weigh a ton. You carrying that?'

Before he can answer, his wife does. 'We use boiled water, filter it, and put iodine tablets in to be safe. There are all kinds of diseases and microbes that . . .'

'Ah yes, I know all about that. Rather carry a microbe in me stomach than that thing on me back.' A Nepalese enters the room. The Irishman stands to attention, clicks his heels together, his right hand sliding out of the protective coat sleeve as if triggered by a spring mechanism: he salutes, his outfacing palm bouncing up and down in front of a grey lock of hair cutely curled on his forehead. The Nepalese boy giggles and puts a pot of tea down in front of him, and salutes back. The Irishman's jacket is pulled up in his greeting, revealing khaki shorts beneath. He has white socks pulled up to his knees and

[62]

well-polished black boots. 'As you were.' He sits down rubbing his hands together for warmth.

The female doctor complains to the boy as he goes out. 'We would like some light in here. It is too dark to read.'

'Go outside, madam. I think plenty of light outside.' Which is true.

This makes her almost apoplectic with rage. 'We are also very cold in here,' she accuses him.

The door opens and Carrot Head with his loose-hanging lower lip peers around the door. 'Don't you dare come in here! Go on, get away with you, shoo!' the Irishman shouts, standing up, flinging his hands at him as if shooing away chickens. The carrot head disappears. 'Obnoxious specimen. He's been following me all the way up here. His parents must have given him money and told him to go away for ever. I would have done the same. Ohh, the stories I could tell you about him don't bear repeating.'

The Canadian doctors inform an entourage of Canadian eager beavers gathered around them, 'We took out student loans all those years to get our medical degrees. Now we can't even earn enough with the lousy British Columbia medical system the way it is to pay back our loans. Luckily the interest rates on student loans are real low so we'll keep them outstanding as long as possible and buy some real estate. If property values keep rising in Vancouver, the way they have, we should be able to do real well. Our profession is recession-proof you know, so we can trade up every time there are bad times. But prices are starting to get out of hand with all the Chinese specu-lators, before we get a chance to get into the market . . .' She pulls the zipper of her Goretex jacket up tight. 'We got a friend to bring our climbing equipment out so we wouldn't have to buy anything here. We'll sell the stuff for what we bought it at, and with the money get some Tibetan carpets in Kathmandu real cheap and send them back by ship unless we meet someone heading to Vancouver before us. Look great on a living-room floor. In Indonesia we got some real deals . . .' She pauses briefly to take a breath. Their travels are defined in terms of what they bought, how they sent it home, and where it will fit in their imaginary home if they can just get into the real estate market in time before the Hong Kong immigrants push the market higher, before they can 'ratchet up'. 'Our friend said prices of real estate back in Canada . . .' She drones on, with an annoying habit of dragging out all syllables with the letter 's', like a snake hissing.

The Nepalese boy comes in again, pushing the door open with his foot, both hands laden with plates of food. The doctors have eaten their boiled potatoes which they have meticulously peeled. 'Close the door!' she directs.

An American woman reprimands her, 'Give him a chance. He can't serve food and close the door at the same time.'

One clear sign of altitude sickness is irritation, and the only ones up here not exhibiting signs of altitude sickness are the Nepalese staff, who have more reason than any to be irritated. With a rising atmosphere of tension, the Canadian group decide to get up at three in the morning to start their crossing of Thorong La. They disappear to their sleeping-quarters.

Like an officer addressing his soldiers about to climb out of the trenches for the final assault on the enemy, the Irishman announces, 'It's over the top tomorrow, me boys. No matter what happens, it's into the land of milk and honey on the other side. Apple pies, pizza, private rooms, real toilets.' He refers to the famous hospitality of the Thakhalis, professional *bhaati* owners along the Thak Khola stretch of the Kali Gandaki River.

We retire to bed early. In the passageway I hear Carrot Head tell his porter, 'Tomorrow we go at four o'clock. No tea, no food. We leave here four, understand? No waiting.'

Shay shows me her trick of cutting the neck off a plastic mineral water bottle so one can pee into it with greater ease. I understand how I can pee into it effortlessly, but I am still not sure how she does it with such accuracy on a dark night. 'Good night,' Shay bids us as Easy blows out the candle.

'Good night,' I reply, 'Don't let the bed bugs bite.'

'Andrew?'

'Yes.'

'If you are Canadian, how come you sound English sometimes?'

'I went to English schools.'

'In England?'

'In Hong Kong, India, Kenya, Scotland, Singapore.'

'So, where are your roots?'

It is dark, we cannot see each other, rendering the conversation once more unreal. 'I don't know. I have a British and Canadian passport. Most of my life I've lived and worked in Africa or Asia. Now I've emigrated to Norway.' I sound, and feel, like a cultural nomad.

'And home is . . .'

'Home is where my head is.'

'You mean your heart?'

'I mean both.'

'You're a Westerner,' Easy offers in the dark, trying to be helpful.

'I'm not even that,' I contradict, contemplating how comfortable I can feel among rural Nepalese, or Bangladeshis, Indonesians and Africans for that matter.

'He's a human,' Shay says protectively.

'I'm a Martian,' I counter. Despite my extraterrestrial leanings, I drink a litre of water to keep me hydrated during the night. My lips, left knee-cap and fingertips tingle after I take the prescribed Diamox tablets.

PHEDI–MUKTINATH

It is cold during the night. The Diamox pills take their effect and I have to urinate urgently. I fumble in the dark for the bottle Shay gave me. The blackness in our room is absolute, as if I am blind. Without getting out of bed, I slide the upper part of my body from the sleeping-bag and pull down my thermal underwear. Leaning prone to the side, I delicately stretch my reluctant penis and point it over the edge of the bottle, tilting the plastic receptacle so there is no splashing sound to wake Shay or Easy. It seems an eternity before anything trickles out of my flaccid member. Lying in bed and urinating is not a habit, and it is hard for my brain to get the message through to my bladder that it is OK, just this once, to pee in bed. I repeat this process several times during the night until it almost becomes a reflex action. Shay amazes me with her dexterity and accuracy, as I hear her urinate sightlessly into her bottle. Easy obviously has an expandable bladder.

At three in the morning, reading the luminescent dials on my watch, I hear the Canadian doctors getting themselves organised. I have to pee again, and I fumble around for the bottle. Half-asleep, I wriggle part way out of my sleeping-bag, pull down my underpants, and tilt the bottle so that I do not wake up Shay and Easy with the splash. This time, however, the bottle is full to the brim, and as I tip it, the contents pour over me, my sleeping-bag and the mattress.

'Damn!' I crawl angrily out of the urine-soaked bag, flip the drenched mattress over and fumble around in my back-pack to extract a dry set of thermal underwear.

'Andrew?' Shay asks, more or less asleep.

'Yes.'

'You all right?'

'I've peed my bed.'

'Oh.'

I brave the freezing cold and empty my bladder against the outside wall, which I should have done in the first place, before returning shivering into our room, and slipping back into a frozen sleeping-bag. Two hours later we wake up and begin packing. The sky outside lightens. I explain to Easy and Shay what happened, and to excuse me if I smell particularly odious.

Today is the big day. Easy will propose to Shay. And by the skin of my teeth, I'm still with them. Inside the dining-area there is chaos as nervous, tired and irritable trekkers simultaneously demand their breakfast orders. 'I want my porridge, now!' insists a German in luminescent green Lycra body-suit, dominated by bubble glacier sunglasses perched on his forehead, waving high-tech collapsible walking-sticks, much as if he were a spectacular praying mantis about to decapitate its prey.

It is a beautiful day outside as we begin our climb. We are determined to take our time and enjoy ourselves and take the whole day 'to go over the top'. Soon we pass the Canadian doctors sitting by the path explaining to a group of compatriot sycophants, 'Urinary tract infections are common. If you experience burning . . .'

Easy has to stop. He has the runs, but endures it stoically. The Canadians leapfrog past us again, still talking medicine. 'Antibiotics should be taken if the temperature is more than one hundred degrees . . .'

Catching up, Easy tells us breathlessly, 'I just saw two human femur bones on a rock outcrop. I wonder if they are from a sky burial. Tibetans sometimes place the body of the deceased on a rock, you know, hack the body apart, and leave it for the vultures to consume.'

It is hardly surprising that cremation is not practised here. There is no wood, there are no trees, just a moonscape of rocks, like a desert, covered in a layer of snow. It is cold, but the effort of walking up the steep path soon has us wet with perspiration. We are surrounded by impossibly huge mounds of glacial moraine. Remnants of glaciers hang suspended from the rock face, massive overhangs defying Newtonian laws of physics, waiting to crash down into the pass. Vulnerable plump birds, white with black striping on their brown bodies, with yellow beaks and legs, flee up the scree. I look them up in my bird book. Tibetan ptarmigan, a mountain-dwelling grouse.

We march slowly. Shay is tired, and suffering a throbbing headache. Easy is weak from his stomach problems. For the first time, I am the fittest of the three of us.

The Canadians leapfrog past us again. 'Hyperventilation can . . .' The female doctor has a cold and a trail of discarded pink toilet paper follows her up the path. At a bend in the track we come unexpectedly across the Canadians clustered around one of the girls, lying on the ground.

The female doctor pulls a stethoscope out from her jacket faster than a cowgirl pulling her six-gun, and checks the heart rate of the prone girl. She fires orders. There is nothing we can do, with two zealous doctors in attendance.

'After priming that group for auto-induced medical problems, the Human Gods finally got their wish,' Easy says cynically.

The sparkle has gone from Shay's eyes, and the spring from her walk, which is now just a lacklustre shuffle. 'This isn't fun at all,' she sighs, despite our intentions to make this a wonderful day. We are higher now than the bottom of the surrounding glaciers. Behind, the Annapurnas glitter in the bright sun. A cairn beside the path is a poignant reminder of the dangers of high altitude:

Richard James Allen
Age 27
Died 24th February 1991 of AMS.
Trekkers Beware

After several false passes, the summit of Thorong La at five-thousand four-hundred metres above sea level appears unexpectedly and anticlimactically. The snow-covered high mountain pass between the Marsyangdi and Kali Gandaki rivers systems is heralded by multi-coloured prayer flags fluttering from stone cairns. From the top of the pass we can peer down into the valley of the Kali Gandaki and the Kingdom of Mustang.

Mustang. Even the name has a magical quality about it. 'We made it to the top of the dreaded Thorong La,' Easy exclaims. Easy and Shay cry, hugging each other tightly in their emotional outburst. I drift away discreetly, not wishing to be an unwitting impediment to Easy's elaborate plans for betrothal and Shay's fervent wishes for the same.

One of the two unfriendly German boys from Tal sits on a rock writing his journal. The other German boy stands a few metres behind him, covertly reading the same journal through a pair of binoculars over the unsuspecting scribe's shoulder. The probable cause of the espionage, the German girl, sits conspicuously, and unaware, by herself.

Shay and Easy are huddled together on a cairn, emotional. I sidle up to them, curious to see if Easy did propose. Kirsten has packed my favourite chocolate which has gravitated to the bottom of my pack. 'Have some real Norwegian chocolate. Carried all the way up here just for this occasion.' I extend pieces of frozen, previously melted chocolate carnage.

'No thanks. I'm not feeling well. Easy?'

'Thanks but no thanks.'

Shay reaches out to me, 'Come here.' As I bend over she pulls me towards her and gives me a bear hug, then a tearful Easy and I hug each other. 'We made it.'

'Yes.'

'We all had our doubts at one stage or another.'

'Yes.' I wait impatiently to hear their big news.

Finally Shay grabs my hand. 'Easy's proposed.'

'What!' I feign incredulity.

'Yeah. He says to me, "Shay do you mind marrying me?"'

'What'd you answer?'

'That I didn't mind marrying him.' She stands up, the romance of the situation overridden by waves of nausea. 'Let's get off of here. My head is banging to bursting point. I'm going to be sick if we stay up here much longer and I don't want to ruin my memories of this place.'

I take a long, last look down the path we have just come up. The incredible view of Annapurnas III and IV and Gangapurna has disappeared behind the walls of closer mountains behind us. We turn our backs on Manang and the dreaded Thorong La and take off, hurtling down the snow-covered, pebbly trail towards Muktinath.

The descent is more difficult than the ascent, and after an hour my bamboo ski-pole becomes indispensable as a means of cushioning the interminable jolting on my cartilage-less left knee, the outcome of a series of operations to reconstruct the ligament-damaged joint.

At a makeshift tea-house in a derelict herders' hut, I catch up with Shay and Easy who lie debilitated on the ground. Strangely, my headache has returned during the descent.

'I can see villages,' Shay points to rusty-hued oases against an otherwise monotonous desert-like brown landscape. 'They seem so far away, and don't seem to get closer as we go down.' The rolling plateaux and hills to the north are Mustang, the Kingdom of Lo Mantang, and after that, Tibet. 'I can hardly believe I'm actually here, as if it were all a dream, or a film,' Shay says.

Descending from the pass on the holy site of Muktinath is an anticlimax; it was not meant to be approached from above. The ragged assembly of temples in a stone-walled compound is a disappointment. Muktinath village, or Ranipawa as it is more correctly known locally, is simply a collection of lodges. Muktinath itself is the holy temple grounds, enclosed within a stone wall, where it is forbidden to camp or stay. Apart from one large historical stone building constructed expressly to house pilgrims, the collection of small *bhaatis* has been built for Westerners since the trekking route was opened in 1977.

A sign proclaims, rather enticingly given my personal hygiene problems: 'Hot shower at 2 mins. far.' In the distance, a lonely path follows the contours of the hill, away from the lodges. Another sign proclaims: 'Hot shower at 1 min. far.' I am reeking, and the lure of hot showers preoccupies my mind far more than the holy site of Muktinath.

Easy finds us a lodge, the Blue Moon: its name alone conjures a different world from that of the other side of Thorong La. The three of us are destined once again to share a three-bed room, but a Swedish boy and an American girl who have just met are in a double, and I ask if they would let Easy and Shay sleep there, while we share the triple. 'They *are* engaged you know,' I say, rationalising my request and using

[69]

Easy's recent marriage proposal as leverage. We change rooms, and Easy and Shay have a room to themselves, at last.

I am both curious to see the 'Hot Shower' and eager to wash. In the dwindling twilight, equipped with towel and soap, I trustingly follow the solitary path away from the comforting tatters of civilisation. I have no idea what to expect; a man sitting outside beside a huge cauldron of boiling water, a roaring log fire underneath? Where would the firewood come from? There are no trees to speak of at this high altitude. Instead of a boiling pot over an open fire, there is a steel pipe, thirty centimetres in diameter, running from the direction of the Muktinath temples above to enter one side of a nondescript cement structure, pass through the building and out the other side and down the valley: a mini-hydroelectric power station.

Two shower stalls fronted by a board with complicated instructions beside a control panel with flashing red and green lights and banks of gauges indicate temperature and pressure and other esoteric information. Sounds of ecstasy and steam emanate from one of the two shower stalls. A diminutive Nepalese attendant appears and explains to me, 'This is hydroelectric power station made from water coming through Muktinath temple grounds to supply electricity to small villages in valley below.'

It is particularly auspicious for the valley to be lit up by electricity derived from the holy waters from the temple grounds. Muktinath has been a pilgrimage site for at least two-thousand years because of holy flames that burn out of the ground, rocks and spring. Now electrical 'flames' light up mud homes. No need to visit the holy temple. Just the flick of a switch, and the holiness inspired by these magical waters casts aside the evil shadows of darkness in the comfort of one's own sanctuary. A British company has designed the newly constructed shower system so excess hydroelectricity stored up during the day is used to heat water. What better use for all that hot water than to shower filthy trekkers who have just crossed Thorong La? At twenty rupees for a five-minute wash in the steaming holy waters, it is a bargain. The occupied shower stall opens, and a naked American girl wrapped in a towel steps out briefly to reach for her shampoo. 'Hi,' she says, and ducks back into her shower.

'Twenty rupees, five minutes. You tell me when you ready,' the ex-Gurkha army soldier informs me. I peel off the requisite bank notes.

In the cold twilight, standing in front of a blinking control panel, I strip off, about to have a steaming hot shower from the holy waters of Muktinath, with the Kingdom of Mustang, one of the most isolated places left in the world, about me. I have five minutes in the steaming privacy of a shower stall, during which consecrated water pours over me, to ponder this auspicious occasion. The shower is hot and as spiritual an experience as I am ever likely to have in the confines of a wet cement cubicle. When my five minutes are up, the American girl is still in her steaming shower and I begin to feel there is some sexism here. Short holy hot showers for the guys, long holy hot showers for the girls. Perhaps her sins are worse than mine for she couldn't possibly be filthier. When she exits, the steaming water is still running.

'That was a long shower,' I say, probing for an explanation.

She smiles radiantly as she adroitly dresses within the privacy of a bath towel. 'I really needed a shower badly. I paid one-hundred rupees to have twenty-five minutes worth. I've been holding back on asking for hot water at the lodges. You know, saving wood and all that. It's so nice to have a shower and not feel guilty about it. Know what I mean?'

The money collected from the showers, which must be a considerable sum in peak season, goes towards building a community school. Considering the lack of showering facilities on the 'Other Side' of Thorong La, and the large number of foul trekkers descending the pass, they should be able to build a university here during the productive life of the shower stalls.

At the Blue Moon, Easy and Shay are already seated around a dining-room-sized 'hot table', with burning coals in a bucket placed underneath. To seal in the foot-warming heat, a blanket is draped over the tabletop, dropping over the sides and wrapping around our laps, as if it were a communal hot water bottle. There is a dinner-party atmosphere in the room. Everyone is happy, having crossed the dreaded Thorong La and surviving Acute Mountain Sickness, pulmonary oedema, cerebral oedema, diarrhoea, freezing temperatures, hunger and unwashed bodies. Although still well over four-thousand metres, we are all acclimatised. Cold beer is served, and a varied menu whets the appetite.

We recount our Thorong La experiences. After a five-minute shower in hot holy waters, I feel sufficiently sanitised to confess to all and sundry my own nocturnal ablution problems at Phedi. A New Zealander, who has a body builder's top-heavy, wedge-shaped frame, tells us about his notable experience on the 'Other Side'.

'When I reached Pisang I was freezing. I can't fit into my damned Nepalese sleeping-bag, it's only big enough for me to pull up to my navel. I couldn't sleep with the cold, so I got up early in the morning and headed for Manang; listened to the doctor-talk-show about altitude sickness. That lecture got the wind up me, but I didn't have enough time on my trekking permit to slow down so I carried on to Letdar to stay at the lodge. Set my alarm and fell asleep. Woke up with a raging headache, and thought, "Fuck! I've got altitude sickness, if I go to sleep again I'm going to wake up dead." I looked at my alarm clock. Five o'clock in the morning, so I thought I might as well get up and go on to Phedi. It was dark outside, and as I walked, I thought, "Hmm, that's funny, it's not getting lighter." Hours later I arrived at Phedi, and it was still dark. I didn't know what was going on. Some trekkers were getting up to climb Thorong La. I asked them what time it was. Three-thirty in the morning. I unpacked my alarm clock. It said three-thirty in the morning. I turned it upside down, it showed ten o'clock. I realised when I had woken up thinking it was five, it must have been ten-thirty in the evening. So I decided to keep going anyway and climbed Thorong La. Basically I walked from Pisang to here in one go, with a three-hour stop in Letdar.'

This is his second night here. He spent the whole day yesterday sick, recuperating and sleeping off his exertions. Having now fostered a beer-inspired conversational head of steam, he goes on to tell us he has been travelling around Africa and Asia for half a year. 'I can tell you about every single day and night during these last six months, right now, without looking at a diary. Before this trip, I taught at a school in London, and I'd have trouble remembering a specific day or night of that whole year.' He contemplates for a minute, and obviously does remember a night or two in London. 'Mind you I haven't had a good bonk in the last six months either and if I don't get one soon I'll be carrying my balls back to New Zealand in a wheelbarrow.' Despite his avowed problem, there are no amenable bonkers around the dinner table to alleviate his gut-wrenching condition.

The Irishman tells us, 'I was coming down from the pass, and me right foot was killing me and me left foot was cold. Couldn't understand it. I took me boots off. Had four woolly socks on one foot, and none on me other foot.'

An orange head with freckles peers around the door. The Irishman sees Carrot Head. 'Oh no. Dear Jesus, not again! The Red Scourge of Asia. Don't look. Maybe he'll go away if we ignore him.' The Scourge is undaunted by the comment. 'He's the bane of my life. There's enough people now in these mountains know about him, they won't stay in the same lodge. Can you imagine, here in Muktinath, with the lodges almost all full, and his is empty? I'm not kidding you. He's the only one in his lodge. No one will stay with him.'

The Red Scourge of Asia comes in and lights a cigarette. A New Yorker instructs him, 'No one else is smoking here, maybe you should ask if we mind.' He squeezes the end of the cigarette out.

Grant, the New Zealander, says, 'Don't just stand there. You're making me nervous. Sit down.' The Red Scourge sits down.

We eat and soon the conversation is interrupted by the orange-head, whose dream is to emigrate to America. He lights a cigarette under the table, and soon the smell of tobacco wafts up.

'I thought we agreed that we weren't smoking,' the New Yorker says.

'No one else says that,' the Scourge replies.

'Does anyone object if we make this a non-smoking table?' the American insists, looking around the table. No one objects. 'So put your cigarette out. Or leave.'

'Hwhy should I?'

'Because, I'll tell you because. Here are some people that will talk to you, and what do you do? You act obnoxious so that they don't like you. Don't you care? If you want to smoke, go outside.'

'It's too cold outside.'

'Then go to your own lodge.'

'There is nobody there.'

'Exactly. Nobody wants to stay in the same hotel as you. These people are polite to you and you are being an ass-hole Think about it.' Under the relentless pressure from the American, the Scourge gets up and stands a couple of metres away, cigarette smoke curling from behind his back. 'Not there. Just go away.' The American is insistent. Finally the Red Scourge of Asia settles against a wall some metres away, smoking. For the rest of the evening Carrot Head stands forlornly, listening, no longer part of the group. He wants to be part of

[73]

the camaraderie, but is unable to extend himself to accommodate the others' wishes.

Despite this incident, there is a good atmosphere by the time we all go to our rooms. In our bedroom the Swede, who cleans nuclear reactors for a living and has half a year off annually with pay, to de-radiate, tells the American girl how great Sweden is. I wonder whether he will glow blue and yellow during the night. Through the paper-thin walls between our rooms, I hear the familiar sound of Shay using her bottle.

MUKTINATH–KAGBENI

Mustang. I can hardly believe I am here.

As children, my siblings and I were brought up in isolated corners of Asia and Africa. At boarding-school in Delhi, both my brother and I, the only non-Indians, came home after the first term speaking a barely intelligible Indian-rendered English. Our inflections were authentic. At eight years old, I was like a parrot. It is an accent I can still assume all too easily when speaking with Indians.

The first taste of the Himalayas had come from spending the summer months on a houseboat in Kashmir. My father, a foreign correspondent, had an eclectic taste for the unusual and the shelves at assorted homes were lined with books from exotic backwaters of the world. A whole section of our movable library was devoted to Tibet and Nepal. One of my favourite modes of escape, as a socially inept and unqualified teenager in Canada, had been reading Michel Peissel's *Mustang: The Forbidden Kingdom*. As one of the first Westerners to go to Mustang, in the spring of 1964, the Frenchman published his account of the trip in 1967. Not so many years later, the same trip can be undertaken by armchair travellers. Having read about this exotic destination so many years ago, I have difficulty taking in that I am really here.

The air is dry, like a desert, but considerably warmer than the other side of Thorong La towards Manang. Snow lies only on the north-facing slopes, protected from the glare of the sun. To the south, east and west, snow-plastered Himals and Just Hills pierce the sky; to the north sprawls the immense Tibetan Plateau.

Shay and Easy sleep in, taking advantage of their private room, and no doubt savouring their new-found status as an engaged couple. I meander alone through the crowded alleys of the fortress village of nearby Jharkot. The fortress's crumbling double perimeter walls are made of packed mud and timber, some metres thick. Sitting omnipotent on the spur of a ridge, with my back to the fort, I have a panoramic view of the surrounding valley. At the bottom of the Dzong Khola, the Fortress River, lies the village of Kagbeni on the eastern bank of the Kali Gandaki River, running south from Tibet through the Himals. At the top of this adjoining valley, Muktinath, straddling either side of the valley, fortress-dominated villages.

Who warred here? The ancient Kingdom of Jumla against the Kingdom of Mustang? Or were the fortresses minor fiefdoms, each one protecting its own section of river valley?

Surrounding Jharkot, brown fields lie fallow now that the harvest of buckwheat, barley and maize has been reaped. Within weeks I have almost witnessed a complete season, from the verdant green paddy growing around Dumre, to the dry fallow fields being prepared for next year's crop before the arrival of winter. Summer and winter collided. Most of the roughly terraced fields have already been ploughed. Unworked fields are dotted with heaps of conical basket *doko*-shaped dung, waiting to be ploughed under. Children, robed in grey Tibetan-style *chupas*, file past with their baskets full of manure, singing as they walk to the fields. A man whistles to his yak-sized *zopkio* to encourage it to pull a wooden, steel-tipped plough through the dusty earth.

As I stand on the ramparts of the old fortress, my shadow is cast long, descending to the fields below. The sun warms my back. How much easier to feel at peace in the awesome nature and simple lifestyle of these mountains and people, far away from the daily demands and pressures of our high-paced, high-tech, stressful and materialistic Western lives. The thought occurs to me, the major reason for the simplicity, and even the attractiveness, of life here is the exclusion of vehicles, of any kind. There are not even any bicycles, let alone motorised means of transport. What would our Western world be like in these circumstances? Vehicles are certainly convenient in many respects for modern life, but with the overabundance of cars and concomitant problems of pollution, the planet could arguably be better off without them. Two little girls disturb my contemplations. 'This my?' she points at my pencil.

'No, this my,' I reply.

She giggles. 'This my?' She grabs my notebook.

'This?' her tiny sister repeats, learning the tricks of the trade. The bigger girl looks for pictures in my notebook. Seeing nothing interesting enough, she gives it back to me. 'School-going-to-pen? Hello, hello, pen.'

A boy joins us. 'Where are you?'

He has got the idea right, but forgotten to add, 'coming from'. Stage fright I suppose.

'Jharkot,' I reply. 'Where are you?'

He laughs, the extent of his English pushed to the limits and he continues happily on his way to the fields. Although I am unable to communicate efficiently with these children, their laughter and humour rub off on me.

A Tibetan mandala painting on the wall of the Jharkot *gompa* depicts the essential aspects of the Buddha's teachings. In the centre are depicted a pig, a cock and a snake, respectively representing the three cardinal faults of delusion, passion and hatred. The Buddha, who laid great stress on moral responsibility, had taught: 'This bad action which is yours was not done by your mother or your father or by anyone else. You alone have done this bad action, you alone will reap its fruit.' Only by overcoming craving, hatred and delusion can one achieve Enlightenment, or nirvana. The main part of the mandala circle is divided into six spheres of existence: the realm of the gods, of the rebel gods, of the ghosts, of the hells hot and cold, of the animal world and of human beings. An inner ring depicts those who deteriorate spiritually and end in hell, and those who advance towards nirvana. The outer ring depicts the twelve links of dependent origination. Holding the whole is the fierce Mara, the personification of death with long canine teeth and a crown of skulls.

I walk through Ranipawa in the morning: late-rising trekkers recovering from Thorong La wait patiently in line for their Holy Hot Showers. The hydroelectric showers command a better attendance record among visiting Westerners than the once-popular old temple grounds with the burning flames.

An oasis of poplar trees in the Muktinath grounds lends a peaceful atmosphere to one of the most sacred sites for both Hindus and Buddhists. Guidebooks inform me the site is mentioned in Hindu writing as long ago as three-hundred years BC. Hindus gave the site significance because of the awesome natural gas flames burning on the surface of the stream, from the earth and out of the solid rocks. The flames were, and still are interpreted by Hindus as an offering from Brahma, the creator.

It is not difficult to imagine the awe of early wanderers after weeks climbing up the Kali Gandaki, on arrival at this remote site at the foot of Khatung Kang, which towers some additional two-thousand-plus metres overhead. The setting does exude a sense of being the home of the gods. The dilapidated condition of the Jwala Mai Temple in which the miraculous flames burn is rather a surprise in the context of the religious significance of Muktinath.

There are three 'windows' strategically placed flush with a worn, cracked, black-and-white marble-tiled floor, directly in front of the statues of deities. I get down on my knees, not in supplication, but so that I can see into the cunningly designed windows at floor level. I draw the curtains back to peer into the cavity. The first window's flames are extinguished. In the centre window I can hear the spring trickling, and see the faint blue of flames burning. In the window on the right, blue flames flicker, dancing from the earth.

The whole temple has been built to enshrine these flames. It is not particularly impressive in the days of television, videos, lasers, CD-ROMS and nuclear bombs, but must have been so to people two-thousand years ago. My own contemporary imagination is ignited by these flames, but there is no religious fervour.

Outside, I wash my hands and face in the waters spewing out of a golden calf's head attached to the base of the temple. It cannot hurt to perform one's ablutions in these waters and indulge in a bit of divine insurance.

Back at the Blue Moon for lunch, Easy says, 'We're heading down to Kagbeni. Coming?'

I feel the peer pressure again. After wanting to get to Mustang for so long, and with so much time on my trekking permit, it seems a waste to hurry. 'I don't know.'

'We'll be staying at the Red House Lodge. If you stay here tonight you could skip Kagbeni tomorrow and meet us in Marpha.' They leave and I make vague promises to meet them later that evening.

I am drawn back to the peacefulness of the temple grounds. Under the malevolent gaze of a four-armed icon of Vishnu strident within a pagoda-like temple, a sadhu meditates mutely, his worldly possessions in a pitifully small cloth sack beside him. Proffered coins glitter on the bottom of two bathing-pools outside the temple. Behind the temple one-hundred-and-eight elephant and cow heads spew effervescent water, giving the Tibetan name for Muktinath, Chu Mig Gya Tsa Gye, meaning 'the one-hundred-and-eight springs'.

The sadhu packs his bag to begin his walk back to India. He prostrates himself in front of the statue of Vishnu, supreme ruler of change and stability. Like many of India's deities, this angry Vishnu exhibits a great variety of characteristics, reflecting the many local cults that have formed him, including incarnations as Buddha. The sadhu kisses the ground before asking me for a donation.

I listen to the trickling sounds of the stream, smell the earthy freshness of the air, open my eyes and absorb the crisp light, feel the rough texture of the wood I sit on, taste the cold water, sense the gentle breeze on my sun-warmed body. This is a spiritual experience for me and has nothing to do with the four-armed statue waving angrily within the pagoda. Sitting in the speckled sunlight under the banyan, peepul and poplar trees, beside the babbling spring-fed stream, I feel a sense of freedom, peacefulness, of harmony within and without, as if my spirit and body are catching up with each other.

A Tibetan-looking woman on the terrace of a Buddhist *gompa* weaves colourful cotton-thread bracelets. She smiles at me, evidently recognising the feelings I exude. She holds up one of the woven bracelets for my approval, and purchasing it I make a wish as she ties the knot around my wrist.

Shay and Easy have gone to Kagbeni. I leave Muktinath and the Blue Moon Lodge reluctantly, but not before talking to Kharma, the lodge owner. 'Is it possible to go into the forbidden "inner Mustang", across the river, to the Kingdom of Lo, without a special permit, using just a local guide?'

'No is possible,' he tells me definitively.

The area north is still a restricted area. There are various reasons given for this, but sensitivity to the Chinese–Tibetan border is paramount. Mustang is a geographical anomaly, sticking into Tibet like a sore thumb as far as the Chinese are concerned. Although linked to Tibet geographically, ethnically and politically, the Kingdom of Mustang during the late eighteenth century became politically indebted to the Raja of Jumla to the south.

Jumla, then a principality on the southern slopes of Mount Dhauligiri, once ruled over western Nepal and its power extended into India and over great portions of western Tibet, eventually sub-ordinating forty-four small Hindu rajas. The many fortresses lining the Kali Gandaki up to Lo Mantang probably originated over five-hundred years ago, during the time of the confrontations between these ancient kingdoms. Mustang paid taxes to Jumla until the Gurkha 'Nepalese' kings to the south in turn conquered Jumla, and thus Mustang transferred its allegiance in 1795 to the Gurkha kings and eventually became part of modern-day Nepal.

The status of Mustang today is unique in Nepal. A token amount of tax is paid by the King of Mustang, but he is allowed in return to collect any amount of taxes and money from his people and to dispose of this sum. Unlike other areas of Nepal, Mustang pays no land tax to the King of Nepal. It is, in effect, an independent principality within Nepal. Now His Majesty's Government of Nepal allows élite bands of tourists into Mustang proper, with a hundred-dollar-a-day trekking permit payable to the government. The trip can be undertaken only under the auspices of an organised trekking outfit from Kathmandu, with an accompanying 'environment officer', dressed in blue police uniform. Political sensitivity of the area is still given as the official reason for its limited access to tourists.

It must be clear to the politically well-connected Kathmandu-based trekking companies that the local people, with their chain of *bhaatis* extending around the Annapurna Circuit, are organising themselves in such a way as to make overseas or Kathmandu-based companies redundant. To survive, they must open up new frontiers, where they still have a virtual monopoly over foreigners trekking. This seems to me to be the strongest reason for the central government's continuing to keep Mustang in enforced isolation.

I walk down to Kagbeni, my vague promises to Shay and Easy getting the better of me. Two Indians ask me, 'How much further is it to Muktinath?' The one asking the question looks as if he could be a fallen sadhu; the other looks more like a wealthy Indian businessman undertaking the pilgrimage to atone for his sins and to guarantee a good reincarnation.

'Maybe four hours,' I reply, judging their pace, and deliberately avoiding slipping into their heavy Indian accents.

I continue descending the well-worn path towards Kagbeni perched on the banks of the Kali Gandaki. Eroded yellow cliffs on the other side of the Dzong Valley are riddled with holes like Swiss cheese. I surmise they must be man-made caves, thousands of them. Who lived in there? Did monks come to pray around this holiest of sites? Do the caves demarcate the limits of two ancient kingdoms, providing protection in case of hostilities? Are they further evidence of the influence of the Mongolian peoples clashing with the influence of the Indo-Aryans pushing up from the south? Despite the natural barriers of the Himals, wars were fought among kingdoms as far away as Gorkha to the east and Jumla to the west, and allegiances changed constantly. For societies dependent on modern methods of transport, a hundred kilometres across the roadless Himals today seems unmanageable. Five-hundred years ago the distance between Jumla and Mustang would have meant nothing. The sun dips behind the mountains.

A young boy trots up the path on a horse. 'Namaste.'

'Namaste,' I reply.

'What time is it?' he asks, stopping.

Time has become meaningless. 'Four o'clock,' I answer, looking at my watch for the first time in weeks.

'Thank you,' he replies, and trots off, bumping up and down in the saddle.

I stare after him, the figure on the horse getting smaller as he climbs up the trail towards Jharkot and Muktinath. Surely he had no need to know what time it is? I have an uncanny feeling I know the boy. He was smiling as he spoke to me, as if he knew something I did not know. Stopping to ask me the time was a way of communicating with me. But what was he trying to tell me? I turn around again to study his form receding into the distance. Something happened between us. In this lofty place it is easy to read significance into the most commonplace experiences. The feeling is unsettling, if only because I am not sufficiently in touch with my intuition, my inner being, to understand the signals.

At a bend in the trail I stop and turn and stare up the valley at Jharkot and Muktinath. Is this the last time I will ever see Muktinath? The thought makes me sad, and I dwell on the moment to take in a last view of this magnificent place where I have felt so much at peace.

No longer protected by the outcropping ridge, I feel the Kali Gandaki wind blowing hard against me. As the air over the Tibetan plateau heats up during the day, losing its density, it sucks the cooler, denser air of the Himalayas with gale force winds up the Kali Gandaki canyon, filling the partial pressure vacuum created over the sun-warmed plateau of Tibet. Two lammergeiers, large as the Himalayan griffin, effortlessly descend unseen currents of wind. The pair dip lower and lower until they are parallel, escorting me to the medieval fortress village of Kagbeni. Kagbeni's buildings, secured within a protective perimeter of walls, are clumped around its red ochre-washed *gompa* and *dzong* fortress.

Just before entering Kagbeni I am hit with the full force of the Kali Gandaki wind blasting up the river valley. The stone walls are not just for fortification against intruders but also clearly offer protection against the relentless gust of the wind. A dozen yak driven wild-eyed through the narrow alleys of Kagbeni force me to take refuge in a dark corridor leading into an enclosed inner courtyard. There is an overpowering barnyard smell. My foot slides as I step into fresh yak dung. It looks too dismal to be a *bhaati*, but this is in fact Red House Lodge. Run by two Tibetan women who cannot stop laughing at the slightest excuse, Red House Lodge has a peculiar charm. Traditional notched tree-trunks have been replaced by steep, rickety, Western-style staircases. The rooms are a jumble of mismatched cubicles. On the roof a glass-enclosed 'conservatory' is filled with trekkers reading in the fading daylight. Easy and Shay are there.

'Seen the Buddha?' Easy asks me.

I shake my head.

Easy leads me to a heavily padlocked room, the door of which is open, and within which a remarkable gold Buddha, two-storeys high, sits surrounded by photographs of the Dalai Lama, and other more ancient esoteric relics. The room is a reminder of the building's origins as a monastery, long before it became a Khampa hideout and then a *bhaati* for Westerners.

Over dinner Shay asks me, not unkindly, 'Andrew? Have you figured it out?'

'All of it?'

'Whatever.'

'I'm getting there.'

'No conclusions yet?'

'Not yet.' It sometimes seems that the more I know, the less I understand.

As I lie in bed, my thoughts and dreams are haunted by revelations brought on by Shay's questions and the ghosts inhabiting the *bhaati*, until I no longer know what is real and what is not.

KAGBENI

'If you could choose one country to live in, where would it be?' Shay asks me. We eat breakfast on the rooftop, bathed in the warm early morning sunlight, the air crisp, cold, dry and still.

'If I had to stay in one country only, for the rest of my life?'

'OK,' she nods.

I think. 'Now, probably France.'

'But?'

'But, I just wish there weren't so many Frenchmen.'

Shay laughs.

'No, I don't mean that. I just wish the French weren't so chauvinistic.' I try to understand where the question is coming from. 'Going to move there?'

Shay looks at Easy. 'Nah, just wondered what you would say. What's Norway like, and the Norwegians?' Shay is delaying their departure, just as I had tried to do in Upper Pisang.

I play along. 'Norway is nice. Beautiful country, especially in the spring and summer. Winters are dark and too long. Nobody's rich or poor. You feel neither envious of others nor guilty about them. They've avoided most of the problems in the rest of the world. There's a sense of community; their nationalism is pretty outrageous, but they haven't inflicted themselves on other people since the Vikings stomped all over western Europe a thousand years ago, so it just seems quaint rather than obnoxious. They can afford not to be part of the European Union, their economy is fuelled by North Sea oil. Eventually though they'll have to wake up, and join the rest of the world.'

'What about the people?'

'Homogeneous society, Lutherans; good people whom some would describe as dull and provincial, inward-looking. Shy and reserved at the best of times, until they get alcohol into their bloodstream, then they can become the opposite, loud and stupid. Hard to get to know them, but once you do, they are friends for life. I like them,' I conclude.

'Going to stay there?'

'It seems too tribal, too insular. I'll always be an outsider there.'

Easy swings his pack onto his back. 'Coming?' he asks Shay.

I say goodbye to them. We have shared an unforgettable experience, and I could not have had better companions. I would choose each of them as friends, and count myself lucky to have had the privilege of travelling with them for a while. Easy has been the model of what a good Buddhist should be – give or take the odd exception, like a strong attachment to a collection of baseball cards secured in a bank vault. 'Thanks for carrying my pack all those times, Easy.'

'Hey. I should thank you. If it hadn't been for you I probably would have struck out way back there that first night.' He hands me his out-of-date Nepali–English dictionary. 'For you. You'll need it more than me.'

'Thanks.' I flip through well-worn pages. 'Good luck with the base-ball-card collection. Hope it doesn't ruin your chances of hitting the Buddhist equivalent of a home run.'

'Nah. Don't worry. Bases are loaded, I'm on third, pitcher's got a rubber arm and Buddha is up to bat. See you in nirvana.' He gives me a high five.

'Thanks for your company, Shay. Let me know how the wedding goes.' I'll miss her acute observations and her company. 'Write!'

'I will.' We hug quietly. None of us feels much like talking. And then they are gone.

The sadness of breaking away from them is compensated for by the freedom I feel to slow down and take my time. There is a distinct twinge of loneliness as they leave, but I am excited to be in Kagbeni, the northermost town in Mustang District I can visit without paying exorbitant trekking fees. I make arrangements to rent a pony for the day. A small boy goes out to the fields to fetch one. The thought of galloping up to Muktinath, for only ten dollars, is irresistibly appealing.

While I am waiting for the pony, a horrible scene in an adjacent inner courtyard is played before me. In an enclosure, a full-sized Tibetan yak is in the process of being trussed up. He is massive, black, with thick hair reaching down to the ground. His forelegs are tied together. Rope is looped over the right horn and fastened around the foreleg. The ropes are pulled tight so the yak's head is pulled down by the right horn to his forelegs. His neck is twisted, one white-rimmed eye staring at the sky, the other eye almost in the dirt. Uncomfortable, he jumps up and down, but soon tires.

Two wild-looking wranglers with braided pigtails tackle the yak. These are outcast tribe members of 'Shembas', scorned because they are the 'butchers' of Tibet and kill animals. Children watch, especially the boys. The yak's back legs are tied together, then front and back legs are pulled tight as possible and the destabilised animal is pulled onto his side. The head is released, twisted, then stretched out on the ground upside down. A man stands astride with a foot placed on the inside of each curved horn. One of the braided men cuts a small incision in the hide behind the shoulder, then plunges the knife through the incision and into the animal's heart. The killing is intimate. The yak does not react at first, but as the knife and the man's fist are plunged deeper into the cavity, and rotated, the yak struggles to get up.

Ten minutes later the animal is still breathing, clouds of dust billowing from around his nostrils as the knife continues to be twisted viciously. Finally the yak exhibits death throes, kicking violently, stiffening, his body shaking, muscles quivering, horrific snorts and grunts emanating from the depths of its Tibetan soul. It sounds as if it is snoring. There is a final, long, drawn-out groan, the body quivers, the legs thrash. The men begin untying his legs when once again it struggles and grunts before a final exhalation of air wheezes from flared nostrils. This time one of the men cautiously flicks its dulled blue eyes with his fingers to get a reaction, before they untie the legs and begin the butchering process.

'Hello!' A little boy distracts me from the bloodbath.

'Horse?' he asks, uncertain. It is the urchin who has been sent out to fetch it for me. We trekkers probably all look the same to him.

My rented pony is an unhealthy-looking specimen. The Tibetan carpet and saddle on its back disguise protruding backbone, ribs and hips. I mount and the small boy leads the pony with the reins, I presume to see me on my way, but surely not to walk me all the way up to Muktinath? At the edge of the village the pony is unco-operative, refusing to ascend the hill. I reach out to pull a branch of a shrub to use as a riding-crop. 'No, no!' The boy indicates the pony will buck even more. I dig my heels into his corrugated rib-cage. 'No,' the boy suggests again, that will further induce the pony to refuse to budge. I am reduced to sitting like a sack of potatoes on the pony's back, while the boy plays tug-of-war with the scraggly beast.

He is so small, there is not a snowball's chance in hell the boy will make headway in this contest of wills. In half-an-hour we have not progressed an inch. The romantic idea of riding up to Muktinath is receding all the time. The fact is, I am watching the struggle between boy and beast as if I had nothing to do with the affair while sitting on the pony's back. Passing trekkers add to my ignominy, asking mockingly, 'Going somewhere?'

I slip off the horse and give the frustrated groom a hundred rupees before another cluster of sardonic trekkers assemble curiously around us. 'I'll walk,' I inform him.

'You go Muktinath?' he asks.

'Yes,' I reply.

'No horse?' he asks hopefully.

'No horse,' I confirm. He seems eternally grateful this no-win situation should have worked out so agreeably. Walking up to Muktinath, on my own two feet, I feel omnipotent without my back-pack binding me down firmly to earth, as if I could fly, or make astounding leaps with just the minimum of effort, like striding about the moon. It is obvious I am acclimatised to the altitude. The steep walk up seems effortless.

The two Indians I had passed yesterday are now descending the path. I ask the talkative Indian, 'How was Muktinath?' His companion, wearing mirrored aviator's sunglasses, stands to one side.

'Oh, good sir, too much beautiful.' His head wobbles emphatically as he talks. 'It is most beauteous occasion to undertake pilgrimage to Muktinath.' Without my asking, he further explains, 'I am having Master's Degree of Philosophy. Many years I am teaching philosophy at university and many years teaching yoga. Now, I am monk for last seventeen years,' his eyes grow wide with the self-revelation. So do mine. My head totters automatically in synchrony. 'I am sponsored by this good gentleman,' he indicates his companion, 'a rich house-holder,' he lowers his voice conspiratorially, 'to accompany on pilgrimage to Muktinath. All expenses, fooding and lodging, paid.' His eyes open wide again, and his head wobbles dynamically with this juicy information. 'I am fifty years old. No family. I am sadhu, but not begging sadhu. Many sadhus uneducated, and only for begging purposes.' His limp hands writhe about him for emphasis as he chews the words out of his mouth.

The air is so pure, clean, dry.

A man with long braided hair riding a horse, accompanied by two yak, a donkey, several goats and three children trailing behind, descends the trail. Their baggy, black-brown robes contrast with the waves of trekkers clad in the bright colours of form-hugging Lycra and windproof Goretex. One of the psychedelically outfitted, a young Japanese man, sits by the wayside looking quite ill. Green in fact. 'You all right?' I ask.

'All light. All titude sickiness.'

The two Canadian doctors approach, perhaps on another mission of mercy, their entourage of Canadian eager beavers intact and still in formation. A quick head-count confirms that none has joined Richard James Allen under a pile of rocks on Thorong La. 'Where are you going?' she demands imperiously, recognising me and taking note of my ascent back to Muktinath.

'To have a shower.'

She looks at her watch. 'You should have left earlier. It's closed between twelve and two.'

Got'cha.

'How's the patient?' I ask, addressing the girl I had last seen lying on her back with a stethoscope attached to her chest, and ignoring the doctor's annoying proclivity to prescribe my day.

'Fine,' the girl answers, 'A touch of diarrhoea. I was feeling pretty weak, eh.'

'We insisted she climb back down to the hostel in Phedi and stay there a second night to be safe and sure,' the female doctor hisses, wiping her nose with a piece of pink tissue paper which she keeps in her hand momentarily.

More trekkers descend, many bypassing Kagbeni in a desperate bid
to get to Marpha. Sadly, I recognise no one now. A new wave of tourists; like going back to school and recognising the surroundings, but all
the old familiar classmates have gone. I miss Easy's reassuring flip-flop
prints on the ground in front of me, and the prospect of bumping into
Shay incinerating a bundle of waste paper. I feel a resurgence of loneliness.

At the Blue Moon, I ask Kharma the owner once again, 'Is it possible to go with you and two horses into inner Mustang?'

'No is possible,' he replies again firmly. Or do I see a glimmer of an
opening? On the rooftop of the Blue Moon are a new group of
trekkers. I look through the lodge's menu.

'Don't get excited by what you read there,' an American warns me,
giving me unsolicited advice. 'The food doesn't taste anything like the
description warrants. The pizza is Tibetan bread with gunk on top.
Pretty fuckin' bad. Lasagne's the same shit. It's like going to a Chinese
restaurant in New York. Different names for the same thing.'

Another adds, 'It's better than the dump over there. Food stinks.' A
Tibetan-looking woman yells at him from the rooftop of the other
bhaati.

'Is she yelling at one of you?' I ask.

'I just moved out of that hotel. She wants me to move my back-pack
but I've told her I'm having lunch, I'll do it later.' He wears nothing
more than running-shorts, wrap-around, go-fast opaque mirror sunglasses, and is preoccupied with rubbing suntan lotion into his white
hairy body.

More grateful than ever not to be part of that group, I indulge my
new-found addiction of a Holy Hot Shower. Illuminated by flashing
lights and dials and goodness only knows what else, I purify myself.

It is late afternoon, past five o'clock, and I should be back in Kagbeni
before dark. I have no flashlight and am without warm clothes.
According to the guidebooks, it takes a minimum of three hours to
walk between Muktinath and Kagbeni. Feeling wonderful after the
holy cleansing shower and without an immobilising back-pack
strapped to me, I traipse through medieval fortress villages as if they
were my own backyard.

The Pen Brigade see me as I exit Jharkot. They run in V-formation,
as fast as their little legs will carry them across an open field to inter-

cept me, but they do not stand a chance of catching me. Without my back-pack to slow me down, I fly down the path, and ignoring their cries of 'Pen, pen,' I leave them behind in the dust. The thought of so easily evading the ambush and outstripping these small yet fearsome members of the Pen Brigade makes me laugh aloud. I keep running. The air becomes colder as the sun drops behind Dhauligiri.

At Red House Lodge, with the resident, giant Buddha just metres away from my slumbering head, I couldn't be more secure.

TREA

❖

KAGBENI

A Belgian group is about to have breakfast, reading through the menu approved by the Trekking Hotel Association Mustang, which includes some rather curious items:

Lynonaise Potato
Croquette
Potato au gratin
Russian Egg Monn Salad

At the bottom of the page is a reminder: 'Nepal is here to change you, not for you to change it.'

There is a wide assortment of guides press-ganged into service during the trekking season. The guide working for the Belgians looks Indian, and hails from the Terai, near the Indian border. He looks, talks and acts like an Indian caricature of himself. He could be Peter Sellers in the role of the Indian in the film *The Party*. Thin and nervous, with thick prescription glasses, a pencil-thin moustache and a constantly mobile toothpick, he wears jeans which he often has to hoist up over his bony hips, despite a wide leather cowboy-belt dominated by a massive silver buckle almost the width of his waist. He looks as if he has just fallen out of bed, which is in fact the case. The Belgian clients have all finished their breakfast.

[89]

'I am sleeping late this day.' He laughs nervously at his own joke and hovers over them solicitously, then sensing their hostility, retires to stand in front of a mirror and back-comb his bed-head into a canopy of matted black hair.

'Are we going?' a member of the group asks, obviously irritated at the tardiness of their guide.

'Yes, yes. You go with porters. I eat first, come later.' He laughs again nervously and replaces the toothpick in his mouth, and the long and dirty pink comb into his back pocket. He has sensed the group's general antipathy towards him but continues to be obsequious, only making the situation worse. The disgruntled group leaves, and seeking allies and possible clients, he sits next to me. 'Where are you from sir?' he asks, trying anew.

'Canada.'

'Oh yes. I am been to America.' He has a small day-pack with him out of which he pulls a bundle of well-thumbed photographs and shuffles through them. 'Here is me in Disneyland. Here is me, in New York City. Here on beach in Florida.' Conspicuously skinny in a swimsuit on the beach, he has an arm over the shoulders of two clearly uncomfortable, bikini-clad girls, pulled in on either side of him.

'Are these your girlfriends?' I ask provokingly.

'Goodness gracious, no sir. Wanting American girlfriends too much, but unfortunately not getting.' He stares at the photos of the girls, 'Beauteous,' and half-unconsciously repeats, 'Most beauteous! And wanting? Oh my god! Wanting! Wanting too much! But not getting.' He closes his eyes better to project his fantasies, then opens them again. 'What to do?' He sorts through the photos and exclaims, as a consolation, 'This is girlfriend, sir!' It is a photo of a very young mountain girl, perhaps a Tamang or a Rai. 'She is girlfriend,' he repeats absent-mindedly, lost in memories of extra-marital bliss, and pulling at his crotch in agitation.

'Will you marry her?' I ask with feigned innocence.

'Dear sir, is not possible. My wife become very angry.' His head wobbles violently at the very thought. He sorts through the bundle of photographs and pulls out one with his family, a wife, and four daughters dressed in their school uniform of white shirts and blue skirts. They stand outside a bricked house surrounded by fields.

'Are you a farmer?' I ask.

'Yes sir, I have rice fields, two cows, two oxen for ploughing purposes, two goats, six ducks, twelve or ten chickens, sixteen or fifteen
pigeons for fooding and one dog,' he proudly tells me.

The lodge owner's children have collected around us to examine the
photos as well. The most popular picture for them is one of the guide,
with baseball cap, sitting on a John Deere tractor lawnmower on a
green and well-trimmed suburban lawn.

'Here is my card sir, you may have it. KC is my nickname sir.' His
title on the business card is *sidhar*. Without prompting he tells me
about himself. 'I am forty-three years, from poor family. Leaving
school eleven years. First I am working repairing roads, then getting
job as porter.' He rubs Chinese Butterfly cream fastidiously into his
face as he talks. The owner of the lodge, a Gurung clearly of Tibetan
stock, stands next to us. The contrast between the two is striking: the
sidhar wears tight jeans and a cowboy-style plaid shirt buttoned up to
the top of his scrawny neck, with his hair combed into a wild bouffon;
the dishevelled Mustangi, loose robes carelessly thrown on, has grime-
covered black hands, uncombed and unwashed hair. KC has to go
through all the photos again to show the owner.

I ask him, 'Isn't that bad luck to have only four daughters, what with
a dowry . . .'

KC cuts me off. 'No sir, dowry is not necessary. Maybe something to
help,' he wobbles his head at the thought, holding one arm up and
twisting the wrist of the other as if wielding a screw driver. 'If someone
wanting to marry daughter, OK, but I cannot give dowry. If still
wanting dowry, maybe I can help. Many people not like dowry system.'
Especially, I think, if they have four daughters and no sons.

KC is a Chetri, the warrior or ruling class, second in hierarchy to the
Brahmins, or priests. Despite coming from a poor family, he has
worked his way up the ladder, ingratiating himself to his foreign clients
with enough success to have been invited at least once to the USA. With
his wages, less than five dollars a day in salary, he has saved enough to
build a brick house on a small farm, with livestock. His earnings are
probably insignificant compared with the 'savings' he makes through
wheeling and dealing. He shows me receipts he has to take back to his
company in Kathmandu, but these are only hand-written notes, given
by *bhaati* owners. There is so much competition among the lodge
owners that having ten foreigners staying the night and eating must be

worth a lot in 'commission'. He tests me out as a prospective customer. 'Do you come to Nepal often sir?'

'This is my sixth time in four years,' I reply.

'Goodness gracious,' he laughs to hide his disappointment that I am familiar enough with Nepal not to need his services in the future. 'Perhaps if you have friends coming sir, I can be of assistance?'

KC burdens me with a dozen more of his business cards and leaves to join his group. Shanti, the owner's daughter, goes to school with her little brother. Pema, the owner, has work to do. I am left alone in the lodge to write my notes among the incongruous posters of Phoebe Cates and tranquil Thai scenes of Swiss-chalet-style buildings in extraordinarily well-cultivated tropical lush settings of ponds, lawns and flowers.

There is another poster. The scene of snow-clad mountains, tranquil lakes and green forests could be set in Canada, Norway, America, New Zealand or Switzerland. The caption reads:

> We all need time
> to be alone . . . . .
> to think . . . .
> to dream . . . .
> to wonder . . . . .

Alone again with my thoughts, I am overwhelmed by a surge of emotions. I feel awkward that my feelings should be so close to the surface. Suddenly claustrophobic in the dark room, I need to get out.

Pema's wife gives me a bucket of steaming hot boiling water and I climb onto the roof to preoccupy myself with laundry. It is sunny and windy, and my spirits are lifted immediately. Most of my clothes are beige except for a bright red T-shirt made in China and bought in Kathmandu. I have not washed it yet and it reeks of perspiration. I put all the clothes together in the bucket of scalding hot water to soak. Sitting beside the steaming bucket of washing, I watch trekkers descending from Muktinath pass by the lodge, between the protective stone walls keeping out the worst of the wind.

Four little girls, wearing tatty traditional *chupas* and carrying *dokos* full of dung to be spread on the fields, have stationed themselves beside a break in the wall. They exit consistently whenever trekkers pass.

They stop the trekkers to show them a cut on one of the girl's fingers. The ice is broken, contact made, the foot is in the door. The girls hope they look photogenic enough; a photo is taken of them, giving them extra leverage when they ask for a pen, or rupees. It is amusing to see the well-rehearsed ruse in action. Nobody ignores them, it's done so innocently. The trekkers get bamboozled. Some trekkers have guides. After the trekkers disappear, the guides, who know what has transpired, hang back and give the girls a telling-off.

The soapy bubbles in the bucket of water containing my boiled washing have turned pink because the dye from my red T-shirt has run. It is a perfect day to explore the caves in the ridge walls leading up to Muktinath. Pema climbs onto the roof to survey his fields. Hanging up my now baby-pink clothes on a sagging clothes line, I ask, 'Pema, do you know who lived in those caves in the valley going up to Muktinath?'

Pema makes himself scarce when there are tourists around, and leaves all communication to his wife or daughter. I had thought it might be because his English was poor. But his English is almost perfect. 'I am born here, my father, my grandfather. My father was lama. No one knows who lived in caves. Always there.'

'Have you been there?' I ask.

'Sometimes.'

'Is it possible for me to go?'

He shrugs. Technically it is in the restricted area of inner Mustang, on the north side of the river. To reach the caves I would have to go past the police checkpoint, unless I take a short-cut through the village fields. I decide to go and explore. I fill a water-bottle and collect a notebook from my room. On my way out of the lodge, I pass through the dining-area. Like an apparition, a tall, very attractive girl is standing in front of the mountain-view poster, reading the caption.

'Morning.' I disturb her as I walk by.

She turns around. 'Good morning.' She has an accent.

'Danish?'

'Dutch.'

The lodge is empty, and it is curious someone should be arriving here at this odd time, late in the morning. 'Are you staying here?' I ask.

'Yes, we came here half-an-hour ago from Muktinath. My friend is sick and doesn't want to walk anymore.'

'Is there anything I can do to help? Medicine?'

'No. We are both nurses. It is not a problem. Just diarrhoea. But thank you.'

'And you?'

'Not now. Before, going over Thorong La. But now I am fine.' She hesitates, then adds 'When I have a problem we go on. When he has a problem, we stop.'

'I am going to look at the caves in the valley. Perhaps you saw them when you came down from Muktinath?'

'I saw them. Do you know what they are?'

'No. I'm going to see for myself. You are welcome to join me if you like.'

'Yes I would like to very much.' She tells me her name is Trea. She goes to their room to get a sweater and we take off, walking through the back alleyways of Kagbeni to the fields, where we climb over stone walls, avoiding the police checkpoint, and cut a direct line up the valley bottom heading towards Muktinath. I am happy to have her company, having been reluctant to wander far off the beaten track entirely on my own; if I had an accident, no one would find me.

The ridge is steep. In places the way entails scrambling up and down rocks. We walk and we talk. It is one of those rare walks and talks when the soul comes out of hiding. 'Do you like nursing?' I ask.

'Yes, very much. I like helping people, I like listening to them, especially old people. They have so much to tell.'

I can imagine she must be a favourite with the patients, her good looks, kind face, apparently generous heart and patience. She is obviously very special. 'Do your patients fall in love with you?' I ask provocatively. She laughs. The question is ridiculous, but she is naive.

'They are patients, I am a nurse.'

We get further and further away from the village until Kagbeni is no longer in sight. The sun in the brilliant blue sky is warm on our exposed skin, and sensuous in the otherwise cool temperature. I am conscious of the surrounding, desert-like desolation. There is no sign of life, no birds, no animals. And it is quiet, as if we were the only living things on this earth. We help each other over deep-sided gullies and along the remains of ancient irrigation canals. It is almost as if we are leaving this world.

There is a rapport between us. 'Why did you come here?' she asks.

The question is simple, but I find myself talking for a long time. My answer has clarified somewhat since Shay asked me the same question some weeks ago. In this rocky lunar landscape, at the bottom of a desolate sun-filled canyon, with the Himalayas on one side and the Tibetan plateau on the other, in a place I have long dreamt of coming to, I am beginning to understand myself better. I talk and there is little of importance I do not tell Trea.

'Was it difficult?' she asks, about my move to Norway, puffing and out of breath from the exertion of scrambling up the rocks.

'Not as easy as I thought it would be.'

'Maybe that is good for you.'

'Yes. Maybe.' I repeat one of Easy's memorised quotations. '"Sometimes it is sorrow that awakens us."'

'Yes. That is true.'

'It was the Buddha who said that, by the way.'

'It is when we are sorrowful our soul stirs, causing us pain,' she adds. We traverse along the rock face without speaking.

'As least you look as if you could be Norwegian,' she eventually continues. 'There are many immigrants in Holland and I do not think they find it easy either. Did you find work?'

'No. I couldn't speak Norwegian then. In the end, I started up a company to provide me with income and a job. But to run a company successfully you have to be motivated by making money.' I think about it for a while. Norway and the business with which I have been all too occupied seems so far away and irrelevant in this different environment. 'I'm not a very inspired businessman,' I admit.

As occasionally happens when strangers sit next to each other for several hours on a plane, we both talk openly, with candour, about things we find difficulty admitting even to ourselves in more normal circumstances, revealing fears, hopes, loves, disappointments, shortcomings, failures. We are both good listeners, we both exploit the need to bare the essence of our souls, not only to each other, but to ourselves. My confessions encourage her to disclose her own. I feel intensely close to this companion whom I have known for only a few hours.

Eventually we reach a point directly below the first of the caves embedded in the cliff face above. Each seems the size of an average room. Some seem to be interconnecting, as if they were dwellings with bedrooms leading off from a main living-room. All hang suspended in the disintegrating wall of loose rock, like so many high-rise apartments. On the narrow bottom of the gorge, crumbling remains of mud-packed walls of buildings bear silent witness to the society once thriving here. We go further afield and examine the ground around the ruins strewn with shards of patterned pottery. I pick up the most interesting. We also find *shaligrams*, and a rock fossil of a crayfish left from when this high plateau was under the sea.

The *shaligram*, a sacred stone found in the area and valued for its reputed miraculous powers, is carefully pocketed by Trea as a reminder of this day. A Himalayan rock lizard darts into a crevice. There is something living here after all.

It is so quiet that my ears ring. I sit up against a parapet and try to imagine who lived here, try to pick up the 'spirits' that might be associated with this lonely place. Despite the silence and my conviction that I would sense something, have an insight into the lives of generations of troglodytes who thrived here, I cannot feel anything. Perhaps their lives are too far removed from mine. If only I could have an indication as to what their daily existence was like, that would be enough, a key to open the locked doors.

Trea sits beside me. We sit in the sun-baked stillness, lost in our thoughts, enveloped in a silence so absolute as to be deafening. Far above, across the stream, in another world, the path wiggles between Muktinath and Kagbeni. Behind us the vertical rock face is pot-marked with hundreds of caves. Fortresses lie below us and up the valley; there is a temple, a pilgrimage site for thousands of years. But who lived here? Why? I want to transport myself back, visualise this place as it was then. But I cannot. 'Let's take a look in the caves.'

'Yes.' Her clear blue eyes are the same colour as the sky. They penetrate mine and for an instant time stands still.

We walk up to the cliff face and scramble beyond the loose rocks at the bottom. A small cave above us seems to be more intact than the others. We help each other up the steep sections until we reach a small opening through which we crawl on hands and knees into a cramped, hemispherical cavity. The caves are indeed man-made. Above our heads a small aperture lets in light, like a window. On the ground is a hearth, and in the wall symmetrical indentations, to store goods, or to place an effigy. One is large enough to serve as a chair. Small moulded votive clay stupas lie half-buried in the dust. Formed from ashes and crushed human bones left from a cremation, mixed with clay, they are moulded into the shape of divinities and scattered in *mani* walls, on the tops of hills or in caves according to the prescription of the lama in attendance. They have been placed here long after the original inhabitants of these caves left.

We shuffle intimately around the small, dark enclosure, the beam of light from above shining on the particles of dust raised by our feet. In the secure womb-like cavity, time again seems to stand still. Soulmates, we say nothing, conscious of the isolation of our beings from the rest of the world. In the strange psychic intimacy of the moment the physical separateness of our bodies seems, at least to me, to be uneasy. Our souls have embraced, but our physical bodies remain separate. We do nothing to dispel this tension and remain there, centimetres apart but otherwise familiar, for an extended period of time, as if waiting for something to happen. Crawling back out into the brilliant sunlight, our eyes adjusting to the intense light, we bump together on the ledge of rock.

'You all right?' I ask, reaching for her. We hold onto each other. The physical contact is a release of tension, but now we are clinging dizzily to a rock outcrop with a long vertical drop below us.

There is a silence before she replies. 'Yes.'

In the ancient kingdom of Mustang, in a cave ages old, so old no one knows who lived there, a thousand years and a thousand miles removed from reality, with a person I had just met, would never meet again, something happened. Yet nothing happened. Not in this world. No birds, no animals, no people, nothing living, can testify. Only the desert wind, blowing eerily through empty high mountains, among abandoned caves and ruined fortresses, has been witness. What was it that happened? There is no need to talk as we walk back to Kagbeni; we understand what has happened between us. For a brief moment, there is no other way to describe it, our souls met.

At the lodge Sybreen, her boyfriend, waits anxiously. 'Where have you been?' he asks her.

She introduces us. 'To the caves we saw on the rock face on the way down from Muktinath.'

'What! You're scared of heights, Trea,' he says, incredulous.

'I know.' She laughs.

'Together?' He looks at me.

'Yes,' she says simply. The two of them disappear abruptly to the privacy of their room.

I thought he knew.

I had invited a Swedish and an American couple from another lodge to come for dinner. The 'hot table' is full, mostly with another organised Belgian trekking group. By the time I arrive with my guests, Sybreen and Trea are already there, and they attempt to manoeuvre to allow us to squeeze in around the hot table, but there is not enough room for all of us. Awkwardly, we sit at another table instead. The mood at our table is zany. After three years living like a monk in Norway, where it is too expensive to go out for dinner, I absorb the dinner-party atmosphere, and the diversity of talent brought to the table. When it is 'late', about nine o'clock, the Belgian diners at the other table have melted away and it is only Trea who remains, alone, writing intensely in her diary. Unsure whether I should disturb her, I half-expect her to join us. By the time my guests break up for the evening, Trea too has gone to bed.

In case I do not get a chance to say so, I tear a strip out of my notebook, and write, 'Thanks for yesterday, Andrew.' I dress in clean but pink co-ordinated clothes and tuck the note in a jean-pocket to be surreptitiously extracted.

Trea and Sybreen join me at breakfast. He tells me he is a nurse at a psychiatric hospital. We have a rapport with each other, despite yesterday's awkwardness. 'Lots of my patients would benefit from doing this walk. Especially the depressives. But not all of them. Some of them have gone too far,' he says.

They are in a hurry to leave early enough to get a head start before the winds of the Kali Gandaki pick up. I shake Sybreen's hand and give him a hug. I 'namaste' their porter. I turn to Trea and hug her. She looks at me with her startling blue eyes and says quietly, locking her eyes steady on mine, 'Thanks for yesterday, Andrew,' and hugs me tight. And I realise that yesterday meant as much to her as it did to me.

They leave, trekking down the path towards Jomosom. She has a gangly walk, like a colt with legs too long for its body. Her arms protrude from her sides, hands gripping the sleeves of her jacket to pull them down for warmth. She looks like a girl setting off for school. The note to Trea remains secreted in my pocket. I watch them for a long time as they walk down the rock-strewn bed of the Kali Gandaki. A rider on a horse passes them heading in my direction, and then they are gone, for ever, disappearing into the vastness of the mountains.

In life we cannot elude change, we cannot avoid loss, the Buddha revealed. Freedom and happiness are found in the flexibility and ease with which we accept these changes.

In the kitchen with Pema and his wife I feel less lonely, part of the family. I repair my pink shorts and pinkish jeans which have been worn through at the hips where the waist strap of the back-pack has chafed the cotton material to shreds. Pema's wife is statuesque and strong. He is very clever, and I think a little eccentric. Both look Tibetan, but they call themselves Gurungs. Pema tells me that his grandfather remembers when the fortress was still used. The resident was not a king, but was 'very powerful'.

'Are you Buddhist?' I ask.

He looks surprised. 'Yes.'

I point to strips of meat hanging from a wooden drying-rack hanging over the fire.

'Yak meat. We eat only in the winter, to keep warm,' he answers, knowing I am referring to a strict Buddhist's pledge not to kill sentient beings. 'It is necessary.'

'What about *zopkio*?' I am curious to know whether their religion is connected to the Hindu worship of the cow. If they eat yak, would they eat a half-cow, half-yak?

'No. In Mustang some eat *zopkio*. Not here.'

'Why not?' I ask.

He shrugs, 'Too many people not like.'

The Hindu influence is great enough in Kagbeni for *zopkio* not to be eaten, but in what he calls 'Mustang', meaning further north, this is evidently not the case.

Kagbeni is riddled with new cement water fountains. 'What about the CARE water fountains I see all over, none of them are working.'

He shrugs. 'Waiting for technicians from Kathmandu.'

Pema leads me to the *gompa* grounds before departing for his fields. The sounds of bells, cymbals crashing, drums and chanting infiltrate through the *gompa* walls. At the entrance a woman smiles, looks back inside and says something. A tall, imposing lama in saffron and burgundy robes fills the doorway. He studies me hard. I smile. '*Namaste*!'

'*Namaste*! Which country?'

'Canada.'

He returns my smile and motions me inside.

'My name is Ngawang,' he informs me hospitably. Sitting on the far side of the dark room, lit by candles, is another lama, who could easily be a Khampa, with two novices next to him. He does not acknowledge my presence, but continues praying. He is fierce-looking, big, with swarthy features, high cheekbones and almond-shaped eyes that turn up at the outer corners.

'Sit down.' I sit on a carpet next to the younger lama who has let me in. The four lamas and I are lined up against one wall. Opposite us are several women. Between sits a man, leaning against a post, with a proprietary look about him. This is his *puja*, an offering to the gods for next year's good harvest.

The Khampa lama holds a water vessel and pours consecrated libations over the proffered offerings beside a beautiful round gilt-silver box decorated with the eight auspicious Buddhist symbols on the outside: knot, wheel, banner, parasol, vase, fish, conch and lotus. I lean against the wall, close my eyes, and listen to the soothing and hypnotic chanting, and am oblivious to the passing of time. The room is thick with incense. The four lamas perform intricate hand and finger movements, *mudra*, visual gestures accompanying the chanting of their prayers. The bells, drums and cymbals crash and boom in an intricate Chinese rhythm, builds to a crescendo, then stops abruptly. The bells, *ghantas*, and thunderbolts, *vajras*, are put down.

Ngawang talks. His English is almost flawless. I tell him I am interested in learning about Buddhism, but know very little. He turns to me as we sit there, smiles enigmatically and says, as if whispering a secret, 'A little learning is a dangerous thing.' I am trying to remember who said that, when he leans over to me again and says, still smiling, 'But something is better than nothing.' He explains to me the bell symbolises the female and wisdom, and the thunderbolt the male and compassion. When held in a variety of hand movements they indicate the way to liberation. Then the ceremonies are over and food is offered to the monks. I take my leave, thanking our hosts. Ngawang asks, 'May I have your pencil?'

'It is my last one,' I tell him, 'but I have pens at the lodge which you are welcome to have.' He asks which *bhaati* I am in. Before leaving, I mention casually, 'I am trying to get into inner Mustang.'

'Impossible without a permit,' he says without hesitation.

Below the orange *gompa* a herd of yak are driven through the ice-cold waters of the Kali Gandaki. In one of the many stone-walled enclosures built for containing transient livestock, another twenty yak, brought down from Dolpo, mill about nervously. They are for sale. Men in the village assess the yak, gingerly feeling at the base of each animal's spine to assess its meatiness. Three yak are selected and their feet bound together, to be slaughtered. They look so forlorn. It is hard to accept that these harmless beasts, having absorbed the spiritual purity of the high mountains all their lives, will be killed just for their meat. It seems such a waste. A massive, shaggy grey yak looks over his shoulder at me, long and hard, his eyes fixed on mine, as if he knew me. I have the unnerving feeling we do know each other. He reminds me of my teddy bear, which I still have. Pema tells me he has paid the equivalent of one-hundred-and-seventy dollars – eight-thousand five-hundred rupees – for one of the yak.

It is a Saturday and the children of the village are out of school and playing in the passageways. Boys in particular are preoccupied with 'marbles' made out of perfectly round and smooth black river stones. Another group of children enact a scene depicting a yak being rounded up. A boy on all fours with a rope in his mouth pretends he is a yak. The other children, smaller, try to tie him up. Whenever one gets too close, the 'yak' gores the child.

In the kitchen of the lodge, over a pot of hot chocolate, I try to forget the soon-to-be-slaughtered yak and distract myself by leafing through one of Shanti's school books. The paper and printing are of such poor quality that the pages look like bad photocopies, the pictures no more than smudges. These depict wax-moustached Nepalese Rana prime ministers with plumed helmets, coats topped with epaulettes and looped with fine braided chain, chests hung with medals, waists adorned with knives and sweeping swords, costumes plainly inspired by European royalty.

Reading by candlelight in my room, I look out of the window to the stars, clear in the black cold sky, and think of the three teddy bear yak outside, especially the grey one, forefeet hobbled, its death all too imminent. I toy with the idea of buying them all and letting them live the rest of their days peacefully in Kagbeni rather than allowing them to be destroyed. I blow out the flickering candle.

Outside, cotton-ball clouds drift by the moon, their sharp edges gilded in a silvery glow. Inside, a fine layer of dust coats everything.

Snuggling into bed, my hands reach under the pillow. I feel an object and hold it in the palm of my hand. In the moonlight shining through the small window panes beside my bed, I recognise the *shaligram* Trea had found in the cave.

MICHEL AND SANGPO

❖

Drums wake me. In the room next to mine is Pema's *choikan*, his private prayer-room, containing a few prayer books identical to the ones I saw in the *gompa* yesterday. I wonder if they have come from there. Pema recites his morning prayers as I listen.

A Belgian group has occupied the lodge. Last night a maverick in the group read aloud from an English guidebook about cultural insensitivity, and the fact that women wearing shorts in Nepal is frowned upon. This morning, despite the cold outside, two of the middle-aged women in the group are wearing short shorts to maximise the amount of skin exposed to the tanning rays of the sun. It is not against the law, but it is culturally insensitive in Nepal to reveal female legs like this.

The sensibly dressed bohemian couple leave. The remaining scantily clad Belgians pour out a vehement torrent of Flemish as soon as they have gone, the two women comfortable with exposed cellulite-riddled legs, unconcerned by the criticism levelled at them. One of the husbands flips on his short-wave radio to listen to the news. The joys of trekking in a group.

Of the three yak in the enclosure, two are still standing. The third yak is on its back, propped in place by large stones on either side of its rib-cage. The hide has almost been ripped away, revealing the muscled chest which has been split in two. The chest cavity holds reservoirs of blood which are scooped into aluminium containers. Not a drop has sullied the earth. Killing the yak through a small incision into which the blade of the knife is inserted to stab the heart, prevents precious blood from being wasted. One of the villagers dips a glass into the steaming pool and drinks it greedily, blood dripping from the corners of his mouth. Children play with the unsheathed penis, tying it around their heads, amid laughter. An old man helps himself to what looks like a chunk of clotted blood; he tilts his head back and swallows it whole. Every aspect of the yak is removed and saved and separated into four distinct piles, to be shared by the four families who have pooled together to buy this animal. Even the stomach is divided into four equal slithery piles and cleaned.

Two middle-aged Americans crane their heads over the stone wall to see what is happening. 'Oh, Martha look! They killed that cow we saw here this morning, with its head tied to its feet,' the man remarks.

'What a shame,' the women replies on looking at the carnage.

I wonder if they think hamburgers ripen on trees? These are two members of a trekking group returning from inner Mustang. Their mules are loaded with camping equipment, tables, mattresses, wicker chairs, food, kerosene containers, back-packs. The élite Sherpa guides are adorned with mirror sunglasses, baseball caps, basketball shoes and fashionable haircuts. The group, outfitted from Kathmandu, spend a week going in to Lo Mantang and come back out again without the slightest benefit to the local population.

The Government of Nepal has stipulated that tourists entering Mustang are not permitted to distribute money or gifts or charity to local residents and students. I wonder what local Mustangi leaders think about these terms and conditions.

Informal efforts to find a guide to take me illegally into inner Mustang produce no results. The quest is hopeless without expensive Kathmandu-issued trekking permits. Reluctantly I decide to give up this thwarted ambition and leave Kagbeni.

On the way through the village I witness two more yak being stabbed to death. One is the cuddly grey one, and I intrude on the scene just as the knife is plunged through the incision in its hide, into his heart. I feel I have let a friend down. I cannot shake the terrible feeling of guilt as I walk back to the lodge and I know it is too late to do anything about it. If only, a couple of minutes earlier, I had . . . But death is so final.

'Andrew! Andrew!'

It is Ngawang Lama. Why is this Buddhist monk calling me? Am I in for a spiritual revelation? Has he found someone who will take me to inner Mustang? 'Can I have your pencil?' he asks.

Disappointed, I can see the irony too. 'Yes. It is my last one, but you may have it.'

I pack, saying goodbye to Pema, his wife and children. With the Kali Gandaki wind sandblasting my face, I descend the dry riverbed towards Jomosom. The great canyon of the Kali Gandaki has been one of the major passageways linking the high Tibetan plateau with the lowlands of India for centuries, perhaps even thousands of years, and as I trace this route I wonder at the historical trade that has preceded me.

Jomosom, the unattractive government administrative headquarters for Mustang District, does not look like a Nepalese village let alone a village in Mustang; its streets are too wide and regular, there is no fortified circular wall protecting the inhabitants. With the only airfield on the Kali Gandaki, Jomosom serves as the outermost staging-point for the more harried visitors' trek into inner Mustang. It is also a major Gurkha military camp.

When the US stopped its military support to the Khampas in 1971, the guerrillas naturally enough continued to fight. The Chinese Government complained bitterly about the Khampa bases in Mustang. The Nepalese Government tried to persuade the Khampas to cease their military raids into Chinese-occupied Tibet. Eventually most of the Khampa guerrillas realised that it was pointless to continue without support from the US, and without tacit approval from Nepal in allowing them to base their operations in Mustang. About one-hundred determined and perhaps suicidal Khampa 'bandits' refused to give in and continued their cross-border raids until the Nepalese Gurkhas caught up with them, and slaughtered them to a man. It was from their Jomosom army base that the Gurkhas hunted down the remaining Khampas, who had refused to stop fighting because the US had changed allegiance in favour of China.

The 'Telecommunications Office': a tumble-down building on the east side of the river; inside, a little man in thick spectacles tinkers industriously, winding one end of a naked copper wire around the element of an electric heater, the other end leading to the source of the electric current. He looks and acts very much as if he is seriously contemplating suicide. '*Namaste*! Is this the communications office?' I ask quickly, before he puts his karma to the test.

'Yes.' He continues to fiddle with the wires, apparently determined to end his assignment in this windblown outpost.

'Can I telephone Europe from here?' I ask hopefully, counting on his sense of professionalism to take precedence over whatever actions his depression precipitates.

'Telegram.'

'I can send a telegram to Europe?' Even this seems unlikely as there is not the slightest vestige of communications equipment in this dusty office.

He looks up at me, his eyes enlarged through his goldfish-bowl lenses, and he puts his hand on a barely recognisable radio half-buried amid the rubble of papers and files. His magnified eyes blink at me. 'At four o'clock I am sending radio message to Kathmandu. In Kathmandu they take radio message and send to Europe. Which country?'

'Norway.' It sounds even more obscure than Jomosom.

'Nowhere,' he repeats, searching under 'N' in a book of tables. He passes me a pink pad. Whoever had written on it last had pressed so hard that I can almost read the indentations of the previous message. In order to make it visible, I rub the lead of the pencil sideways on the pad and read: 'CANCELLED FLIGHT FROM JOMOSOM STOP MISSED CON-NECTING FLIGHT KATHMANDU TO EUROPE STOP TRYING TO GET OUT STOP.'

'How much is this?' I ask, showing my own less frantic message, with Norway, as distinct from Nowhere, written clearly at the top.

He sits down and takes out a pencil. As he calculates the cost he murmurs aloud like a lama chanting a *puja* for my telegram to soar successfully through the ether. 'Pibe hundred rupees.' Ten dollars. I am amazed, and wonder whether the telegram will ever arrive.

Walking through the eastern side of Jomosom, I cross the suspension bridge over the Kali Gandaki. The wind howls through the cables, the bridge sways violently. Prayer flags tied to the bridge stand horizontal with the force of the wind. I would be late landing a plane here too, if I landed it at all.

Jomosom's main street is another replica of a windswept cowboy town. The wind blasts down the wide thoroughfare, scouring dust and debris. A horse tied up outside a lodge seems to be a promising sign of hospitality, and I open two sets of double swing-doors to a relatively clean Thakali lodge. A woman asks, 'You want room?' She is squeaky clean, having just come out of the shower. Although she has Mongolian features, she wears a Hindu tika on her forehead, and a red and gold sari. Within a two-hour walk I have left one world and entered another.

She flicks an electrical switch, which activates a naked bulb hanging by its wire from the ceiling, revealing the contents of a room. A ram standing immediately outside the window looks balefully in. 'Meat for tomorrow,' she laughs heartily, acknowledging the condemned beast. I close the door after her. The ram's neck is tethered tightly to the exterior of the window-frame. He looks at me with golden eyes, not ten centimetres away from the glass pane. The rope is so short that he has no choice but to stare pleadingly at me, scrutinising my every move as I unpack. This unnerves me and I have to leave the room. The grey yak is still on my conscience.

In the dining-area I barely recognise myself in a mirror. I have not seen my face for a month. My hair is a dust-encrusted mop, my beard full. I look a mess. Despite several attempts at washing my hair and beard with soap and subsequent rinsing in the shower, the dust and grime remain stubborn. I give up trying to unravel the knots in my hair, which I have not combed since Kathmandu. I resemble a *bhotia* character, one from the butcher class. Now I know why they braid their locks.

The relative sophistication of the lodge, and the people running it, are not what I came for. I do not look forward to descending the Kali Gandaki to a world catering increasingly to Westerners. I want to get back into that desert-like, primitive world where it is so easy to imagine oneself taken back five-hundred years or more.

I do not sleep well during the night. The sheep staring through the window continues to give me the creeps. In this land of incarnations, his mute plea to get him off the butcher's hook is too real and significant and I still feel guilty for letting the grey yak get the chop.

JOMOSOM–JHARKOT

The first Nepal Airlines flight arrives from Pokhara. A few minutes later the swing-doors of the *bhaati* crash open and a lanky Westerner strides in, eyes bright, an all-encompassing smile, and a wool cap pulled over his balding head. '*Bonjour*,' he says with the aplomb characteristic of those French who assume that everyone should be able to speak their language.

'*Bonjour*,' I reply. He is followed by a *bhotia* companion, long black hair inter-braided with decorative red strands curled on top of his head. The *bhotia* sidekick has the appearance of a North American Indian. I guess he is a Khampa.

In the otherwise empty *bhaati*, we introduce ourselves: Michel, a French doctor living in Nepal now for six years, and his shadow, Rinchen Sangpo from Dolpo and Tibet. I am reminded of an unmasked Lone Ranger and Tonto. Sangpo is not only a Khampa, I soon discover, but a Bon, a member of one of the oldest religions in Asia, originating long before the Buddha, and even extending into pre-Christian Europe.

'We are going up to Muktinath.' When he talks, he pulls the few long strands of his moustache into mouse-like whiskers. All he needs is a beret and a stick under his arm to live up to the clichéd caricature of a Frenchman.

'Can I join you?' Like an autumn leaf fluttering in the wind, a recalcitrant gust blowing the other way takes me with it.

Michel and Sangpo look at each other. Sangpo shrugs, Michel says, 'Sure, you are welcome.' Sangpo falls behind us, unable to understand our conversation.

Walking back up to Muktinath, my new companion tells me something of why he is here. 'When I came to Nepal I was posted as a medical doctor in Tatopani, a village two days' walk further down the Kali Gandaki, for a three-year period. I was assigned there with another French doctor. We fell in love and two years into our contract we married. Now we live in Kathmandu. I work for Swiss Aid, in charge of their health-care programme in Nepal, and Agnes, my wife, looks after our two young children. We intended to come on this holiday together, but our older son fell sick; we decided I should continue alone with Sangpo, rather than abort the entire trip.' He is evidently ecstatic to be here again, an area he visited frequently when he was based in Tatopani. Like fragments of litter, we are flung up the rocky bed of the Kali Gandaki, the fierce winds blasting us from behind.

Despite Michel's positive attitude to virtually anything and everything, his cynicism for Nepalese bureaucracy knows no bounds. He
tells me loudly over the blustering gusts how difficult it is to get anything done. 'If you want an appointment with a Nepalese Government
employee, the only time is eleven o'clock. Before, he is either not in the
office, or drinking tea and reading his newspaper. After twelve o'clock
he has gone home, or to his other private job.'

Marching up the riverbed we face a wave of trekkers descending, the
morning rush-hour traffic of Get There People struggling against the
prevailing winds to reach Jomosom from Muktinath. Most have not
bothered to divert through Kagbeni.

Michel's long strides enable him to cover ground easily, but weeks
on the trail have conditioned me, despite my heavy pack. The high altitude no longer has a debilitating effect. We walk non-stop to Khingar,
where we pause, warming ourselves in the sun; we watch a man producing sausages from the blood, gristle and intestines of a yak.

Most of Michel's work is administrative. But one medical topic has
him boiling. AIDS. 'The problem,' he says, 'is catastrophic if the
government continues to avoid the issue. There are thousands of AIDS
cases in Nepal. If you think AIDS is a major problem in under-
populated Africa, it is minor compared with what Nepal has in store.
You have three-hundred-thousand young Nepalese girls sent to India,
to cities like Bombay, as prostitutes. When they get sick, they come
back and infect their local villages. *Bhotia* traders go up and down the
valleys to India, Thailand, Hong Kong, and many of them come back
infected. This problem is compounded by sexual promiscuity among
the mountain people and prostitution among the Hindus. But talk to
the average Nepali about sex? Impossible. There are six-million
condoms stored indefinitely in warehouses in the Terai, in southern
Nepal. These have been donated by US AID and the World Health
Organisation, but have not been distributed because the cost of distribution is too high, and also because it is not a government priority.'

I tell Michel about Easy's description of the *bhaati* owner's strange
death in Shyange. 'No question about it,' Michel says, 'He died of
AIDS.'

At Jharkot Michel tells me, 'This is as far as I will go today. I am
exhausted, it has been a long day.' We find ourselves rooms at a tradi-
tional-looking *bhaati*.

Leaving my back-pack at the lodge, I continue to walk on up to Muktinath to talk to Kharma at the Blue Moon. He is surprised to see me again, and calls his wife over, as if I were a novelty. He says, 'Maybe possible find guide into Mustang. Come back one hour.'

I pass the time in the Hot Holy Showers, then walk through the temple grounds again. At the pagoda temple the same woman offers to sell me a woven cotton bracelet. I show her the one I had already bought from her, but buy another one anyway. On this one, which she also ties with a knot around my wrist, I do not make a wish. I shall give it to someone else, someone special, to wish on. I lie down beside the stream within the temple grounds, and listen to the sounds, once again marvelling at the beauty and serenity of the place. I throw a coin into each of the ponds reflecting the evening sunlight. The woman with the bracelets has been watching me. We smile simultaneously, and in that brief glimpse, share an effortless sense of joy and happiness.

Kharma has set up our trip into inner Mustang. 'We leave five in the morning, from here. I rent horse for you, I myself am your guide. We come back day after tomorrow, in evening.'

When I see Michel I tell him in confidence, 'I have found someone to take me into inner Mustang. Want to join me?'

He pulls at the strands of his moustache, looking north, towards inner Mustang. He looks at Sangpo and says thoughtfully, 'I've wanted to go in there for a long time.' I can see him playing with the idea. 'But I risk far more than you. I would lose my job, we would have to leave Nepal. That for us would be a tremendous tragedy.' He shakes his head, common sense prevailing. 'I'll wait for you here to make sure you return.'

JHARKOT–INNER MUSTANG

Muleteers in the courtyard noisily make tea and prepare their mule train. It is still dark. I fumble in the darkness of my room, dress warmly, and leave the lodge as quietly as possible, my over-designed, triple-layer sleeping-bag under my arm. It is well below freezing and I am able to walk over a shallow frozen pond instead of around it. The ground is covered in white frost, the black sky filled with stars. I continue past the empty police checkpoint to the Blue Moon where two horses stand outside the *bhaati*, but there is no sign of Kharma. I hammer on the locked doors of the *bhaati* until eventually he appears, bleary-eyed, to open them.

'Sorry. Yesterday too much *chang*. We have tea, breakfast, first.' Kharma, with his wife and children, sleep on one mattress, close to the warmth of the stove in the tiny kitchen.

It is almost dawn by the time we are in the saddles and trotting out of Muktinath. I leave first, some minutes before Kharma. The pony has a peculiar gait, with small, quick dainty steps, which makes it impossible to post while trotting. I imitate Kharma's style instead and jiggle in the saddle which is so well padded that the ride is surprisingly comfortable. Well-worn leather saddle-bags full of food for the ponies and us hang heavily from our saddles.

We pass the village of Dzong on the other side of the valley, over ground covered with autumn-coloured leaves from poplar, banyan and peepul trees. Exiting the village, we climb out of the Dzong Khola towards the rounded pass which is as high as Thorong La, but leads north. Several times we dismount to walk the ponies over narrow, slippery rock ledges, covered in frost and ice. With dawn the morning sunlight hits the summits of Nilgiri and Dhauligiri. We are now illegally within 'inner' Mustang.

As I am wearing only lightweight boots and only one pair of socks, my feet begin to freeze. Already they feel numb. I am tempted to tell Kharma, but he looks as if he might be asleep. He is slouched forward in his saddle, his quilted Chinese army jacket and woven hat giving his figure a Michelin-man form. The chiming of the bells on the horses' necks soothes and I too feel drowsy. Doves streak overhead, the wind whispering in their wings. The sun peeks through Thorong La and down the Dzong Khola towards Kagbeni. From the vantage point of Kagbeni, it must appear as if the sun streams straight out of Muktinath. The autumn leaves of the trees in the oases of the valley below absorb the intense morning light, colourful against the brown of the surrounding rocks. Soon the sunlight hits us. It is not warm, at least not immediately, but psychologically it makes a difference to see the ground around reflecting the warm light as we ride through a deserted, lifeless moonscape.

I mimic Kharma's posture, my feet relaxed, legs hanging loosely down, my back slumped, the reins so loose I may as well let them go. Periodically I wave my riding-crop at invisible flies, as Kharma does, so the sleep-walking pony stays awake. We climb slowly but consistently higher and the ponies sweat profusely. My shadow, with the pony, is cast far down the mountain slope. Sometimes the shadow is a recognisable but elongated outline, sometimes it skips and bounces drunkenly over boulders or gullies. The only sound is the clicking of the ponies' hoofs and the tinkling of their bells. I would not be anywhere or anyone else.

Since leaving Muktinath, I have not exchanged a word with Kharma who rides ahead of me, nursing a hangover, half-asleep. At the crest of the pass, an unobstructed view of the Kingdom of Lo. Kharma points out the lay of the land. To the right a path leads to the upper route through Dhi, an alternative way to Lo Mantang and little-used passes into Tibet. The path leading down takes us to our destination, the three villages of Chhuksang, Tetang and Tangme. The landscape is devoid of any evidence of human habitation: just rocks, cliff faces, gullies, ridges in shades of beige, brown and red. And silence.

We dismount to walk the horses down the other side of the pass. Kharma stops and shows me footprints in the ground. I cannot identify what the animal is. They are large dog-like prints, with claw indentations. 'Dangerous,' Kharma tells me, 'killing cattle, yak, sheep, horses. *Chongu*, very dangerous.'

Himalayan wolf. Is he joking? We follow the tracks for some distance before they diverge.

Kharma tells me, 'I do this trip many, many times. But now is first time with foreigner. Sometimes foreigners tell me they give me one-hundred, sometimes two-hundred dollars. But I no like. Too dangerous. You is OK.' I am left wondering what has inspired him to have confidence in me for we have agreed on a far lesser fee.

In places we ride over the loose rock of recent landslides, sometimes beside a sheer drop hundreds of metres into the gully below. Areas still in shadow are white with the frost covering the rocks. Often the path is so narrow and tortuous and the drop so precipitous that we are forced to dismount. We descend to a plateau at the foot of cliffs with caves set in them, like the high-rise apartments I had explored with Trea. I wish I had time to inspect them.

Worried that we might be seen on the open plateau, Kharma wraps a scarf around his face, puts on a large pair of sunglasses designed for women and his oversized Chinese army hat. He looks unrecognisable. We ride fast, at a gallop, across the open plateau, pock-marked with semicircular stone shelters, the protective stones facing south towards the source of the withering Kali Gandaki winds. At a shallow depression we stop and Kharma ties the reins around rocks, putting the feed-bags over the ponies' noses. Removing the saddle-bags with our food, we climb out of the depression and walk to a point overlooking the Kali Gandaki. Prone on the high crest, we scan the Narsing Khola directly below, to the three clustered villages of Tangme, Tetang and Chhuksang. We have ridden a distance almost a quarter of the way to Lo Mantang, bypassing the village of Tangbe.

The villages are similar to Kagbeni, but in better condition. The red *gompa* is taller, perhaps four storeys high, the mud-packed *dzong* looks to be in better shape, higher and bigger than those in the Dzong Valley. But most dramatic of all, the village is entirely enclosed by high solid walls some ten metres high, with few windows facing the outside. 'You want to go down?' I ask hopefully.

'No. Too many people know me. My father is lama. I come here many times as boy with my father. If they see me, maybe I have problems after. Many friends here. They no problem. But sometimes Brahmin teacher at school, not friend. Then he can tell police.'

I do not want to get Kharma into trouble. We sit on the ridge surveying the three medieval fortress villages, eating our dinner of boiled eggs and Tibetan bread. In the distance a canyon of fluted organ pipes lies astride the riverbed, stained red in the saturated colours of the evening light. I am living a dream come true. I am exactly where I want to be. The way itself is the goal, there is no target.

INNER MUSTANG–JHARKOT

Early morning light wakes us, illuminating the spectacular landscape around and below us with a warmth and clarity that will be indelibly etched in my memory. I have rarely felt more elated. The air is palpably fresh and clean, the sky immaculate and immense.

We are camped high on a ridge, and the sunlight poking over the mountain peaks is soon upon us. Eating leftover Tibetan bread and boiled eggs in the luxurious warmth of our sleeping-bags, we patiently watch the salt and pepper colours of a herd of goats, driven by three goat-herd from the villages below, up to the plateau. Kharma watches their approach with increasing alarm.

'We must go,' he says nervously. The goat-herd is wandering closer to where the ponies are hidden. They may not recognise Kharma, but they might identify the ponies or their saddles.

'I am going to talk to the villagers. You go to the ponies and wait for me. I'll come in five minutes.'

We split up, Kharma moving with our belongings in a direct line to the ponies to load up as I stride purposefully to three villagers, one man and two boys, who are partially concealed in one of the semi-circular stone enclosures. When they see me and recognise me as a foreigner, fear creases their faces. Why would they be frightened of me? I smile deliberately, and 'Namaste' them when I get within hailing distance, then squat with them in the shelter. I am surprised when one speaks to me in English.

'Where you come from?' he asks.

'Lo Mantang,' I lie to confuse him. That is not what he meant, but that is what I tell him. He clearly wonders where on the face of the earth I have come from. 'Where you come from?' I ask instead, to put him on the defensive.

He laughs and points down. 'Tetang. Where you go?'

'Kagbeni.'

'Why you no group?' he asks. The other two boys sit there listening but not comprehending.

'I no like group. Sometimes I go away from group maybe one day. Group there,' I lie again, and point vaguely down to the Kali Gandaki.

He nods.

'What are your names?' I ask.

'Pema, Tochez, Nomkai,' they answer one after another.

'How did you learn to speak English?' I ask the one communicating.

'Taiwan.'

Taiwan? The word slips so easily off his tongue, but why would anyone here even know of that faraway place? Was he working in a factory? Surely there is enough cheap labour there already without recruiting from this outpost of human civilisation? Or was he one of the Khampas trained clandestinely by the Nationalist Chinese regime in Taiwan? Many Khampas were recruited into the Nationalist Chinese army and then flown and parachuted into Tibet even well after the US had withdrawn its support.

This clump of villages was one of the strongholds of CIA-supported Khampa fighters. We sit there in silence studying each other. For them too, the encounter must seem otherworldly. As the conversation has reached a standstill, I say goodbye and walk towards Kharma who is waiting half-a-kilometre away. Looking back, I see the three villagers huddled immobile in their stone windbreak, eyes peering bleakly over the protective wall, watching me disappear mysteriously out of their lives.

Kharma and I remount in the gulch and canter back across the desert-like plain to the foot of the cliffs and the narrow gully that will take us up to the pass again. On the cliff face the shadow of a soaring bird bounces crazily about the rocks, ducking into crevices and out again. I spot the bird, a lammergeier, gliding effortlessly on invisible currents, before it disappears from sight some kilometres along the wall of rock. Kharma tells me that someone, a hermit or a monk, lives up in those apparently inaccessible caves.

As we climb back up the steep-sided gully, the horses sweat again, and by the time we reach the pass they are blowing like locomotives. The wind picks up as we come out from the protection of the ravine. The Dzong Valley lies far below, beautiful in the evening sun, which catches the colours on the trees and the ochre *gompas* of the villages of Jharkot and Dzong, and the lush oasis of Kagbeni far down the valley. Cutting directly to Muktinath, we traverse the Dzong Khola. On the steep defile I dismount, leading the horse by the reins, when the edge of the path gives way under his right foreleg. He somersaults down the side in a heap, to a ledge some five metres below. He struggles upright and stands quietly but unhurt. If the same thing had happened on certain sections of the route we did today, and if I had been riding, we would have dropped some hundreds of metres down into the precipice of a gorge.

For discretion's sake, we separate going back into Ranipawa. Kharma rides in front of the police check-point. I sneak around the back, tying the horse up behind the *bhaati*. As previously agreed, I continue to the Hot Holy Showers before meeting Kharma later in his kitchen where we sit on the floor, in front of the fire. The ice-cold bottle of beer tastes better than any beer I have had before.

I have experienced two days riding into inner Mustang. I have washed my outer body, and quite possibly my soul, under an auspicious Hot Holy Shower, and my more mundane physical innards with two large cold bottles of beer which have gone straight through my empty stomach to my head. Skipping merrily and haphazardly down to Jharkot, I meet a group of well-to-do, portly Indian pilgrims on their way up to Muktinath. They are exhausted, out of breath, unhappy, and sprawled out astride the path as if expecting a picnic to arrive up the trail on the backs of their porters.

'Is it how far to Muktinath?' one gasps, holding in an ample belly.

'You're almost there,' I reply to the exhausted crew, my feet still not touching the ground. But I am wrong. Distances have shrunk with familiarity. For the five fat Indians, it is still another couple of hour's struggle away, or at their current rate of progress, another lifetime.

JHARKOT–KAGBENI

'Souf? Souf?' The little girl's eyes light up every time she comes through the doors to serve us food. She is a *bhotia*, a highlander, her hair uncombed, dirty, her *chupa* an indistinguishable colour. But her Mongolian face is alive and full of vitality. 'Pibe souf?' she asks hopefully.

We are all in love with her. Last night's meal had been confused and nothing we ordered actually came out of the kitchen. But Michel and I are easy-going, taking the muddle in our stride. Besides, we are despairingly enamoured of the little girl, as are two Dutch girls and Yanzeh, the American whom I had met at Tal whose path I now cross again. His trekking permit is as extended as mine.

The little girl has brought in five 'soufs' for breakfast. None of us ordered soup. But we each take a bowl and thank her graciously. She is ecstatic that she has apparently managed to get the order right again, and hurtles into the kitchen screaming her consistent success rate to the owner-cum-cook. I wonder whether there is in fact a conspiracy between the proprietors and the little girl, to serve us what they have, regardless of what we order; or whether in fact the owners genuinely have no idea there is often no connection between what we request and what the girl brings.

She returns, carrying pots of tea. 'Milik tea? Milik tea?' I ordered hot chocolate, but I take the milk tea, just to see her eyes light as she chalks up another success. She seems to take real pride in her work. Late last night I saw her, too small to reach over the sink, hence squatting precariously on the edge of the cement basin to wash the dishes. The pile started off much higher than her own tiny body.

I'd stay here just for her. In a stone enclosure behind the lodge, seven yak from Tibet are slaughtered. Piles of meat accumulate. The tiny 'souf' girl, barely able to walk with her burden, staggers away from the carnage, four yak feet tangled obscenely in her arms. I dread to think under which menu item the yak feet will reappear through a conspiracy of confusion.

She asks for the kerchief that is wrapped around my neck. 'No is possible,' I tell her. I found the neckerchief during a mountain climb in Norway, and it has sentimental value for me now.

'Everything possible,' she replies coyly. She is right, everything does seem possible up here. And to prove the point I symbolically unknot the memory and give it to her. She laughs in pleasure, eyes flashing.

Despite her charms, we continue, down towards Kagbeni through the semi-terraced fields of Khingar, listening to the singing of the men as they plough their fields. Their voices waver in the breeze, interspersed by sharp whistled commands to their *zopkio*. The pastoral sounds are disturbed by the unusual sight of a large, ground-hugging army helicopter, flying low over Jharkot, across the Dzong Khola and up and over the pass I had traversed yesterday on my way back from inner Mustang. I watch open-mouthed as the helicopter disappears over the pass.

Michel observes, 'They are looking for you. The goat-herd must have mentioned it to their village police post and they radioed the information to the army base at Jomosom.'

'Just for me?'

'They have a strong economic incentive to stop trekkers going into inner Mustang without a permit. Don't underestimate that. They

[117]

would love to catch someone doing what you did and put him in jail just to set an example to other foreigners thinking of doing the same thing. You were lucky. Nepalese jails are not fun, nor are they easy to get out of. There are quite a few Westerners languishing in them, mostly for selling drugs, and you're guilty until proven innocent.'

There have been stories of other Westerners secretly entering into inner Mustang without permits. Some have been stoned by the locals, some have disappeared. In a way I am not surprised that the Khampas, who sacrificed so many lives against the Chinese with the prodding of the Americans, should be bitter over the sudden removal of that support, and subsequently display open hostility to vulnerable Westerners.

Sangpo's first wife's Tibetan family have extended an invitation for us to stay with them. Sangpo insists we visit and stop overnight. Their abode is a typical Kagbeni building, entered through a door which leads off an outside alley into an open private courtyard surrounded by stalls for animals. We climb up a notched log to the second floor. This is the living-area, which includes a ground-level hearth, with no duct for the smoke; on the sides are mud benches, covered in Tibetan carpets, which act as beds. The roof is cross-laid by wooden rafters superimposed by smaller branches mixed with straw and mud. With so little rainfall, there is no need to slope the roof. The walls are decorated incongruously with posters marketing Indian movies. The cosmetically pale faces of Indian actors, clones of Rambo, appear heroically amid flames, guns, women and hurtling cars.

We are served Tibetan tea, a savoury drink combined with salt and yak butter. I have occasionally found it undrinkable, but this time it seems acceptable. Then we are served *chang*, a home-made brew of fermented barley, by a woman with no fingers on her left hand. Sangpo sees me looking at this misshapen fist. 'Eaten by cat, when baby,' he explains. She coughs persistently, but laughs as often. I wonder at the misery and hardship these Tibetan refugees suffered before and during their escape into Nepal. Thousands died of hunger *en route*.

The room fills with family, and the curious, as it becomes dark outside. The fire gets fiercer, providing heat as well as light. More *chang* is served. In a display of comradeship which transcends the language barrier, Sangpo instructs me how to dip my right ring finger into my drink and splash the liquid drops into the air three times: the first time to honour the gods, the second time to friends and the third to family. Finely ground *tsampa* flour is spooned into the *chang*, to make a messy mixture of alcohol and roasted barley flour. There is enough nutrition in this concoction to sustain a binge for some days.

We are crowded around the fire, grimy faces lit by the orange flames. A pretty girl with a shaved head huddles next to me for warmth. She wants to be a monk, she explains in Nepali. She is fourteen, her face full of hope. She shows me a treasured photo of the Dalai Lama which she pulls out of the folds of her clothes. Michel is able to translate, enabling me to find out more about her.

It is traditional for the second daughter to become a monk, but she wants to do so 'from her heart'. I believe her. She alternates between staring into the fire, hope written all over her face, and smiling broadly at me. I cannot help but remember Michel's awful statistic of three-hundred-thousand young Nepalese girls sent to India to work as prostitutes. With her pale complexion and ruddy red cheeks, she would be attractive to Indian men. I hope she fulfils her wish to become a monk, her face is so kind. She tells me her name is Nima Tolma.

The old man, the father of the woman whose fingers were eaten by a cat, enters the smoke-filled room. Another Khampa. His weather-beaten face breaks into a smile, revealing toothless gums. He cannot speak Nepali. He is followed by his grandson, about twelve, wearing a yellow baseball cap obtained from a passing tourist, mismatched with his traditional red and blue yak-wool and leather knee-high boots which his grandfather made. He holds up a trophy, a ball-point pen, for all to see. It is strange to see the other side of the Pen Brigade. The boy squeezes in with us, staring at the fire, and frequently at his cherished pen. Michel has a baby on his lap. We all sit on low stools, or on carpets on the floor, the firelight drawing our collective attention during conversation. Eyes sparkle, reflecting the flames, amid frequent smiles etched on dirty faces.

Born in Tibet, the 'old' man is now sixty-one. He looks much, much older. He had three sons and four daughters, of whom the woman with no fingers on her left hand is the only one still living. This old Khampa warrior is now reduced to looking after the house we sit in, on behalf of a rich trader from Kagbeni, living in India.

Sangpo tells us he had eleven siblings. His father, a lama, had four wives, all of them sisters. Sangpo's previous wife, belonging to this family, died. Many other members of his family perished in their flight from Tibet. Those who survived the initial escape died fighting as guerrillas after crossing back across the border into Tibet to attack the Chinese soldiers. I do not question him on the details of how, or why. The occasion is not right. He beams his pride at having Michel and me sharing the evening with his extended family.

Garlic cloves frying in the pan sharpen my appetite. A mixture of spices adds to the aroma. The children stretch their hands out to the fire. Their noses drip from chronic colds, their eyelids close slowly as they get tired, but at the slightest noise or change of speaker the eyelids jump wide open again in fascination. The old man smiles contentedly. He does not understand the Nepali conversation, but he is content to see his family around him.

After drinking so much Tibetan tea and *chang* mixed with *tsampa*, I have to go to the toilet. Understanding my need, Sangpo leads me down the notched trunk to the animal stalls. He indicates the dung-laden straw. Swaying together, we relieve ourselves in the steaming heap. The act itself is a rite of passage, a measure of the bond of friendship between the two of us, despite our inability to converse effectively with one another. A half-moon shines brightly over the courtyard and on the Just Hills across the river.

Sangpo says simply, 'I am happy you are here,' as we pee copiously into the pungent compost. The urine-soaked straw, along with the human and animal excrement in the animal stalls, will be dug out next autumn and carried in conical baskets to the fields, ploughed into the earth to fertilise the crops, to be eaten and excreted and re-ploughed, cultivated and harvested in an endless cycle. Climbing back up the notched tree-trunk, demonstrating we are mates, Sangpo thoughtfully, although probably unnecessarily, guides me up.

We eat *tsampa*, a gruel made of ground roasted barley, mixed with hot chilli and spices, and potato stew with dried mutton. The boy with the pen is sitting up, almost asleep, but every once in a while he opens his eyes and pulls his pen out from his trouser pocket and admiringly scrutinises its shiny plastic surface in the firelight. The old man encourages the boy to speak English to me. 'What is your name?' I ask him.

'My name is Pantzang Tolma.'

'How old are you?'

'I am twelve years old.'

The boy writes out the numbers one to one-hundred, painstakingly, then reads off each of the numbers, his little brother's big-eared head in his lap, almost covering the notebook and nodding approval at each number recited. The old man's lined face beams pride as he watches his older grandson's performance. The mother feeds her new-born baby with food she masticates first, then spoons into the baby's mouth with the fingers of her good hand.

Pretending to be more drunk than I am, I let my eyes close and my head flop to one side, or backwards. The boy with the pen and his brother with the big ears copy me. They mimic a drunkard, their eyes rolling backwards, head falling forwards. Their imitations are perfectly realistic. I cannot stop myself laughing at these two urchins, perfectly caricaturing themselves forty years from now.

I too am content to share this evening with these *bhotia*. Perhaps it is the smoke-filled room irritating my eyes, but I am deeply moved by the evening's intense feeling of generosity and comradeship. They are materially poor, and yet they have a spiritual affluence and strength of inner being few of us 'wealthy' Westerners could match.

KAGBENI–JOMOSOM

Michel agrees that instead of walking the regular trail back to Jomosom, we should climb on the other side of the Kali Gandaki Khola to return via the mountain ridge perched over the village. Sangpo likes this idea too; it is in the direction of his adopted homeland Dolpo, and he still has friends in the villages where he used to work as a labourer during the winters.

We climb higher into the desert landscape, the silence periodically disturbed by a sound like that of a train approaching, warning of a violent gust of wind that seems to have a life force of its own. Men plough their fields, singing hauntingly as they work. As we walk through the village of Dangorjung, a villager becomes belligerent, thinking we are common tourists straying off our permitted trekking route. His eyes open wide as Michel heaps fluent Nepali abuse on him, and within minutes they are holding hands.

Half-a-dozen fearful white-eyed yak are herded through the narrow passageways and we are forced to take refuge in the doorways of houses. Over the doorways, goat skulls covered in cloth and a back-drop of crossed sticks and a spider's web of coloured threads ward off evil spirits. The white threads of the *zor* are for the gods. The coloured threads are for the *tsen*, the evil spirits which lie in wait everywhere, ready to do harm. The exorcists call the evil powers into the *zor* where the gods represented by the white threads can keep control of the entangled spirits bound in the coloured threads.

Rooftop prayer wheels, with three wind 'cups' attached, effortlessly spin silent prayers into the wind. Tibetan-looking women in grey robes with aprons wrapped around their waist go about their household chores. We are invited by our former belligerents to a dark abode for *chang*, which none of us resists.

Staggering slightly inebriated out of the shadows, we pass a school on the outskirts of the village. Classes have ended for the day and children are leaving the school building. When they see us, however, they flee down the hillside as fast as they can. By contrast with the fearless members of the Pen Brigade, they are clearly terrified of us. We are only several kilometres above and away from the well-beaten trekkers' path, and yet we move in a different world. I wonder why these children are so frightened of us. What have they been told about Westerners?

From the fields far below, the sound of the men singing as they work their ploughs wafts on the wind. We must be higher than Muktinath and yet I no longer feel problems with the altitude, or the weight of the back-pack. We pass through areas with small clumps of junipers and Himalayan cedar and delicate purple gentians. At the top of a ridge I pick up a stone and place it on the cairn, which grows higher as each traveller who chooses to do so makes a contribution in thanks to the gods of lonely, windswept crossings.

We take mandatory photographs of each other. God-like, omnipo-tent, we have a magnificent view of the Tibetan Plateau to the north and the Himals all around us. Sangpo is so happy, he laughs and sings and dances as the wind blows through his unravelled hair. We are about four-thousand metres above sea level. The Kali Gandaki and Jomosom lie some thousand metres directly beneath us.

I suck in a deep breath of this pure mountain air and hold it in tight, willing it to become a part of me, the oxygen flowing in my veins, igniting my spiritual self with the same physical energy that my body feels. Sangpo's joy is infectious: I let out the air and soon I am laughing and dancing with him. Michel stands back, delighted to see his two companions so infused with the energy and beauty of this place.

The ridge is dotted with evergreen trees. Gnarled branches lopsidedly hug the leeward side of tree-trunks for protection against the howling Gandaki winds. Stumps testify to recent deforestation. We scramble down the scree slope like skiers in deep snow. The mountainside is so steep that just a small hop projects one far down the incline, and we must scramble frantically to keep upright, legs like windmill blades cutting through the loose stones that are thrown up to our calves. Wind gusts, blowing upward, are violent enough to knock me back into the hill against the force of gravity.

Michel hurtles past at breakneck speed, leaving behind him a long trail of dust. At the bottom he skids onto his back, his legs spread apart, and bursts out laughing. Not to be outdone, Sangpo charges by, almost out of control, yelling. It is amusing to see this friend who has been so quiet, now so exuberant. We catapult ourselves further, down to the bottom of the valley where it is strange to be walking on flat ground again, akin to a sailor back on a motionless shore after long rocking out at sea.

The sun sets down the broad main passageway of Jomosom. Gusting winds pelt dust and grit into our faces, thrown up from the hoofs of a moving caravan of two-hundred mules. I am transfixed by the sight of the somnambulant mules with blowing yak-tail head-tresses back-lit by the setting sun. The ringing of thousands of bells mixes with the roar of the wind as the mules meander timelessly through Jomosom's barren main drag.

JOMOSOM–MARPHA

My mind is a maelstrom of eddying memories from childhood. Although I was born in Toronto, my British-born parents uprooted the family when I was three, so that my connections with Canada often feel tenuous. I find myself more at home in settings such as this fly-blown outpost. A childhood spent in Asia and Africa makes the simplicity of rural life in exotic places more natural in many ways than the intricate complexities of the Western world, although I have learnt to cope with both.

These thoughts have been brought on by memories of boarding-school in Singapore where my best friend was Jhalak Rai, the son of a Nepalese Gurkha soldier serving in the British army. He instilled in me a curiosity for Nepal, the recollection of which is triggered by the sight of the Gurkha base here in Jomosom.

Michel stays in Jomosom to visit friends. I head out early and alone, for Marpha and then Tatopani, where we agree to meet again.

The sun's rays penetrate through gaps in the mountains, hitting the valley on the opposite side, where the inevitable *chorten* or small *gompa* would seem to have been built specifically to benefit from their position: the hot sun warms the ground, and the white coating of frost melts quickly. Well-worn paths ascend into the tree-line, leading only to the forest, the source of firewood.

A flight of doves twists and turns overhead, the wind hissing through their wings as they pass. Where do they have to go in such a hurry? Destination seems unimportant here. Alpine choughs cavort, squeaking noisily as they execute aerobatic manoeuvres. Perhaps there is no purpose to their spectacular flight after all; perhaps they are all flying just for the sake of it.

At this early hour of the morning there is no Kali Gandaki wind. The air is perfectly still and pure; every tiny detail of rock, leaf, pebble and blade of grass is revealed in the crispness of the morning. Not only is the exterior world in absolute focus but so am I. The night's dreams and morning's thoughts have put a sometimes convoluted life into per-spective.

The stark mountains rise extravagantly into the heavens, drawing myself out of redundant introspection. The rarefied air provides no protection from the brilliant sun.

A well-preserved *chorten* on the outskirts of Marpha signals the whitewashed village everyone on the Other Side talked about. Clean beds and delectable food are advertised along the main, intricately pat-terned, flagstone-lined passageway, devoid of dirt and rubbish. A conduit of water runs hidden under the flagstones, like a modern sewage system.

Signs on the Thakali *bhaatis* proclaim: 'Hot shower – Best food in cheap rate. Italian, Mexican, Continental Food.' All the lodges lay claim to culinary expertise, hot solar showers, reasonable rates. Shops sell everything from Tibetan souvenirs to toiletries. There is a cobbler, a community 'library', a post office, a boys club, and 'Freshme Beauty Parlour – Ladies and Gents Haircutting, bleaching, facial, body massage, Marpha, Mustang.' It is not exactly what I associated with Mustang, but I wouldn't mind a haircut.

In one of the stores I buy toothpaste, a red toothbrush and a red comb, all for less than a dollar. The red toothbrush and comb are Chinese. I wonder if, like my Chinese red T-shirt, the colour will come out and stain my teeth and hair a pink to match my pink clothes. Apart from an unsuccessful attempt in Jomosom, I have not combed my hair for over a month; I have not brushed my teeth for some days either. I am tempted to visit Freshme's for an overhaul.

The plump, Indian-looking, sari-clad woman owning the beauty parlour is the wife of the government doctor assigned to this outpost, probably much to their chagrin. I suspect that her income from the salon is greater than her husband's as a government doctor. 'Can you cut my hair?' I prise up a slab of my tangled, dust-encrusted mop.

She wobbles her head yes, and indicates a chair for me to sit on, facing a poster portraying twelve effeminate Thai boys. Each has a preposterous coiffure, ranging through the colours of the rainbow, excluding my own dirty blonde-brown. 'Which one you like?' the doctor's wife asks enthusiastically, pointing to the various faces that look like criminal mugshots.

I select the least scandalous. 'That one,' I point out hopefully. She tries to comb my yak-like tresses, but they are a semi-permanent tangle of dust and knots. She makes a few unsuccessful stabs, but my helmeted head proves quite impossible to combat. I offer to wash my own hair. Anything to stop the tear-jerking pain of her pulling my scalp out by the hair roots. She shakes her head in approval, and I escape to a nearby lodge.

'Do you have a shower?' I ask the *bhaati* hostess. She shows me. 'Hot water?'

'Yes, solar-heated.' Then she adds, 'Now is a good time, otherwise trekkers come and hot water is finished.'

There are two sorrowful-looking trekkers sitting morosely at a table who overhear this advice. The female of the couple wears an amply filled and unbecoming dirty sweat-suit. He by contrast is severely underweight, wearing spectacles which overwhelm his delicate face. I fetch a towel from my room, arriving back just in time to witness the woman slip into the shower cubicle.

Annoyed, I sit down at a table, and practise being a good Buddhist, eliminating all negative thoughts from my head. She is in there for a steaming half-hour, followed by a changing of the guard, as he slithers surreptitiously in and she waddles guiltily out. I wait and practise Buddhist-inspired patience another interminable fifteen minutes before his skinny wet body emerges.

Surprisingly, the hot water is still hot. I shower, wash my hair as best I can, and get back to Freshme Beauty Parlour. She is sitting on the doorsteps pouting, having given up on my returning.

She does not want the chair to face the mirror, which I take as a bad sign, so I am confronted again by the poster of the twelve Thai boys with their hairstyles encompassing the range from punk, rocker, Elvis Presley and Michael Jackson. She starts whittling around my head, I wonder whether I should remind her of the hairstyle towards which I had hoped she was vaguely imitating. A rumbling on the flagstones on the narrow pathway outside the parlour provides me with an excuse to disengage myself from her undivided attention. I jump out of the chair to witness scores of yak running through the village, like so many bulls in Pamplona.

'Meat!' she shouts gleefully, recovering her composure. 'From summer pastures in mountains. Now all come down for making meat.'

She continues chopping. I am surrounded by detritus, as a fresh me takes shape. She pats things into place on my head, rather suspiciously, before I am allowed to see myself. She holds up a mirror. I look like the boy in the top right corner of the poster, not the one in the middle, on the left. My hair is almost uncut on top, with very short back and sides.

'Not bad,' I say politely, gritting my teeth, 'for a first time. Now, how about we just cut all this off?' I unfold the cockatoo feather imitation on the top. 'Make it short like this.' I hold up about an inch of hair.

'No is beautiful. Here is fashioning.' She flips back and coddles the cockatoo feathers.

'I realise that, but there is so much dirt flying around, and it's so difficult to wash my hair. So . . . please . . .'

She reluctantly takes up the scissors again and gives me a crew-cut. It is not fashionable, but it will be easier to keep clean.

'Now, beard,' she says vengefully. I hesitate as a result of recent experience. 'No charge,' she adds. I give in to her enthusiasm and my thriftiness and let her massacre my beard in retaliation.

'Too much beautiful,' I pronounce, wobbling my chiselled head appreciatively at its reflection in the mirror.

I am still in her firm grip when she shows me her colour TV, connected to a satellite dish, pulling in Indian stations. 'You see TV with me?' she smiles suggestively.

'Thanks, but no thanks.' I am not at all sure that her husband would appreciate this offer of hospitality.

While I stroll through the streets of Marpha in the evening, showing off my haircut, the moon rises over Nilgiri, even as the sunset reflects off white summits. Venus appears on the other side of Nilgiri peak. The mountain tops are pink, the sky steel-blue, another spectacular Himalayan sunset. Back down on earth, Marpha's streets are quiet. A dog curled up on itself licks its extended cock. At the end of the village, in an enclosed area below the path, four huge black forms of yak stand quietly, engraved on the flagstones by their own distinct moonlit shadows. One grinds its teeth audibly. The animals are nervous. Tomorrow Marpha will resemble a battle scene, with seventy yak to be slaughtered and butchered, their bloody parts laid open around the village.

The moonlight is intense, casting silvery-white reflections off the wooden shingle on the rooftops; I am reminded of an old-fashioned Hollywood film set, shot at midday, with special dark camera filters to simulate night. Moonlight filters through the leafy foliage of a banyan tree, dappling the flagstone path like one of the fairy scenes in *A Midsummer Night's Dream*. I walk back to the lodge, gingerly skirting the dog who is no longer captivated by his cock. There are few trekkers, despite the fact it is high season. Walking past the open windows of a home, I vaguely hear the BBC World Service news.

Inside the lodge the couple who had delayed my shower are talking to others. I ask for dinner and eat by myself, musing how the Annapurna Circuit is the least sexual holiday one could possibly undertake: sleeping in common dormitories, or at best in private rooms with paper-thin walls; massive amounts of garlic in the food;

chronic diarrhoea combined with lack of showers and toilet facilities; persistent stomach upset; altitude sickness; fatigue. All this mitigates against the lustful vacation.

I am wrong.

Late that evening voices of the couple in the cubicle next to mine wake me. Their electric light bulb is switched on. Spying through cracks in the thin planks that separate their sleeping-quarters from mine, I recognise the showered couple moving aimlessly around the confined space. After some minutes they undress, she out of her soiled sweat-suit. The light is turned off. She coughs, intimately, as if in my ear. I try to sleep. Their voices become more subdued, down to the level of pillow-talk, then whispers, in a guttural language I recognise as Hebrew, but cannot understand.

His breathing becomes heavy. The inevitable creak of the bed follows. I hear every detail of their copulation. His breathing becomes heavier still, and then there is a gasp. Fortunately for me, and probably for her too judging from her chronic rattling cough, his sexual act is over in a matter of minutes, followed by the rustle of cheap toilet paper against skin. It is hardly an erotic performance, but it is, I conclude ruefully after taking note of my own physical celibacy, at least a performance.

MARPHA–GHASA

I want to avoid the wholesale slaughter of seventy cuddly yak.

It is too late. Of the four yak I saw last night in the nearby court-yard, two are already on the ground. One is dead, his head severed and propped glumly over a huge aluminium container to catch each drop of blood. They are about to kill the second, his neck is outstretched, his head upside down. But they do not kill him with a knife through the heart as they did in Kagbeni. His throat is unceremoniously slit like a goat. Blood spurts out in a gush and a lid is used to deflect the pulsating blood into a container. The head seems almost severed from the body yet the animal breathes, no longer through its nose, but through its severed windpipe. The basin fills up with blood and another container is brought alongside. The yak's bound legs kick, as if he is trying to run away. The second basin is almost full and his legs are still straining at the ropes, his deep blue eyes blinking from a virtually decapitated head. A dull blue film covers the eyes, the legs quiver, the wheezing gasps from the windpipe stop, and the animal is dead.

A Frenchman takes dozens of photos, from all angles, seemingly unable to get enough. Two other hobbled yak look on. How must they feel knowing what is happening? I cannot look on these animals without equating them with teddy bears; loved and cherished confidantes. Again I am tempted to say, 'How much is your teddy bear yak? Eight-thousand rupees? I'll give you ten-thousand, if you let him go.'

But I don't. I turn my back on the two remaining yak, standing so forlorn, and I walk out of the village. On the day of reckoning, whether it is my karma or heaven and hell, I am convinced that these moments of callousness and indifference will be brought to account.

The hotel owner told me last night that yak are killed because the protein is needed to help people survive the winter. He had also told me that most of the well-off villagers of Marpha spend their winters in Pokhara or Kathmandu. I am moving out of the realm of Buddhism.

The village of Tukuche, further downstream, is a sad remnant of the extensive trading business that was once the lifeblood of the people living on the Kali Gandaki. This was the principal trading-post on the Kali Gandaki for hundreds of years, where *bhotia* from the north brought down Tibetan rock-salt carried by yak and sheep, and returned with rice and other grains and goods. Goods were bartered, or sold for cash, the mule trains from the south meeting the yak caravans from the north. Now many of the previously grand trading-houses stand empty. Some have been converted to lodges, but I do not see a single trekker.

The wind picks up, composing notes as it blows through the chir pine needles, sounds I have not heard since Upper Pisang. I search for Easy's footprints on the ground but they have long gone with Shay. Grasshoppers and dragonflies flit about again. I am descending through the deepest canyon of the world, bounded on either side by the Himalayas. Winter recedes confusingly almost before we have got used to its arrival, and summer scenes once again charge the senses.

Annapurna I pokes its peak over the summits of Just Hills, with

Dhauligiri towering eight-thousand metres or almost five miles above sea level, some three-and-a-half miles above and across the river. The distance between the two peaks is less than ten miles. The guidebooks tell me that the deep Kali Gandaki Valley through the Himalayas provides a significant bio-geographic divide, both north and south, as well as east and west. The wetter mountain slopes to the east are more densely forested than those of the west, with a corresponding greater variety of flora and fauna. The valley also marks the limits of the Palaeartic and Oriental regions of distribution of animals as well as the extreme range of several European and Asiatic species of plant and bird life.

The north-south divide is more obvious, descending from the limits of the arid, desert-like Tibetan Plateau of the Alpine and sub-Alpine zone to the north, through the temperate zone and into the dense jungles of the sub-tropical and tropical zones to the south.

A caravan of mules knocks me about as they pass. They seem to do this purposely, and I have learnt to stay on the inside of the track. Cicadas drone. The roofs of houses are occasionally sloped now, an indication that I am moving out of the rain shadow. Prayer flags still flap from the occasional flat rooftops, but they are fewer than before.

I descend the gorge forged by the Kali Gandaki through the Himal upheavals, via the desolation and gloominess of the shadowed world created by the overhanging jungle and canyon walls. There is no one else on the track. To heighten my sense of unease, I see the lumbering shape of a dog, a Tibetan mastiff. Alarms ring in my head as the bear-like creature ambles towards me, with no apparent purpose. He has a bell around his neck, and yet there are no sheep or goats anywhere around. The path is steep, a confining cliff face on one side, a precipice on the other, and I have no alternative but to walk within a metre of him, or stop and turn around. I stop, and he turns deliberately to look at me. Not wanting to reveal my fear, I continue walking, terrified, my anti-rabies device bamboo ski-pole cocked and ready to lash out. But he stalks on, as if he had not seen me. As I tread by, I see he has a huge head wound, a plate of his skull is missing, his brain laid bare.

Having already been savaged by a dog on the face which necessitated seventeen stitches to close the ripped cheek, I am not interested in repeating the experience and I accelerate nervously away as fast as I dare, and it is not long before I reach Ghasa, where the vegetation is almost tropical. Banana trees again; guavas; lime trees; some kind of cherry tree with pink blossoms. I stop at a quiet lodge, and sit inside the dark, cool dining-area sipping a cup of tea. It has been a long walk. A trekker couple stride in.

'Do . . . you . . . have . . . a . . . room . . . for . . . three?' he asks me, enunciating clearly in perfect English.

'For . . . you . . . pibty . . . rupees . . . each,' I reply equally painstakingly.

'What!' the trekker exclaims. He turns to his girlfriend and says indignantly, 'That's bloody ridiculous. More than twice what we paid last night.'

'Oh Ian! Don't be silly. He's not the owner, he's just another trekker like us,' the girl tells Ian. My deep brown tan, pink outfit and Freshme haircut are apparently a good disguise.

'How . . . come . . . you . . . talk . . . like . . . that?' he asks, leaning towards me to see me better in the gloom, still not convinced.

'Because . . . you . . . are . . . talking . . . like this,' I answer truthfully.

Ian . . . doesn't . . . think . . . I'm . . . funny. So much for the British sense of humour.

The scene in the kitchen is one of bedlam. Bobby, who runs the lodge, is only sixteen, and is helped by her younger brother and sister. The parents are away managing another lodge, leaving their children to run this one. They resemble mad scientists. The clay oven has three 'burners', over which a concoction of brews is bubbling merrily. Nepalese music plays from a battery-powered radio. Food lies scattered carelessly over the kitchen; used pots and pans, dishes, glasses lie in a pile on the dirt floor.

Bobby, the oldest and most presentable of the three, takes orders from the trekkers: pizza, lasagne, Mexican burritos. Chunks of wood are thrown into the fire to stoke the orange flames licking fiercely through the burners. Eggs are cracked open and the discarded shells thrown on a growing pile. Dilapidated vegetables are cut up for egg spring-rolls. The boy digs his hand into a variety of tins pulling out a handful or a pinch of spice, like magical ingredients to a secret potion. A chapati falls on the ground, is quickly picked up, and blown on forcefully to remove the dirt. An omelette is ripped apart by hand and added to the fried rice. The youngest girl has a terrible cough. She hacks discretely into the brownish towel hanging over her shoulder, which she also uses to wipe the plates clean before putting food on them for Bobby to serve to the guests.

I am struck by the equanimity with which the trekkers order their dinners, fully expecting recognisable meals to arrive out of this medieval, teenage-run kitchen. And surprisingly, they do. Despite the chaos in the scullery, pizza, fried rice, spring-rolls, burritos and lasagne are served in identifiable form. The two different worlds, Nepalese youngsters labouring in their archaic kitchen and Western trekkers on holiday, fuse together with each mouthful eaten.

Ian and I have both asked for fried rice. He eats his with gusto, smacking his lips with the enthusiasm of a gourmet. I am more circumspect, playing with my food, looking for gastronomic infringements, rather than carelessly gulping it all down. Ian licks his spoon and claps his hands in satisfaction.

The younger sister comes out of the kitchen, coughing. She has the brown dish towel wrapped around her head like a scarf, against the cold, and sporadically coughs into an end of it. Over tea I notice on the opposing dining-room wall a typical poster with a Thai scene of tranquil manicured gardens: 'Happiness is the everyday sunshine of your life.' It takes me some time to decipher the Thai-inspired English, but when I do, I realise the significance of the statement.

After dinner I quietly reflect on the poster's subtle truth and wonder whether I have been far too ambitious through periods of my life, and have not enjoyed the way, and its simple pleasures, as much as I should have.

I start a new notebook devoted to 'Everyday Sunshines'.

GHASA–TATOPANI

A mynah bird sings, a chorus that reminds me of sleeping in on tropical Sunday mornings in Dar es Salaam. I worked there for two years with the United Nations Development Programme before in effect dropping out, and starting a safari business in the Selous Game Reserve in southern Tanzania, the largest game reserve in Africa. In that five-year period there was not a single occasion when I did not wake up, usually well before dawn, looking forward to the day. I felt intensely alive. There have been times, after all, when I have enjoyed life along the way.

I savour lying in bed, reminiscing. Too often we, especially in the Western or Westernised world, race through life without having the luxury of time to appreciate it fully. On this new day, I practice what the poster preaches.

My bedroom window overlooks the mynah's garden and the river gorge. Mist hangs over the valley. The first mist-covered sky since Tal on the Other Side. Yesterday, I was in the rain shadow of the Himalayas, in a desert-like winter landscape with yak, Buddhist prayer flags and wild-eyed *bhotia*. Today I am surrounded by dense jungle, fruit trees, mist, water buffalo and signs of Hinduism.

Physically exhausted at the end of the day's trekking, I am usually asleep before nine in the evening and wake up between five and six in the morning. I have never in my life slept so much or so soundly for such extended periods. My dream world has the luxury of overtime.

Last night, as with most nights in these mountains, I dreamt, and woke up remembering my dreams. In last night's dreams my previous job in Ottawa, travelling eight months of the year evaluating development aid projects in Africa and Asia, was offered back to me. I declined.

A tidying-up process is going on in my head. Without the pressures of everyday life, I have eased myself into another rhythm. There are few constraints to a day of walking with a heavy back-pack for six to twelve hours. Each day's success is of my own making. In the rarefied atmosphere of the Himalayas, under cloudless skies, with food and shelter easily available and affordable, anything seems possible. I can make out of my life what I want, shaping my own destiny, casting aside expectations.

In addition to hiking the Annapurna Circuit, I am tracing another circuit: going back to beginnings, to who I was, who I am, perhaps even to who I will be. It is a meditative process I do not have to work at; it is taking place spontaneously, subconsciously, with minimal effort from myself.

At mandatory school choirs, I was asked to mouth the words silently because I sing hopelessly out of tune; trekking, I catch myself humming, despite in-built inhibitions, *Smile, and the world smiles with you*. Confirming there is no one around, I sing the words diffidently at first, then with increasing confidence and volume. Finally I belt out the song as loud as I can, forcing musty air out of my lungs, and stale metaphysical complacency out of my being. It feels good. No wonder there is lots of singing here among the locals. Porters under heavy loads appear unannounced around a bend in the trail, smiling, infected by my off-key crooning.

A man with a crippled leg, probably a result of polio, hobbles by, greeting me '*Namaste*'. He proceeds at twice my pace, despite his affliction. As he rounds a turn in the path carved out of the precipitous rock, he is silhouetted momentarily against the bright sky. The image of the man limping resolutely onwards hits me emotionally as I realise the awful implications of being a cripple in this countryside, with no vehicles, not even a chance of using a wheelchair with any degree of practicality.

Tatopani. The village is famed for its hot springs and Thakali *bhaatis*, although here it would be more appropriate to call them lodges because they are so sophisticated, with private rooms, communal hot showers and flush toilets.

There are two natural hot spring-fed pools at Tatopani. The water is a metre deep in each pool. Half-a-dozen partially submerged trekkers' faces float amid the swirling steam. At the upper pool a heavily built Westerner stands naked. The other tourists in the pool smirk selfconsciously. Nepalese porters and guides, and village women washing their clothes in the effluent from the pool, avert their eyes. An English girl exits the other pool with her boyfriend and climbs into ours. 'He'd be locked up if he did that at a public pool back home. What makes him think he can act that way here?'

As the day progresses, dozens of trekkers arrive and immerse themselves in the pools. The water gets murkier, but we are Westerners, addicted to the fix of a shower or hot bath, and clean bodies. An American girl confirms this generalisation saying, 'I can't get used to not washing everyday, wearing dirty clothes, and hairy legs.' She shows off her newly shorn limbs.

An American lawyer with his heart still in the 1960s tells all and sundry, 'I was in Pokhara thirty years ago. You should have seen it. Those were the days. No concrete, few tourists. But poor? Boy, Nepal was poor. Now look at the country. More than half the Government of

Nepal's revenues come from foreign aid. Britain. The United States. Scandinavia. China. India. You name it. Hundreds of millions of dollars a year. Where does all the money go?' he looks around at us all. No one responds. 'Into the hands of the rich, that's where the money goes. It's the same families who own this country as thirty years ago. Nothing's changed. The poor get poorer, the rich get richer. It's still the same Ranas, Singhs and Thapas who own the place. What has the average Nepalese gained from the revolution? Fuck all. This country was a poor dump twenty years ago, and it's a bigger dump now. The corruption is astronomical, and it's my tax dollars going into creating this fucking mess. Look at the place. Shit everywhere, poverty . . .'

It is not a convincing soliloquy, although his longer-term view is interesting enough. No one argues with him and eventually he climbs out of the pool followed by his girlfriend who glares back over her tattooed shoulder at the unsympathetic fellow bathers.

Michel and Sangpo had agreed to meet me this evening at the lodge. I sit at the outdoor restaurant and wait patiently, absorbing the holiday resort atmosphere of Tatopani. By the time Michel arrives it is almost dark. He flashes me that all-encompassing smile of his, but he looks exhausted. He sits at the table and wraps a worn natural silk scarf around his shoulders like a Ghandi impersonator.

'What's the matter?' I ask.

'I didn't sleep all night. Got news from villagers my son was very sick so I left early this morning to go to Beni where they have a telephone. I spoke to my wife in Kathmandu, and now I am back.'

'And your son?'

'He is fine. He had typhoid. Agnes almost left with him to go to Europe, but he is better since yesterday.'

I can imagine Michel did not sleep.

Sangpo arrives, smiling.

I order three glasses of orange juice freshly squeezed. Within seconds I have finished mine, Sangpo has started his, but Michel does not touch his. He has walked virtually non-stop today for twelve hours, without eating and with little to drink. He can intensify the small pleasure of quenching his thirst by waiting patiently to savour what will be an exquisite experience, giving himself an Everyday Sunshine of his life, on an otherwise inauspicious day.

In the evening we soak in the hot springs before walking up to

Dhauligiri Lodge. A large satellite dish sits on top of the stone building's slate roof. Western pop music blares out of speakers below. A glass counter encloses chocolate cakes, apple pie, lemon meringue pie, apple crumble, cheese cake, coconut cake, strudel, brownies, chocolate chip cookies. We could be in Bali, Greece, the Caribbean, Goa. I am introduced to the owner, Bhuwan Gauchan, a Thakali, and a member of one of the richest families in Tatopani.

'When I say rich,' Michel tells me, 'I don't mean in just Nepalese terms, but in Western terms. He owns real estate in Kathmandu, Pokhara, a trucking business, import-export business. He is worth millions, in dollars.'

The 'millionaire' is dressed shabbily, in canvas shoes with no shoelaces, a dirty and stained brown jacket, dishevelled hair. Bhuwan puts a bottle of brandy on the table, then excuses himself to watch the weather report on his satellite television. After the news, Bhuwan rejoins us and sings absent-mindedly to the accompaniment of Dire Straits. Tucked into the folds of the Just Hills, I have little concept of where I am, divorced from the reality of the villagers living around. The Thakali *bhaati* owner watches the Indian television weather report so he knows whether to put his dining-tables outside or inside in the morning. The display case of desserts, the Westerners chatting on the patio, the electric lights, the Western music; it all seems so out of place.

There is a certain symbolism in my having circumambulated the Circuit anti-clockwise. It has been a progression of the development of the peoples living along the Circuit. From those primitive first nights on the Other Side, to the Western extravagance of Tatopani, I have witnessed within weeks the kinds of changes taking place in Nepal over a generation or two: from the original Nepal to the blending with the Western world; what has been and what is coming.

'It is not something we can stop, or should stop. Who are we to prevent it? This is an aspect of Nepal now, and it is not up to us to condemn it. We have to accept these changes just as we have to accept the backwardness of Nepal,' Michel says. He is ever the optimist, always positive, open and accepting.

We order the dinner special: 'Tomato macaroni cheese soup and enchilada de chicken mushroom, cheese rice and salad'. Italian, Mexican, French and English influences are included in the daily special, but nothing Nepalese.

[136]

Bhuwan does not stay up with us. 'I am tired tonight, I was up late last night watching *Private Benjamin* on the video.' Left to our own devices, we drink the brandy with dinner, and talk well into the night. Michel is blowing off steam, he is so happy that his son is well. Last night, he had imagined the worst.

TATOPANI

I spend the day with Michel, visiting his friends at the government health post at the other end of the village. '*Quelle bordelle.*' Bottles of medicine lie scattered everywhere. 'There is no backup, no system of support from the Ministry of Health. Medicine is brought up here and then for months, nothing. Some of the medicine is out of date by four years, although most of it is just all-purpose antibiotic, aspirin, tuberculosis agent. The medical assistant, she is a dedicated woman, working conscientiously, despite the difficulties. She fled her abusive husband years ago, then trained in primary medical care, and now runs the post despite the lack of backup from the ministry.' Michel looks at her admiringly, knowing she cannot understand his comments. 'You know, the sad thing is the Ministry of Health cannot absorb all the money donated by foreign aid agencies. There is plenty of money, but not enough capability to translate the money into programmes. So they create new administrative departments with more positions, jobs for friends and relatives to the growing list of officials, most of whom have very little to do.'

Back at the lodge, over lunch, a dishevelled Bhuwan explains why he has chosen to live the life of a semi-recluse in his home village. 'I suffered from an identity crisis having been educated at a Jesuit school with North American teachers, and foreign, mostly Western, classmates. At the end of my schooling I did not know where I belonged. For a while I lived in Kathmandu, started businesses there, made lots of money in land ownership, trading, industry, and had many Western friends and girlfriends. But in the end, I realised that I belong here. I have come to accept that I am a wealthy Thakali from Tatopani. No more, no less.'

A buffalo walks into the restaurant. Western music plays, trekkers stroll by carrying towels, on their way to the hot springs. Bhuwan chases the buffalo out of the restaurant and rejoins us. 'Many foreigners come here to discover themselves, searching for something, which they will never find. Why? Because they do not belong here.' He glances at me conspicuously. 'On the other hand, my Nepalese friends from Kathmandu, they come here, see me living in this little village, and they say "Bhuwan, how can you live here? Come, we are going to New York, or London, come with us." That is not for me. They are searching for who they are. They are no longer Nepalese. But who are they? They are not British or American. They do not belong there either. They will not be happy. Here, I know exactly who I am.' He pauses to ruminate on his thoughts. 'Have you ever read *Tao Te Ching* by Lao-Tzu?' Bhuwan asks me.

'No.'

'I thought you said you studied philosophy?'

'I did. Four years. Studied the Western philosophers. We didn't study Asian philosophy, or Tao.'

'What kind of philosophy did you study?' he asks sceptically.

'The gamut of Western analytical philosophers. Aristotle, Plato, Descartes, Hume, Locke, Russell. You name it. I can't even remember them all, it seems so long ago. They were all rationalists, logically working out the Truth, Right and Wrong, the Meaning of Life, God. But each philosopher debunked the others until there seemed to be no Truth but the truth I felt intuitively, and this truth could not be argued or even expressed. At the end of four years I didn't know what to believe. Whatever intuition I had started with had been pummelled out of me. I switched to a graduate programme in economics, and then worked for the Canadian banks as an international economist and got on with life instead of thinking about it all the time.'

'And now?'

'Now I'm thinking again. But I know my thinking won't resolve all the questions I have. To many of them, I don't believe there are absolute answers. Now I'm relying on my inner feelings again, my intuition.'

'But?'

'But, like muscles, they haven't been used for so long that they have atrophied.'

He looks up at the mountains enclosing Tatopani. 'So these mountains are your spiritual ladder to reach your inner being?' Bhuwan asks, again with scepticism.

'Yes.'

He nods. 'But it isn't easy?'

'No. There's a lot of accumulated crud I have to peel away. Doubt. Scepticism. Cynicism. The lingering need to have everything proven to me. I have to learn to accept. To believe.'

'That there is a God?'

'That there is a God.'

'Whose?'

'It doesn't matter. One I feel comfortable with. Do you have a God?'

'Now you are asking me the questions, with the same Western mode of dialectic I too am trying to forget. I too want to accept. For myself. Not for anyone else.' There is silence at the table. We have persuaded ourselves not to engage in any dialectic process. It seems as if Bhuwan is about to say something, but holds himself back. Finally he breaks the awkward silence. 'You should read Tao. You would gain a lot from Taoism.'

'I will.' At midnight I am awakened by voices in the compartment adjacent to mine. I wait interminably for the intruders to hush and go to sleep, then in desperation I get up and knock on their door to ask them to keep their voices down. A skinny man in owlish spectacles opens the door. In the background I see a familiar, ample, reclining form filling a soiled sweat-suit. She coughs.

'Yes?' he says, adjusting his glasses.

'Please, do me a favour, not tonight,' although he probably wouldn't keep me awake for long anyway.

TATOPANI–GHARAMDI

Tatopani must have the cleanest villagers in Nepal. Well before the water gets murky with the sweat and grime of scores of Western trekkers steaming their otherwise unwashed bodies, the local villagers come to soak in the pools which have been emptied, scrubbed and refilled with fresh hot water during the night.

Porters, guides, villagers and trekkers pose in front of a mirror on the corner post of the tea-stall, appraising themselves. The men are the most narcissistic. They flick their clean hair, twist contorted faces from side to side, pulling cheeks down, rubbing hands over chins testing for stubble, standing so close to the mirror that they seem to be trying to reach their own reflections.

Westerners join the Nepalese washing clothes in the effluence from the springs, the Westerners dabbing daintily and ineffectively at their clothes with bars of soap. A young couple squabble, no doubt washing clothes by hand together for the first time ever.

Michel is looking forward to getting off the tourist track, to visit some of the Magar villages he worked in for three years, setting up health posts, training health extension workers, generally educating the hill people in health matters. He invites me to join him and Sangpo.

We diverge off the main trekking route past the turnoff for Ghorepani, head down the Kali Gandaki, then up a tiny path which is steep and narrow, and soon we are in among evergreens. Women harvesting grain in the fields sing and their young children play. 'They seem so happy,' I comment on the idyllic scene.

'On the contrary. Many Nepalese women have severe psychological problems because they feel hopeless in their poverty. Marriage, children one after another, working all their lives. They are responsible for the homestead, children, animals and crops while their husbands are either away for much of the year trading and gambling or at home getting drunk with other men. You would be surprised how high the suicide rate is among these people who outwardly seem so happy.'

We climb almost vertically over the Thak Khola and lose the thin path, so we force our way through bushes to emerge along a cliff line dropping precipitously a thousand metres into the river. I cannot look below without feeling panicky. An intersecting sharp gully stops us traversing any further and we begin scrambling on all fours up what appears to be an almost vertical rock face. The gravitational pull on my heavy back-pack seems to draw me backwards into the sheer drop, and I experience vertigo and have to fight the panic and instinct to freeze.

Eventually we break into the open again. The hamlet of Gharamdi lies on the opposite side of a shallow valley. Stone buildings are surrounded by a patchwork of gold, pink, yellow and brown fields. The semi-terraces are a three-dimensional maze, dotted here and there with pink-blossomed cherry trees. The sun reflects off the flagstone path which winds its way through the colourful plots and becomes lost in the slate-stone rooftops of village homes.

Two young local boys with fashionable Freshme-style haircuts and Lacoste T-shirts stop to stare at us. Michel greets them but they do not reply. They simply stand and gawk. Michel reminds them, 'I am the doctor that worked in your village'. There is no response. When Michel asks them questions, they turn away. When Michel talks to me in French, they are curious enough to listen.

Michel tells me, 'They come from a privileged background, their fathers are probably Gurkhas in the British army. They go to the local school on the heavily tourist-trafficked Tatopani to Ghorepani route where they have learnt to disdain trekkers, especially Westerners. When I ask them what they want to do after school, they don't know. They want to be Gurkhas like their fathers, but have little chance with the British army demobilising their existing Gurkha units. Their other possible aspiration is to work in a factory in Japan, Saudi Arabia, Korea or Taiwan, where in two or three years they can make more money than they could save in a lifetime here. Maybe they invest in a lodge, or a business, and don't have to do physical work again.' Michel can always find something positive about anybody, but he seems defeated as the two boys strut away.

The local *bhaati* in Gharamdi, which does not cater to tourists at all, is dense with smoke from the cooking fire, and I must sit by the door to escape the choking fumes. Children and young adults crowd the doorway and stare at us. Four men inside are already in advanced stages of inebriation. After we eat *dal bhaat* we walk around the village. Michel is clearly disappointed that there are few people he recognises. A boy in the passageway screams when he sees us and runs away crying. Smoke escapes from out under the sooty eaves of smudge-filled homes. There are no signs of the health education extension programme Michel and Agnes spent three years implementing. There is not a single toilet, none of the houses have exhaust pipes from the cooking stoves, the alleys are full of rubbish, there are no pit latrines.

Just outside the photogenic trekking corridors, poverty lurks. The scenic appeal of simple lives in picturesque villages is contradicted by the appalling poverty lying beneath the surface, and just out of sight. 'Nepal still has one of the highest death rates among children under five years old of any country in the world,' Michel reminds me. 'By many standards of measurement, Nepal is one of the poorest countries in the world. A fact conveniently forgotten when we become seduced by friendly and apparently happy inhabitants of Rousseau-like idyllic villages.' We head back towards the *bhaati*.

'No one wants to live here. The young want to work abroad. This village is relatively rich. Look at some of these new, well-built traditional houses. They are owned by Gurkha soldiers. But the family house they put most of their money into now is in Pokhara or Kathmandu. There is nothing to show for all the work Agnes and I put in here because after one-and-a-half or two years, we were only just beginning to learn enough about the local situation to begin to understand. By then we moved to Kathmandu. But part of the reason also is because they simply do not care.'

The conversation back in the *bhaati* is minimal, the men too drunk to make sense, and the others never getting beyond asking how much our boots cost. Crestfallen and strangely quiet, Michel calls it a day.

GHARAMDI–GHOREPANI

We sleep for twelve hours. When I wake up Michel smiles at me from the flimsy mattress he shares on the floor with Sangpo. I now recognise that Michel's smile has the quality of a baby's smile turning to laughter in response to someone pulling funny faces. It is all-encompassing and involves every muscle in his face, his head rolling ecstatically in a paroxysm of delight. Looking at him lying on his back, I almost expect him to start kicking his feet in the air. It is a new day and Michel, the eternal optimist, is back in form.

He gets up to order us breakfast. Sangpo meanwhile practices his French on me. '*Je suis crevé!*' I'm exhausted, he wants me to tell Michel on his behalf, so that Michel will slow the pace down a bit and let him sleep in during the mornings.

I sit close to the door to avoid the smoke as we eat *dal bhaat*. A hen with chicks comes in and is immediately chased off by a dog who stares at my every move, her eyes following my hand from plate to mouth. The dog's eyes fixate on my fingers as I move the food around the plate on the mud floor. Slowly, she moves even closer to me, one step at a time. Soon we will be eating out of the plate together. I selfishly try to shoo her off, but Michel thoughtfully passes his half-finished plate to her, and she gulps the rice down greedily and noisily slurps the dish clean. The hen pecks at the rice scattered on the dirt floor by the dog in her haste.

The cost for all three of us – our accommodation, six meals of unlimited *dal bhaat*, several mugs of tea, three packets of biscuits – is seventy rupees, less than a buck-and-a-half. Two chocolate brownies at Dhauligiri Lodge in Tatopani cost the same.

Sangpo sings for us as we walk. To my ear the rich melody strikes me as more Chinese than Indian. Encouraged by our enthusiasm, he plucks stems from a rhubarb-like plant and splints two stems together. He cuts a couple of notches, then blows. A sound closely resembling that of a trumpet emerges. He astounds me by playing tunes on it. We walk on, Sangpo leading the way, playing his improvised trumpet, like an exotic pied piper.

We enter Ghorepani, the 'horse watering place'. This is the limit of the short trek I did four years ago with Kirsten, and I am interested to see what the difference is. I am unprepared for the developments that have taken place.

Three-storey lodges cling to Deurali Pass almost like Hong Kong slums. The buildings are made out of stone, wood, aluminium sheeting, glass, corrugated tin. A sign in the middle of Deurali, erected by the Ghorepani Lodge Management committee, depicts the routes to Annapurna Base Camp, Tatopani and Jomosom, Poon Hill, Birethanti and Pokhara. 'I cannot recognise the place,' I tell Michel.

'There are three or four new lodges since I was here a year ago,' he admits. Sangpo knows the owner of the first lodge, a lesser one, and we stay there.

Walking through the conglomeration of lodges of Deurali and Ghorepani, we are accosted by two Nepalese women. 'Hello, hello.' They start giggling.

Michel speaks back to them in Nepali and we are invited into their home for tea.

'What is your name?' the more vocal one asks me.

'Andrew,' I reply. 'What is your name?'

'Lakshmi Pun.' She is a Magyar, Mongolian-featured, about thirty, I guess.

'What do you do?'

'I am training manager for ACAP.'

I vaguely remember ACAP from four years ago, but cannot remember anything more than paying the 'entrance' fee of two-hundred rupees. 'What is ACAP?' I ask, to jog my memory.

'Annapurna Conservation Authority Project.'

'A non-governmental organisation?'

'Yes.'

'What do you do as training manager?'

'I talk to villagers about development and conservation, what they think they need and what they should do.' Her friend pours kerosene over sticks of wood and lights an instant fire on an open hearth. Smoke and kerosene fumes fill the room.

'You mean you talk to villagers about health and such things as smokeless ovens?' I ask. She nods. 'Then why don't you yourselves use a smokeless oven?'

She shrugs, then turns to her friend and laughs, embarrassed. They sit hunched by the fire. It is overcast outside and cold, we are almost at three-thousand metres. Sitting by the open fire, hands outstretched for the warmth and atmosphere it creates, I can understand the lack of appeal a closed clay oven represents. The rafters above are blackened with soot and smoking-racks above us are strung with meat, to cure. I cough as the smoke thickens. A steel cage is put over the open fireplace to support the teapot.

I comment in French to Michel, 'Even in a *bhaati* home set up as a lodge in remote Upper Pisang, the woman had a smokeless oven. In all the *bhaatis* there have been smokeless ovens. But whenever we stray off the Circuit, the smokeless ovens disappear.'

Michel agrees. 'The better health standards set up in the lodges to attract Western trekkers can in some ways be more effective community development education than having a doctor like myself work in a village, even for five years. Eventually I will leave. But the economic incentive of the lodge owners to have clean toilets, boiled or filtered drinking water, smokeless ovens, is something that is not temporary, as long as there are tourists. The process will continue indefinitely. Eventually word will spread to others about the intrinsic benefits of smokeless ovens, boiled water, toilets. But this kind of development is a slow process. We cannot expect it to happen overnight. Perhaps in ten years the *bhaati* we slept in last night will have a smokeless oven, no doubt after the current woman running it has already died of tuberculosis.'

When I was in Ghorepani four years ago, I could hardly breathe at night, the smoke pervading the lodge and even the bedrooms was so thick. 'What is your name?' I ask the other girl.

'Mamata Pun, I am the headmistress of Poon Hill Primary School.' She turns to Michel. 'I have medicines sent to our school by donors. I do not know what they are. Can you look at them and help us?'

We arrange to see them in the morning, but he says to me, in French, '*Putain*! These tourists mean well, but what is the use of sending medicine to a school? How can they properly dispense it?'

'But you yourself said the health posts were hopeless.'

'Yes, but the solution is not to send medicine directly to the school.'

'What is the solution?'

He gives me one of his smiles, and shrugs his shoulders.

'You want to see the ACAP office?' Lakshmi asks.

'Yes.' We drink our tea and then walk through Ghorepani, Lakshmi flirting overtly with Michel. At a lodge we stop to see the hot water system, a cunning device with a 'back boiler', a steel barrel with pipes that pass through the clay cooking oven; when the oven is in use for cooking, the water circulates to heat the water in the barrel. The hot water rises, the cold water sinks and is re-heated in the pipes. The water is used for washing dishes or for hot showers for tourists, either by bucket, or with connecting pipes to a shower stall. This too is a big conservation improvement over the old system of open fires lit underneath barrels of water.

The pressure of competition keeps each lodge striving to offer better facilities. Personal cleanliness requirements of foreign visitors make the service of hot showers almost mandatory for lodges, and the ultimate casualty of that demand has been the rhododendron forests, which have been decimated in the constant demand for fuel wood. But with rising awareness of the deforestation taking place, many trekkers give their business to conservation-conscious *bhaatis*, those with solar-heated showers, back boilers and space heaters. With the support of ACAP, these 'appropriate technology' systems for fuel conservation have been transferred from Ghorepani to other areas with deforestation problems.

Lakshmi shows us around the ACAP office. Signs inform us that this is the most heavily trekked route in all of Nepal. Twenty-thousand visitors pass through Ghorepani each year. Fees collected from hikers entering the Annapurna area fund ACAP to the extent that it is self-financing.

Back at our modest *bhaati* we ask for *dal bhaat*. On the wall of the kitchen is proudly displayed a certificate with a recognisable picture of the cook who is preparing our food. But this one is not from ACAP.

Counter Insurgency and Jungle Warfare School
Platoon commanders course 1987.

With a Gurkha soldier as a cook, at least we are safe from attack, and the food isn't bad either.

That evening French trekkers who are camped outside come into our lodge to eat. One of the Frenchmen talks incessantly to the group about his '*bagnole*', car. Everyone half-listens but when they discover Michel is 'the French Doctor from Tatopani' he is overwhelmed with questions, particularly from the women, who have been hearing about '*bagnoles*' for the last two weeks and are starving for intelligent conversation in a language they understand. Michel is a hit. Here, among the French especially, he has a film actor's pull. I leave him to the succession of questions I have already asked him myself.

Outside, one of the French women exits to join me and complains bitterly, 'My tent is so cold at night. The cold and humidity comes from the ground through the mattress and sleeping-bag. I cannot sleep, maybe only three or four hours.'

I suggest that she should think of using the *bhaatis* next time she comes out here.

The evening view of the Himals is a constantly changing kaleidoscope of clouds disguising golden-pink snow-covered peaks. Tired of the questions, Michel extracts himself from the confines of the lodge and sits beside me on the wall. 'It's like watching a woman partially

clothed, revealing portions of her body here and there. It is more allur-
ing than a clear sunset on the stark mountains.'

We sit there for an hour, until the sun has long gone and the stars
have come out. I teach Michel, so he can teach his sons:

> Star light, star bright,
> First star I see tonight,
> Wish I may, wish I might,
> Have the wish, I wish tonight.

And together we wish.

GHOREPANI–TADAPANI

Michel sorts through the medical supplies at the local school. 'It's not
as bad as I thought. Nothing esoteric, just Band-Aids, aspirins, that
kind of thing.'

We leave, and soon Sangpo and Michel have outpaced me.

Banthanti is another collection of *bhaatis* built expressly for
trekkers. Sangpo and Michel bask in the sunlight waiting for me at a
bhaati, beside which Nepalese porters and kitchen crew are preparing
lunch for a mobile camping group. The cooks, guides and porters are
all singing or whistling. The six paying tourists sit subdued at a blue
metal table covered in a chequered tablecloth waiting patiently for
lunch to be served. They have paid one-hundred dollars a day for this
exclusive experience. The sound of laughter and the whistling and
singing of the camp attendants permeates the atmosphere of the camp
as they enjoy themselves thoroughly, quite in contrast to the more
restrained paying clients.

Fresh salad, a hot meal, freshly baked bread. The tourists eat
politely, no one says anything. 'They have everything, but they are not
so happy,' Sangpo observes.

Michel sits thinking about Sangpo's comment for a long time, then
he stuns me with his next revelations. 'When Agnes and I worked in
Tatopani as doctors, it was as volunteers. We were paid virtually

nothing, and we were happy that way. Then my contract with the French non-governmental organisation came to an end. I did not want to leave Nepal. Agnes felt we were just beginning to understand the country. To leave would be a waste. I applied for other positions, and found one with the Swiss Development Corporation. They offered me a job, to handle all aspects of their health programme in Nepal. It was challenging, just what I wanted, to be my own boss, with as much travel into the rural areas as I could manage. There was just one draw-back.'

'Which was?'

'They wanted to pay me three-hundred-and-fifty-thousand rupees a month.'

I do a quick mental calculation. Almost one-hundred-thousand dollars a year, tax-free. To hear it put into the context of Nepalese rupees per month is obscene. 'What did you do?'

'I talked about it to Agnes and my Nepalese friends. We did not want to become typical, well-paid expatriates. Eventually I agreed to take the job, but I resolved with Agnes that we would not save anything. We would spend it all, in Nepal. No bank account in Switzerland. No mortgage on a property in France.'

'But how can you spend three-hundred-and-fifty-thousand rupees every month in Nepal?'

Michel gives me his smile, hunches his shoulders, raises his hands out to his sides, palms uppermost. 'It is not easy. I support a lot of friends. Some come out to visit from France. Some are in Nepal. A group of Newari friends are musicians. I help them get international exposure. Friends like Sangpo. He has no job. I help him and his extended family in Kathmandu.'

'But three-hundred-and-fifty-thousand rupees a month?' In the two-and-a-half months I will be in Nepal, I will have difficulty spending fifty-thousand rupees.

He shrugs.

It does not surprise me that Michel would not only not want to save money, he would go out of his way to avoid doing so. He has the free spirit of someone who is affluent, without owning anything. There is nothing in Michel's happy life he needs, least of all the worry of a property in France. Unlike so many other aid workers paid fantastic salaries helping the poor of a Third World nation, Michel has opted out of the acquisition trap. And he seems perfectly happy with that decision. Easy would have been proud of him.

'It's not so different from decisions that you too have made in the past, Andrew,' Michel reminds me. Over the last weeks we have talked so much. Michel worked in West Africa for some years before he took the posting in Nepal. We have compared experiences on that continent, and what we have done since.

I had told Michel of how I had worked for the United Nations in East Africa for two years and then quit to start the safari operation, which fell victim to its own success. The Government of Tanzania decided in one of its schizophrenic swings between encouraging private business and following an aid-subsidised state-run economy to take over the safari camp facilities. Although flush with Tanzanian shillings, and with assets including several Land Rovers, boats, safari equipment and a Cessna 182 aircraft, there was no possibility of converting the currency.

Without any foreign exchange, I returned to Canada broke. In my second day back, I was hired by Merrill Lynch to be trained as a stockbroker. I worked in New York and Toronto. It was a bull market, and just about anyone could make a good living in the business. But I opted out after four years, having reached the financial goals I had originally set myself. The collective motto of the stockbrokers in the industry tended to be a variation of the bumper sticker: 'He who dies with the most toys wins.' However, it had become clear to me that the marginal return in happiness for every dollar we earned and spent, decreased consistently. Satisfied with the financial security I had behind me, I joined a Canadian aid agency funding projects in Africa and Asia; the annual salary was equivalent to my last month's income as a stockbroker. Like Michel, I never regretted the move.

We walk again through thick forest and occasionally we are afforded views to the south, along valleys crimson with the autumn colours of rhododendron forest. I am jubilant and begin humming, then singing Edith Piaf's *La vie en rose*. I sing not just with full voice, but with all my being. Somewhere in the forest below Michel hears and joins in, confirming I am on the right path. Soon we are singing as loud as our voices are able, and as we descend into a steep valley Edith Piaf's songs and our voices echo on the valley walls. I doubt if it is possible to find two more ebullient individuals. Sangpo laughs merrily at us, then ad-libs as best he can, and soon we hear porters on the other side of the valley singing too. From the depths of the rhododendron forests the valley reverberates with voices joyfully affirming our collective existence to the void.

At a notch in the mountains, on a ridge looking down the Modi Khola, lies the hamlet of Tadapani. Our paths separate. 'From here I divert up to Annapurna Base Camp.' I look around, 'And I think I'll stay here the night.'

Once again friendships are curtailed by deviating paths. I cannot regret this disconnected fraternity. Despite Sangpo's tumultuous and difficult background, he is one of the gentlest people I have met, and he taught me much in his quiet way. Michel has been a model of open-mindedness, generosity and compassion. Both of my companions have infused me with their enthusiasm for the mountains, its people and way of life, and their own quiet spirituality. Michel has set an example of how to avoid becoming ensnared in the materialistic world. His lack of attachment to material things is going to put him, and Agnes, on the fast track to nirvana. Our physical paths diverge, although our spiritual paths have converged. Michel and Sangpo have conveyed some of their spiritual energy to me, which I will not be so easily separated from. They leave for Ghandrung, another two hours' walking. I promise to phone Michel when I am back in Kathmandu.

'Really?' Michel asks.

'I promise. My love to Agnes.' I feel I know her, he has talked so much of his family. 'And to the two boys. I hope Alex is better.'

Sangpo promises to show me around his *bhotia* neighbourhood of Bodhnath in Kathmandu. I am surprised that both Sangpo and Michel seem almost sad as they dissolve into the forested mountains.

The Fishtail materialises and evaporates behind puffy vapour. From the uppermost lodge, I spend the rest of the afternoon in splendid isolation, in the lodge's watch-tower, admiring the clouds perform artful tricks over mountains. The full moon rises quickly over the silhouetted hulk of Machapuchare the Fishtail, and then hides itself behind a stationary black cloud with a silvery lining.

ANNAPURNA SANCTUARY

❖

TADAPANI–CHOMRONG

I continue our discussions from the previous evening in the kitchen, with the owners, Sita and Siney Gurung, two attractive spinster sisters. Their considerable lodge was built over several years from profits earned from a smaller establishment, a loan from their Gurkha soldier father, and money from a brother working in a plastics factory in Korea. They have the most advanced stove I have seen in any of the lodges. A mud smokeless oven, with a steel plate on top and three variable-sized ring 'burners' and a steel latched door on the front. The exhaust chimney pipe passes through a steel barrel heating up the water contained therein.

'This,' I am told with evident pride, 'is the latest model of water heating system, donated by ACAP as a prize for having the cleanest lodge in Tadapani. Otherwise the cost would be ten-thousand rupees.'

We discuss conservation in the Annapurnas. 'Are there any deer left here?' I ask.

'More than before,' Sita tells me enthusiastically. 'Before villagers hunt them. Now we know they are good for tourism. Nobody can hunt deer in forests now. If so, we report them.'

'To whom?'

'To Village Committee. Then hunter is fined.'

'What about the trees?'

Sita replies, 'Village Committee says no trees can be cut now. Only dead tress. If villager found cutting live tree, he is fined two-thousand three-hundred rupees.' The villagers are taking responsibility for their forests again. Decades ago, traditional management of forest exploitation kept cutting and growth in balance. The disruption to this indigenous management was the 'nationalisation' of all the forest lands. Villagers no longer cared. The police, who were not locals, theoretically monitored forest cutting on behalf of the Government of Nepal. But in practice, the scattered police stations could not possibly control the use of the forests.

I talk with Sita in the kitchen. Despite her considerable charm and beauty, she considers herself too old to get married now; for all her claims of freedom from the oppression of married village life, she seems sad about this. 'Promise you will come back here from Chomrong,' Sita commands as I pack to leave.

Tadapani is not on my route when I come out of the Sanctuary from Chomrong heading directly for Ghandrung. 'I can't promise, but maybe, anything is possible.' I do not have the heart to say goodbye. These two women have charmed me effortlessly, and I feel sad to be going. I ask for my bill.

'Nothing,' Sita says with a determination underlying the generosity.

'I have to pay you, and if I don't, I'll feel guilty and definitely will not be able to come back,' I insist.

'OK,' she concedes reluctantly.

I pull out the brand-new rupee notes from my bag. 'Untouched, from Kathmandu.'

She counts out my change in dirty, torn, creased notes, their colour and denominations barely recognisable.

'I give you new money and you give me back this used money?' I joke.

'Maybe I too am used when you come back!'

'What do you mean?' I ask innocently.

Sita covers her face with her hands in embarrassment.

It is tempting to stay, but the allure of the walk ahead persuades me to move on. These women, who meet hundreds of tourists during the trekking season, made me feel special, as if they cared for me, as if I was the only person passing through their lives. Walking late out of the trekker-deserted village I feel a tug of loneliness, but the negative feelings are counterbalanced by the onset of another perfect day when once again anything seems possible. I descend immediately into the cold and shadowy forest. In a clearing full of irises, covered in melting frost, I stumble on five buffalo lying in the sun, chewing their cud. For a split second I am back in Africa, and frightened. My response is an out-of-synch reaction to the formidable African Cape buffalo. Taking advantage of these more docile beasts I lie down, fascinated, in their midst. The sun drenches us in its hypnotic warmth until they become accustomed to my presence and close their eyes against the brightness of the early-morning sunlight. I am tempted to fall asleep with them, their relaxed composure is infectious.

Walking under the thick canopy of foliage, I hear a noise and stop to listen. An animal? The forests are full of monkeys and deer. I walk towards the direction of the sound, then hear another noise, behind. I hesitate and listen again for more sounds, but there is nothing. I continue walking and hear the same noise again, to the side. I become paranoid. Are people, animals, following me, surrounding me? I stop again for a longer period and listen intently. Then I hear the rustling sound again. This time I identify it: a large brown leaf floating to the ground, the sound as it brushes against the branches of trees amplified by the stillness of the forest. Another leaf falls, catching the sun as it drops through a speckled patch of light. The fall of leaves, like so many giant brown snowflakes descending gently but noisily through the forest. I am totally alone.

In Chomrong, under Siley's advice, I go to the Moonlight Lodge and ask for the owner, Bhuvan. He responds to my query, 'We are fully occupied'.

'Siley from Tadapani said I should come here,' I counter hopefully.

'OK share a room?'

'That would be fine.'

I follow him into the dining-room, where several trekkers are sitting around a 'hot table'. He asks a young blonde, 'OK share room?'

She looks at me. I cannot be a very inspiring sight: sweaty, clad in co-ordinated grimy pink clothes, a Freshme crew-cut, a few days growth of an untrimmed squelched beard, underweight, with an over-stuffed back-pack, knobbly knees, and two left-footed flip-flops protruding inexplicably from the top of my pack. All eyes around the table appraise me.

There is something about these Annapurna 'trekkers' I have not seen before. They look too well fed, clean. Among them are two swarthy men, with red bandannas tied around their foreheads, Rambo fashion, and cumbersome necklaces made of fist-sized Kenyan wood carvings hanging pendulously from their necks. A Chinese-looking girl looks as if she could be a model for the Thai posters we see everywhere as she brushes her immaculate tresses. Four other girls, their backs to me, turn around to give me the once-over. One man looks as I feel. His hair is uncombed, he has several days' growth on his face. He is the only one who does not bother to look up. His face nestles in the crook of his arm bent on the table.

After what seems like an eternity of scrutiny, the girl says, with a recognisable Swedish lilt, 'Yes, that's OK.' I am led to the bedrooms.

This is the last opportunity to wash properly before entering Annapurna Sanctuary. I launder my pink clothes and sleuth my grime-creased body as a brief rain-shower intensifies the colours of hundreds of marigolds lining the property. Clouds above swirl in a confusion of light and darkness.

Sitting alone on a chair on the terrace, I lean back, balancing on two legs of the stool, and like a lunatic with my slack mouth wide open, stare up at the fluid exchange of colours and shapes, against a background blue of an intensity I have never seen before. I greedily absorb the celestial performance and realise there is a pain within me, the pain of falling in love with something perfectly beautiful and unattainable. The first star appears, and I wish on it. A mynah bird's song from somewhere in the jungle echoes my thoughts.

'Dear sir, excuse for interruption. We are teaching local primary school and seeking donations.' Three Brahmin teachers approach me in my faraway state. From the heavens I come crashing back to earth. They hand me their donation book, full of official-looking stamps.

'I am sorry, I do not have my wallet with me.' I manage successfully to avoid slipping into their cadence.

'Oh, that is all right sir.' Their heads wobble in synchrony.

I reach into my pocket, and find twenty-six rupees in change. 'Here at least is something.' He hands me the book to sign with the amount of my donation. For the sake of the audit, I write my name and nationality, and the amount.

'Thank you sir,' and the Wobbly Heads follow one another into the crowded dining-room for richer pickings. To ask for a donation in those surroundings might yield richer pickings than from one gazing alone and insanely at the open sky.

At dinner I listen to the men with bandannas and giraffe-and-rhino necklaces. 'I don't understand hwhy tourists spend so much time looking at these mountains. Hwhy? You see them, you see them. OK, so I can see them from here, hwhy I should go any further. Mountains are mountains. So hwhat?'

The others sit listening. Or maybe they are not.

He continues, taking his fingers underneath his bandanna and around his forehead to ensure that there is not a hair out of place. 'Another thing I do not understand. Hwhy this country is so poor?' Nobody answers. I assiduously pretend to be reading; then, my nose blocked, I pull out my handkerchief.

The Australian girl next to me asks, 'Got a cold have ya?'

'No, not really.'

'Bin sick long have ya?' she persists.

'I hadn't really thought of myself as being sick. You been sick?'

'Na, just the usual. Diarrhoea, Giardia.'

'What was that like? Giardia, I mean.'

'Ah, pretty wicked, ya know. Burps and farts stink like rotten eggs. Hate farting a giardia fart in a sleeping-bag on a cold night. Ya could've usefully lit me up for a blow-torch.'

CHOMRONG

My body, after a month's hard exercise, refuses to respond to the physical output required to climb into the Annapurna Sanctuary. I can't even get myself psyched up to re-pack my back-pack. Having no ambition to move on, I decide instead to stay another day and crawl back into my sleeping-bag in a sunlit corner of the flagstone terrace of the *bhaati*. Surprisingly, I sleep soundly most of the day until the evening when drums beating a rhythm and Nepalese voices singing wake me.

CHOMRONG–TIP TOP LODGE

The morning is still fresh. Frost lies on the ground. Despite the loneliness, I am happiest to start out and travel on my own. It is impossible to walk and admire the mountains simultaneously. They are so high and the path is so rough that I must deliberately stop and look up, otherwise I am liable to trip and fall. I cross a small suspension bridge over a stream full of rounded, smooth rocks. Stopping to rest in the middle of the bridge, I listen to the sounds of the rushing stream. A brown dipper flits to a rock, its tail flicking up and down, and then dives into the fast-flowing current and amazingly feeds along the bottom before it disappears beneath shards of sunlight reflecting off the rippling waters.

The simplicity of the scene, its absolute beauty and peace, move me to tears. Am I becoming unhinged, or am I just becoming more in touch with my feelings? I examine a harmless moth. It is pure white until I touch it, when it slides its wings wide, and two enormous black eyes appear threateningly on the unfolded wings.

At Tip Top Lodge I slip inside the simple structure made out of bamboo wicker, lined with plastic sheets under the wicker roof to make it waterproof. A tiny girl cooks over a kerosene pressure stove. She runs towards me with a skip and grabs my hand. '*Namaste*!' Her smile is devastating. She has chubby red cheeks, a toothy smile, and Mongolian eyes that sparkle with humour. 'Lemon tea?' she asks.

'Yes, thank you.'

'Soup?'

'Yes, thank you.'

'Come!' She pulls me to a wooden bench beside the stove to keep her company and puts her finger over her mouth to indicate that I should be quiet, then motions to a wicker partition where I can see a woman is lying down, breast-feeding an infant. 'Baby,' she says, and puts her head to one side, palms together under her chin.

I nod.

She expertly mixes packaged soup and spices and stirs the concoction as I drink a glass of hot lemon tea from a thermos. She looks at me, smiles, her eyes little slits, squeezed together by chubby pink cheeks. Her slightly protruding upper teeth give her all-encompassing grin an extra dimension. When her eyes open again, they sparkle. The mother gets up to help, but the little girl has everything in hand. The mother looks as if she is a Gurung. The girl looks distinctly Tibetan.

'Is this your daughter?' I ask the mother.

'No mother, no father.'

'How old is she?'

'Nine years old.'

'How long has she been with you, helping you?'

'Five years.'

I ask the girl in Nepalese, 'What is your name?'

'Krisna, Krisna Gurung.' She flashes me a smile and her eyes disappear in red cheeks swollen by fits of giggles. I give her my pencil and notebook and she writes her name: 'KRISNA GURUNG'. She writes it again in Nepalese Sanskrit, and the number nine, for her age. She is constantly jumping up and down to do this or that: singing, laughing, skipping to the other side of the kitchen to peel potatoes, wash dishes, soliciting clients outside the *bhaati*, checking the baby. She cannot slow her pace down to a walk, but skips wherever she goes. Despite the hardship of her existence, she is happy. The girl entices me to stay for the night, although it is still morning. I take off my sweat-soaked thermal undershirt and hang it up to dry, then sit myself in the sun.

Krisna follows, holding my hand. When she discovers my Dictaphone she sings into it, apprehensively at first. When she hears her own voice played back she beams happily, teeth flashing, eyes dissolving in her fleshy dimpled cheeks. Within minutes she has worked out how to play the machine and is tirelessly singing and giggling, recording and replaying.

About mid-afternoon I feel nauseous. I pull my thermal undershirt off the line where it has been drying. I enter the simple 'bedroom' with two narrow beds, partitioned from the other bedrooms with a wicker wall, and lie down. When I am overcome by chills, I crawl into my sleeping-bag.

Krisna locates me, pulling aside the curtain serving as a door. She stands there beside my pillowed head, with her infant brother, and sings. Her little brother can hardly stand, but the two of them perform a Nepalese folk dance for me, swaying and pirouetting. The dizzying activity makes me even more nauseous. 'Krisna, I'll come and play later.'

Her mother arrives, concerned, Krisna obviously having told her I am not well. 'No good?' the mother asks.

'I am fine, just tired.' I do not want her to feel responsible for my stomach upset.

'Nice girl come? Sleep here.' She pats the extra bed.

I am feeling very nauseous. Can it be altitude sickness again? I am shivering, even in the over-designed sleeping-bag with layers of clothes on.

Voices wake me. Sure enough, Krisna's mother has found me three nice girls, all nurses. One moves into my 'room'.

'Are you all right?' the nurse asks as she unpacks.

I try and smile. 'Just tired. Where are you from?'

'Switzerland. And you?'

'Norway.' A chameleon, I change colours to a flag of convenience.

They go outside for dinner. I fall asleep again, and vaguely hear voices, as more trekkers take up the remaining beds. The nausea becomes worse and, knowing that I am going to be sick, I sprint outside just in time. A torrent of vomit spews out of my mouth with such violence that it forms a rainbow arc over the fencing to the terrace below.

At the outdoor dinner table, conversation stops. All eyes are on me: a mutant Linda Blair performing a Himalayan rendition of *The Exorcist*, projecting another stream of half-digested food far over the ledge. Lemon tea and Krisna's soup exits the way it went in. I lurch inside and lie down. The dinner conversation picks up again, in French, followed by laughter. The nausea builds up a head of steam once more, and I just manage to run outside to the ledge again before another torrent comes out of both my mouth and nostrils. Feeling marginally better, I join those sitting around the table. They stare at me. It wouldn't surprise them if my head rotated three-hundred-and-sixty degrees.

There are three Swiss nurses, a middle-aged balding and paunchy French doctor accompanied by a middle-aged French girl friend, and two dyed-blonde Jewish American girls, who live in Israel, with three drooling Israeli men in escort.

The French doctor's gonadotrophin hormones are working overtime as he flirts shamelessly with the two American girls, with not a word of condolence or interest in my health or lack thereof. Where are the overzealous Canadian doctors when you need them? He says to the

Swiss nurses, in French, not knowing I will understand, 'The Norwegian, he is a little fragile.'

One of the nurses asks me, 'Are you all right?'

I reply in French, 'I'm fine. Feeling better now, at any rate.'

'Are you still nauseous?' she continues in French.

'Yes.'

She goes inside and brings out a toilet bag full of medicine. She gives me a suppository, and I leave the table for the privacy of the night, but I cannot open the indestructible plastic package. Chagrined, I return to the table. 'Everything OK?' she asks.

'I can't open the package,' *sotto voce.*

She opens it blatantly with a pair of nail scissors.

'What's that?' one of the American blondes asks and I mentally curse her inquisitiveness.

'A suppository,' I reply softly, hoping she knows what that is so I do not have to explain in detail. She obviously does know, for she turns back to the French doctor for a less intimate conversation.

I skulk once again to the privacy around the side of the *bhaati*, and drop my trousers, and delicately slide the suppository up my rectum, pull up my trousers and return to the table. As I sit down the suppository slips out. I get up from the table, and the nurse whispers to me, 'It's better if you stand up for a while.'

I exit backstage again and shove it up a second time, good and proper, then return to the table and stand around nerdishly in my pink clothes as the suppository melts messily inside me. 'Sit down,' the doctor orders. I could kill him. Instead, I introduce myself and proffer my hand in greeting. Surprised, he accepts it.

'Where are you from?' one of the American girls asks. I take the course of least resistance and stay Norwegian.

The French doctor asks, in French, 'Why do you speak French?' he sniffs. He smells of cheap cologne.

'Because I went to university in Grenoble.'

'I am a doctor in Chamonix, at a ski resort near to Grenoble,' he proclaims in English grandly, for everyone's benefit.

'How old are you?' I ask in English, for maximum effect.

He hesitates and replies, rather subdued, in French, 'Fifty-five. Why?'

'Fifty-five you say?' I repeat in English. 'Hmm.' I adopt an Easy pose, scratching my head in a show of slow-witted calculation, before unleashing my version of Easy's brand of wicked humour. 'You would have been a doctor there when I was studying. As foreign students at the university in Grenoble we used to ski up at Chamonix. We were told by the university administration for foreign students that if we had a ski injury, under no conditions were we to go to a French doctor for medical treatment.' I sit at the table and squeeze my buttocks tightly together to stop the suppository from sliding out. My mouth makes up for the anal contraction. 'We were given written instructions on how to get into Switzerland where we would get proper medical care . . .'

The doctor's Gaelic mouth drops open at my insolence. His eyes draw tighter.

Like Easy on a roll, in for a penny, in for a pound; if you're not going to make it to nirvana you might as well enjoy it. I give the doctor an equivalent of Easy's *coup de grâce* administered to the Mountain Travel guide. 'Of course, I am sure it has all changed; younger French doctors nowadays are probably as good as the Swiss were reputed to be then,' I inform him diabolically in English as a secreted Swiss suppository proves the point and I start feeling a lot better.

TIP TOP LODGE–ANNAPURNA SANCTUARY BASE CAMP

Without appetite, and wanting to avoid another bout of food poisoning, I avoid breakfast and say goodbye to Krisna and her mother, and promise to stop on the way back.

The sides of the gorge are impressive vertical rock faces with numerous cascading waterfalls. The path, on the other hand, is no more than a goat trail, with rocks and exposed roots providing ample opportunity to twist one's ankle. Unlike the Kali Gandaki and Marsyangdi River valleys of the Annapurna Circuit, this trail was never a historical trading route. The only people using this gorge, before Western mountain climbers and trekkers, were the few local herdsmen who took sheep up to the higher pastures during the summer. There is little indigenous cultural merit to the route.

Not until ten-thirty does the sunlight begin to shine into the shad-owed defile. The vegetation thins out, and with the sun overhead, it becomes warm again, warm enough to wear only a thermal T-shirt. Where the path clings closer to the river, I take off my thermal under-clothes, rinse them and hang them on the back of my back-pack to dry. As I climb higher into the Sanctuary, out of the narrow defile of the Modi Khola gorge, I am once again spectacularly surrounded by the Himals, although I am not sure which peak is which, for I have never seen them from this angle before. I thought I knew the shapes of each mountain so well now, but the only obviously recognisable mountain is Machapuchare, with its fluted fishtail columns of snow.

Annapurna Base Camp is at the centre of this huge amphitheatre of Himalayan mountains comprising Annapurna South, Machapuchare, Annapurna I and lesser peaks. For well over a month I have been cir-cling these mountains on the outside. Now I am intimately familiar within the bosom of the Sanctuary. As I keep ascending I am sur-rounded by an apparently seamless caldera. A plaque bolted on a stray boulder the size of a house is a poignant reminder of the dangers:

Hellenic Alpine Club of Athens
The first Greek Mountaineers
Klimis Tsatsaragos
Takis Boudolas

Who came to the Himalayas
and stayed forever
22–10–85

I tramp up a path towards one of three large hanging glaciers and find myself unexpectedly on a ridge overlooking a valley of glacial moraine resembling a massive construction site. Mounds of rocks look as if giant dump trucks have unloaded them.

Despite the bone-penetrating cold, I cannot stop watching the trans-formation of these mountains as the clouds disappear from the peaks, and the angled, softer evening light reveals every detail on the moun-tain walls. The yellow light turns to orange, then pink, then red. I am almost getting blasé about this celestial pageant of changing shapes and colours. My breath freezes in miniature clouds in front of my face.

[161]

The mist slightly veiling Annapurna I renders it monochromatic, like an old-fashioned daguerreotype photograph.

The first star comes out and I make a wish. Or are these wishes an excuse for long-forgotten prayers? In bed I try unsuccessfully to reconstruct the Lord's Prayer from childhood memory.

ANNAPURNA SANCTUARY BASE CAMP

The tide of bright yellow leaks into the craggy dark mountain faces, draining the shadows. Within a short time the mountains radiate white so strongly it hurts the eyes.

Four trekkers arrive. They argue about whether to have breakfast. 'Food is more expensive here, hwhy we should pay more, hwhen is cheaper in our lodge?' one of them tells the Nepalese kitchen help.

'OK,' says the Nepalese and walks away.

'Hwait! Hhow much if all of us eat? Hwhat discount you give?'

'One, four, same price.'

'Hwhy? Should be group discount.'

I had been sitting quietly by the lodge reading, savouring the atmosphere, looking up occasionally to satiate my visual senses with the splendour of the surroundings and trying unsuccessfully to put it all down on paper. Peace has been disturbed by these tourists arguing over the price of eggs.

Recognising classic symptoms of high altitude irritability, I walk away, and begin climbing up the steep moraine ridge leading directly up from the tranquil Alpine meadow of Annapurna Base Camp. The climb is steep, and I am surprised to register how tired I am. I must stop every ten metres. Yesterday I had no problem walking with my backpack on. Today I am out of breath, without my back-pack. I want to stop and rest, but I can still hear the voices from below, arguing over the price of food.

'Hwhy one egg omelette is not half price of two egg omelette?'

I keep walking, unable to shut their mundane lives out of my own. I must be one hundred metres above them, yet still their embittered voices carry up to me. I am more focused on the fracas than I am with the impeccable panorama of mountains displayed around me. I climb even further away until I have to sit down and rest. The sun has risen up over the mountains and its warmth and brightness make me drowsy. I lie down and within minutes, I am asleep. Haggling voices wake me.

'Hwhy you bring me one egg omelette? I hwant two egg omelette.'

'Hwhat! This is not two egg omelette!'

I get up and keep ascending, until the dispute is no longer audible. Once again I lie down, wilfully forcing their voices out of my hearing. I feel so tired, and soon I am in a slumber, feeling the warmth of the sun on my body. A slight breeze blows, the air temperature is perfect. Occasionally, portions of glaciers break loose, with a crack like lightning, followed by the rumble of thunder.

The crowd in the lodge is young. The conversation is dominated by comparisons of places to stay in India, Indonesia, Thailand, what to do, how to get there, what to avoid. This is definitely the 'back-packing around Asia' crowd, wearing disposable 'Tibetan yak wool' sweaters made in India, the kind that disintegrate after two weeks, or roughly equal to the time the sweaters are needed during their owners' sojourn in Nepal. Someone picks up a guitar to play, marijuana joints are passed around. Most of those in the room would have to think very hard to remember which country they are in.

Conversations become disjointed. The distinctive aroma of marijuana smoke fills the room. A girl says, 'I think I saw a mongoose, or a beaver, or an otter today. I'm not sure. What does a mongoose look like?'

A young English boy replies, 'A mongoose, that's like a big deer.'

Mike, my room-mate says, 'You're thinking of a moose.'

'Well, what are those big things then, buffaloes or yaks?'

I retreat to my semi-private room and undress down to my thermal underwear, remove my socks and throw them at the foot of my bed before sliding into my sleeping-bag. I blow out the candles.

My room-mate's voice, moments after he enters the darkness, gags, 'Hey, I don't mean to be like, impolite, but would it be possible to put your socks outside for the night?'

I hop around the room in my sleeping-bag, find the offending culprits, open the door, and throw them outside where they bounce beyond olfactory sensory range. Muffled Tom Waits tunes thump dully from my room-mate's Walkman earphones. 'Thanks,' he says too loudly.

ANNAPURNA SANCTUARY BASE CAMP–CHOMRONG

A breeze awakens me. Through the door, which is wide open, I can see a beautifully clear, starlit, ink-black night. And there is something else out there. A presence. Otherworldly. Nothing to be afraid of. Something magical. Nice. Friendly.

In the morning I reach for my water-flask next to my head. It is frozen solid.

Machapuchare looms way overhead again as I slip back into the claustrophobic confines of the gorge. Then the intimate view of Annapurnas I and South are gone as I descend and disappear into the wall of mountains. Three exhausted young Nepalese boys, inadequately dressed, lie curled up and asleep beside the path, their baskets of vegetables beside them. The cabbages are already brown, the onions sprouting.

A constant file of burdened porters slowly winds its way into the Sanctuary, carrying tables, tents, wicker chairs, mattresses, cooking equipment, food for their Get There People clients. Another stream of porters goes down, singing, whistling, leaping from rock to rock, with minimal weight on their backs. I too am descending so rapidly through the gorge that I must equalise the pressure on my eardrums: just as aeroplane passengers and scuba divers occasionally have to do, I periodically hold my breath, pinch my nose and blow hard.

Back at Tip Top Lodge, halfway down the gorge, I risk a hot chocolate and discover I am not the only one to be charmed by Krisna. Three Germans try to take her picture, but she recognises me and hovers about holding my arm, ruining the Germans' photo opportunity. She wears a newly acquired fluorescent-pink baseball-cap emblazed 'Kick Butt'.

After hot chocolate, and a few more giggly songs on the tape, which I keep, I say goodbye. 'Thank you very much. Good bye. Good Love.' She waves, her little brother strapped on her back. She made me happy.

The jarring descent and twisted roots and rocks take their toll on my knees. At Chomrong, I check into the police checkpoint at the bottom of the village, then for the fun of it, gallop up the long bobsleigh-run of stone steps in a final manic burst of energy, all the way to Moonlight Lodge at the top of the village. I arrive soaked with perspiration but full of the vibrant well-being instilled by weeks of hard exercise and mobile meditative contemplation. Depleted of one form of energy, I am renewed with another.

Knowing I would arrive back today, Bhuvan has saved me a room to myself, though his lodge is full. I wash my soiled pink clothes in buckets of warm 'back-boiler water', then shower. Refreshed, I sit in front of the kitchen, with a cold beer and my notebooks. I feel so physically fit as to feel omniscient, high on endorphins.

CHOMRONG–GHANDRUNG

I spend most of the morning conversing with Bhuvan and his wife. He repeatedly serves me cups of tea, saying 'No charge, no charge.' Before Bhuvan built the lodge he had seventeen mules with which he transported goods along the Kali Gandaki between Pokhara and Lo Mantang. From that small business he saved enough money to start this lodge.

Sitting with Bhuvan I feel a sense of equality, despite the differences in our lives. He has a quiet strength, an inherent understanding of the ways of the world, bridging the gaps in our education and experiences.

Classic pillars of Jesus Rays reach from the clouds to light up the valley. I almost expect Him to appear between the billowing sunbursts before once again, I am drawn back into the mountains to unshackle the pedestrian bonds of humanity, and become closer with the awesome nature surrounding me.

As I descend the steep, twisting path to Kuldi, a porter is labouring up and slips on the loose rocks. He falls forward, dropping the *doko* over his shoulder in a crash of bottles. I rush down to help him but already he is on his feet, his legs shaking violently. He is about to cry. His ankle and shin are scraped, and blood is beginning to form in thick globules. He points to his legs, but there is little I can do. It is only a surface wound, but he is nevertheless in shock. I grab him by the shoulders and make him sit down. I ask him in Nepali, 'Where are you coming from?'

'Pokhara.'

That seems a world away. 'Where are you going?'

'Chomrong.' Another hour up the trail.

After a while he gets up again and I help him put the basket of bottles on his back. He begins the slow climb up the path. His trousers are split, he has no underpants, and his bare buttocks add to his indignity. As he walks away, liquid drips out from the basket. He feels the drops on the back of his legs, he reaches behind his back, and his fingers confirm what must be a porter's nightmare come true. I put down my back-pack again and help him unload his. We sort through the bottles. The liquid is water from a burst plastic mineral water bottle. I take the bottle out and give him fifty rupees, more than what it would cost me to buy in a lodge in Chomrong. He does not understand what I am doing. 'I'll take the bottle, you keep the fifty rupees.' There is a brief look of appreciation, before he puts the basket on his back.

Continuing down the path, I am struck by the absurdity of carrying this bottled water all the way up here, when filtered, boiled and treated water are all available. Besides which, the waters coming off the upper, uninhabited slopes of the Himalayas are just as pure as the bottled water, although not conveniently packaged.

The settlement of New Bridge has significantly altered the trekking pattern of the Annapurna Sanctuary. Before, the route was primarily through Ghandrung. Now with the new Chinese road passing close to Birethanthi, it is easier to take a truck from Pokhara directly to the Modi Khola and walk straight up the valley, past Birethanthi, into the Sanctuary. Four years ago getting into the Sanctuary was still a physical effort, needing a minimum of ten days from Pokhara.

When I reach New Bridge, I realise I have missed the turnoff for Ghandrung. On my map, which I have learnt to mistrust, a red dotted line suggests that I should be able to walk up from New Bridge to Ghandrung. There does not seem to be any way in which the path could ascend through the densely packed contour lines, unless something on the map is wildly inaccurate. Nevertheless I follow a narrow path which climbs steeply, then peters out. I find myself in under-growth, ascending narrow, tunnel-like goat trails. The heat of the day builds up and I sweat profusely with the effort of the precipitous climb and the heavy pack. Eventually I break out onto terraced ground. Stupidly, I have not eaten since last night and have climbed arduously up some thousand metres carrying a very heavy pack. I finish the contents of my water-flask.

Thousands of little swifts twist and turn agitatedly, feeding on a profusion of insects that flit about; the sun reflects on the tiny wings of these darting, feathered projectiles so that they look like shooting stars against the shadowed cliffs across the valley. By contrast, a Himalayan griffin floats serenely alongside me, effortlessly catching the thermals as I struggle against the bonds of gravity.

Around a ridge lies Ghandrung; it does not look terribly far as the griffin glides, but with another valley that I must walk into, down and up, the village is still some hours away. The red dotted line delineating a path, drawn from New Bridge to Ghandrung, definitely exists only in the addled mind of the over zealous, Kathmandu-based 'Annapurna Circuit' cartographer.

Because Nepal was forbidden territory until 1950, detailed information on the geography of the land was gathered secretly by British-sponsored secret agents who called themselves Pundits. The British-trained Pundits secretly mapped these mountains a century ago. In disguise, with notebooks hidden within prayer wheels and sacred rosaries containing one-hundred beads instead of one-hundred-and-eight, to facilitate counting their paces and measuring distances, the Pundits would not have been so treacherous as to add fictional foot-paths to their measurements. Or would they?

The first lodge I encounter in Ghandrung is good enough. I don't have the energy to check the options. I unload my sweat-stained pack and collapse, face down and fully extended, on the warm flagstone terrace, dehydrated, devoid of even an ounce of energy. The sun heats the back of my soaking T-shirt. A foam mattress materialises unso-licited beside me. 'Where from?' the owner of the lodge asks.

'Chomrong, via New Bridge.'

'Difficult,' he acknowledges, with a lovely smile. He reaches into his *bhangra*, a cloth tied over his shoulders and hanging behind his back to form a large pocket, and hands me a tangerine.

'Do you have more?'

'Plenty more.'

'Can I have ten more, a cup of tea, and is it possible to have *dal bhaat*?'

'Yes, is possible. You stay here?'

'Let me eat lunch first.'

'No problem.' He gives me the tangerines and tea. I eat four tangerines immediately, drink the tea, roll onto the mattress and fall asleep in the warmth of the sunlight, totally debilitated.

When I wake up, he is squatting next to me with a steaming plate of *dal bhaat*. A signboard on the edge of the terrace informs me that this is Sangri La Lodge. It is slightly eccentric, like the owner I suspect. I eat a second and third helping of *dal bhaat*. The owner is so pleasant, skipping effortlessly backwards and forwards with the food. There is something cheerful and likeable about him. He shows me a room, and I take it and he closes the door discreetly behind him. An inevitable poster on the wall reads:

> Everything happening,
> Great and Small,
> is a parable whereby
> God speaks to us,
> and the art of life
> is to get the message.
>
> Malcolm Muggeridge

I sit on the edge of the bed and think about it. In these awe-inspiring, spiritual mountains, the ubiquitous posters in the *bhaatis* themselves are a pre-destined fluke, sowing seeds of faith among vulnerable souls. I tug my fertile thoughts back out into the sunlight.

Ghandrung is the best-preserved Gurung village on the Circuit. The lodges are on the outskirts, leaving the original village itself intact. Villagers pursue their traditional daily life, in the pleasant sunshine, which makes it easy to observe them. Walking through the village, I meet a blind trekker, led by a Nepalese guide, who greets me, '*Namaste*.'

'*Namaste*,' I reply as we pass by each other. Connected to his guide by a stiff pole, the sightless man lifts his head at my salutations, rotating it. I stop, look back, and watch as he is guided over the path he cannot see. I feel as if someone has both punched me in the stomach and is gripping me by the throat.

With a renewed sense of vision I look at the magnificence of Annapurna South and Machapuchare and the mountains around, the stone buildings and slate roofs of the village, the terraced hills extending down to the river far below, the reflections of sunlight everywhere. And for the first time, I overlook the visible beauty of these mountains, close my eyes and really try to see.

Sitting on the terrace of the Sangri La, admiring the evening view with my eyes open once again, a young man approaches me to sell tangerines contained in a *doko*. He is shivering, his naked legs shaking uncontrollably. He is barely clothed in tattered rags. He attempts to smile at me, revealing rotten teeth. I buy two dozen tangerines and tell him to keep the change from the notes I give him. Drubar, the proprietor who has been observing, tells me, 'He is very poor man, from village one-and-a-half hours walking from here.'

'He is walking there now?' I ask incredulously. It is almost dark and getting cold and his scruffy rags barely cover his malnourished body.

'Yes.'

GHANDRUNG–BIRETHANTHI

Indistinct shapes of this idyllic Gurung village take form as night and the cold mist disappear with the daylight. Occupants stir under the pagoda-like roofs, struts supporting the heavy, overhanging slates. Shuttered windows closed against the cold night air are opened. Someone coughs and noisily expectorates. The buffalo stops grunting and I hear the pulsating squirts of milk striking an empty metallic pail. Villagers wrapped in scarves to ward off the chill silently perform chores, bringing in firewood from the store room, lighting the hearth, leading their buffalo out to the fallow fields to feed.

Tiny birds, dark-breasted rosefinches and blue-fronted redstarts, fly from millet-head to millet-head, twittering excitedly. The roses and marigolds lining the terrace have an intensity brought out by the melting dew and the sun. My attention is drawn to a tiny bird hovering in front of the marigold. It has what appears to be a long beak and tongue which it extends into the flower-head. It looks and behaves like a hummingbird, but is far smaller than any hummingbird I have ever seen, not even as large as my small finger. I creep closer to the creature only to realise that it is a moth, with a long proboscis, not a beak. It looks virtually the same as the European hummingbird hawkmoth. How can this insect develop so similarly to a bird but on such different evolutionary paths? Can there be any scientific explanations to the mysteries and complexities of creation?

A deaf-mute, carrying a loaded *doko*, joins me in watching the moth. When it flies away he extends his hand out for money. I do not have the heart to ignore him so give him ten rupees. This amount is entirely meaningless to me, but for him it is money with which to buy cigarettes, maybe something more useful. His hands are huge, out of proportion to his body size. He smiles when he receives the note and ambles off happily.

It is time for me to go too. Walking through the village, I am jolted by an enthusiastic '*Namaste*.' The unexpected greeter has flashing eyes, a broad smile, his hands are raised and pressed together.

'*Namaste*,' I reply, again touched by these genuine, spontaneously offered greetings.

There are many everyday sunshines of my life. They make me happy and I find I am smiling a lot, as I walk, or even at night as I drift off to sleep. The physical act of smiling not only changes my countenance, but the way I feel inside.

Leaving Chandrung village, through what I suspect is the last Buddhist prayer wall of the trek, I spin the prayer wheels and make a wish, a sort of prayer, the same one I have made as I have progressed through this trip. It is bound to come true. I have prayed for it, every night. It is something I have wished for as long as I can remember. The conversation with Trea, talking with such clarity on the day walking up to the caves, has reinforced the desire, and made me realise it is all possible.

It is a short distance to Birethanthi, and I am relieved to see the settlement is unchanged from four years ago when Kirsten and I walked down from Chandrakot to do the loop up to Poon Hill and back. The village then seemed hundreds of years removed from our world, and a hundred miles from Pokhara. Good memories flood back. Because I do not want to rush back to civilisation, I stay at Birethanthi for the night in a *bhaati* overlooking the river. Through the gorge flanked by mountains covered in jungle, a tropical sunset settles into the opaque river, reflecting the pastel sky.

Voices sing. Three trekkers have almost completed the Annapurna Circuit. Their entourage of porters, guides and cooks are celebrating, all quite happily drunk. The trekkers' downcast faces contrast with their Nepalese crew who are happy another trip is over, and their pockets are once again full of money.

DIPAK

❖

BIRETHANTHI-HILLE

Two trekkers arriving in the morning tell me they have taken a truck to a point just twenty minutes' walk downstream from Birethanthi. The truck had let them off at the newly expanding corrugated tin settlement of Haijung, sprouting up where the road meets the Modi Khola, before it turns south for a stretch across to the Kali Gandaki. Already the Chinese-financed road has bypassed Chandrakot and has reached Baglung and soon it will reach Beni.

I look up and see the village of Chandrakot perched on the steep-sided mountain. The same Chandrakot had taken two full days' walk from Pokhara, so isolated and full of promise four years ago. The intensity of the memory of walking into Chandrakot then is indelibly etched in my psyche. The steep flagstone path descending from Chandrakot to Birethanthi is a nostalgic reminder of Kirsten.

I had received a scholarship to study economics for a summer term at the univeristy of Oslo. Kirsten and I had met during my last weekend that summer. We were both hiking in the Norwegian mountains and literally bumped into each other at Memrubu on Lake Gjende. The setting, a classic glacier-fed, turquoise-coloured lake overshadowed by one of Norway's best-known peaks, could not have been more romantic. Over the next year I travelled a lot, from Ottawa to Mali, or Bangladesh, or Indonesia, or Southern Africa, always via Oslo.

A year after we met, we were married at the exact spot of our meeting, on the rocks beside the lake. Four days later I was in India for a month, and then we met in Delhi and flew to Nepal together. A sort of delayed honeymoon. It was also the Festival of Lights, and most offices were closed in Nepal for a ten-day period. During the holiday we walked a loop from Pokhara to Sarankot, Chandrakot, Hille, Ghorepani, Tadapani, Gandrung and back to Pokhara.

We had arrived in Chandrakot, after a long walk from Sarankot, on a clear, full-moonlit night. The experience had been magical, and I remember clearly walking through Chandrakot to turn a corner on the flagstone path and looking up the Modi Khola valley towards Annapurna South, its blue snow-covered slopes bathed in the moonlight. We felt far from the cares of the world, in a setting more exotic than our expectations. We could not have been happier, or more in love. Ensconced in a room at a lodge, we laughed when a tiny mouse with huge ears peered at us benignly from the rafters of the ceiling.

Chandrakot appears diminished now, lying within half-an-hour's walk of the road. The memories are shattered. Maudlin thoughts dominate.

By normal standards, the massive investment in the nearby road infrastructure would not be economically feasible to service a total population that cannot exceed more than ten-thousand permanent residents. Costs of construction must range in the tens of thousands of dollars per capita, in one of the poorest countries in the world, where such a massive infusion of capital could be better spent in health care or education. International politics and the military hegemony between China and India have more to do with this road being built than the welfare of the communities living alongside it. The destruction of the fragile environment and the culture of the indigenous people is not in the hands of the people most directly affected. Even with the possibility that their perceived wishes are indeed to have a road built, the inhabitants of the Kali Gandaki would never be able to implement such an awesome project on their own.

The next village to be reached by the road will be Tatopani. Once it reaches the Kali Gandaki it will be relatively easy to continue up the valley. And what country's engineers would not like to have the technological honour of constructing 'the road that runs up the deepest canyon in the world'? The thought of busloads of tourists being taken to Kagbeni and Muktinath and eventually Lo Mantang is awful.

One key aspect of tourism in these mountains now is the lack of vehicles. No matter how rich the tourists, we all have to use our own two feet to walk in this mountainous environment, just as the local people do. It is the great equaliser. With a road, a different kind of tourist will invade, in even larger numbers, sitting safely insulated in their coaches, staring indifferently through barrier-like windows.

A mule train passes through the village. The lead mule pulls back its ears and I know that it is going to brush by me aggressively. Sure enough I am knocked aside. I relish the smell, the patter of hoofs on the stones, the tinkling of bells. Instead of diesel fumes, the bitter-sweet smell of the mules' dung, warm and wet, is an insignificant hazard. I step in the middle of a tennis-ball-sized lump of dung, to demonstrate to myself how innocuous it is. Not only harmless and biodegradable, it is also an asset to flora along the route.

Within twenty minutes' walk I could be back on a road, with vehicles, on the fringes of civilisation. The narrow sides of the river shelter the village of Birethanthi from the visible and audible aspects of the civilised world. A familiar sight as a trekker staggers down from Hille, his arms outstretched in an attempt to keep balance as he swivels straight-legged and painfully down the stepped path.

On an impulse I decide to reverse direction. Rather than head straight back through Chandrakot, Naudanda, Sarankot and Pokhara as was my original intention, I shall climb up to Hille, and retrace the loop I did with Kirsten four years ago.

A British couple enter the same tea-house and sit at a table next to me. 'Which way have you come?' I ask them, innocently enough.

'Down from Chandrakot,' she answers lyrically in an Irish accent.

'Took the truck?' I ask, disguising the rising tide of belligerence.

'Yes.'

'How was that?'

She does not understand the question, or where it is coming from. She has no idea that I feel primed for a confrontation. 'It was all right. A truck ride, not much else.'

'You know that road goes to Baglung and almost to Beni, and will eventually go up the Kali Gandaki? Four years ago it didn't even go to Lumle.'

She looks at me, 'So what?'

'Four years ago you could walk all the way from Pokhara to

Chandrakot without coming across the road,' I say, trying to impress upon her the insidious encroachment of the communications infrastructure. 'Now the road comes here, and soon it will go further into the mountains.'

'Enjoy it while you can,' she says cynically, and turns away to ignore me.

I bury my passion and bite my tongue. My attachment to the old route is also for personal sentimental reasons. This is not the place to take out my frustrations. I am where I want to be. Why ruin it with an unnecessary and fruitless argument?

Enamoured of the mules and their drivers, I follow patiently behind them, ruminating on my thoughts as I climb up the steep path to Hille. The ascent is not the obstacle I remembered it to be. I recall waiting for Kirsten at one stage, then unloading my pack and descending the path again when she didn't appear. I found her slumped against a wall crying. 'I can't make it,' she sobbed, exhausted.

Now I am accompanied by an unknown man wrapped in a *lungi* who sashays barefoot, a split bamboo pole over his shoulders with two flat swaying trays full of tomatoes and cauliflowers suspended on either end. He looks for all the world as if he had been transplanted from the plains of India.

As I approach Hille I try and remember the lodge we stayed at. There was a boy, about eight years old running the lodge. He created such a distinct impression on us I can still remember his name: Dipak.

Hille has changed, there are more *bhaatis*, four of them. Some of the terraced fields have been turned into camping-grounds for Westerners, others have been converted into holding areas for mules to spend the night on their way through. Then I see Dipak Lodge and simultaneously I recognise young Dipak, standing on the terrace soliciting business, just as he did four years ago. He has not changed much. The set of his jaw gives him a determined, bulldog look. 'You want room?' he asks automatically.

'Yes, I want a room. Dipak, it's great to see you again!' His eyes open wide. 'Can you remember me?' He admits he cannot. 'I remember you.' I want him to remember. I pull out my wallet and extract a photo of Kirsten. She looks more exceptional, with her white-blonde hair and deep-set blue eyes.

'Wait,' he commands, and disappears into the lodge and exits again with his sister in tow. 'She remember,' he says. She looks at me. I look like another generic, scruffy trekker but she diplomatically shows signs of remembering Kirsten.

'The lodge is bigger, no?' I ask. I walk in to the ground floor. 'This was your family room before, for sleeping and eating, yes?' They both laugh in agreement. I walk into the kitchen. 'This is new.' They agree. 'Show me the rooms upstairs.'

We walk up an outer stairway, which is an innovation, to the veranda under the overhanging slated roof. Dipak gives me the room next to the window, the very same one we had before. I unpack to put on some dry warm clothes. In the kitchen, I meet the parents. They still do not speak English, which is why Dipak 'runs' the lodge. They seem friendlier. I had thought of them as being aloof before. The last four years have been hard on them. I suspect that they have been adversely affected by the decreased tourist traffic along this route as a result of trekkers diverting on trucks going to Baglung on the Kali Gandaki.

Even in Dipak's modest lodge, there is a back-boiler system, conserving wood. The Indian with the trays of tomatoes and cauliflowers enters the *bhaati*. I ask for two *rakshis*, and offer one to the Indian. He accepts, dipping his ring finger on his right hand three times into the drink like Sangpo. Dipak gives me a 'no charge' plate of fried potatoes smothered in chilli powder. He is generous, but also smart. I order a relatively expensive beer to quench the fire in my mouth, and another as a precautionary measure against further signs of generosity.

'I am so happy to be here,' I tell Dipak again, although I am walking beside my shoes again. My mind is half with Kirsten back in Norway, half on those halcyon days when we shared the same experience here four years ago. I can almost feel her presence.

Sitting in the kitchen with the parents, the Indian and the sister, we laugh a lot while waiting for dinner. I do feel very happy, and as time goes on and as Dipak catches on to my good humour, he warms to me. Soon he is sitting propped up against me. As night sets in drums beat from a terraced field below: a camping group celebrating the end of their trek.

'Come, we dance.' Dipak grabs me by the arm, and pulls me outside. It is crisp-cold, and dark, despite the stars. Below, in one of the terraced fields converted to a camping area, pressure lamps light an area in front of tents where Nepalese porters and guides dance and sing. Dipak leads me down the steps. Once in the field, there is no stopping him. He is a superb dancer, rotating and twisting, his hands held high, his body swinging one way and spinning the other. Someone beats a drum, another plays the harmonica. Soon they are all clapping as Dipak struts, his gyrating shadow cast on the whitewashed stone wall of a nearby home, a giant cavorting silhouette, a Norwegian troll let out for a night's fling.

> *Resham phiriri, resham piriri*
> *Oorayna jauki*
> *dara ma basnay*
> *resham piriri*

I translate the middle of the verse to what I think I hear:

> *Resham phiriri, resham piriri*
> I am a monkey
> You are a donkey
> *resham piriri*

Dipak finds this hilarious. He has soon made friends with all the Nepalese guides and porters. It almost seems as if he had met them before.

Back at the lodge he asks me, 'You want hot chocolate?'

This is better than being at home. 'Sure.'

'How big?'

The parents, sister and Indian are all still sitting on the floor around the smokeless oven. 'Big pot.' And when it is ready, we all share it, laugh and talk. Dipak sits huddled up against me, his hands knitted together over my forearms. He makes me sing my version of *resham phiriri*, and everyone laughs together, then we all sing it.

Dipak turns to me, 'I be your guide? OK?' The others stop talking to hear what my reaction will be.

I am not sure how serious he is. 'To Ghorepani?'

He nods emphatically. It is cold up there. We might be walking through snow now. 'Have you been to Ghorepani before?'

'One time before. With Israeli friends.'

'Have you got warm clothes, good shoes?'

'Yes.' He runs off to get them. I feel at home, part of this family, sitting on the mud floor, around a fire, drinking hot chocolate together.

'Have you been to Kathmandu?' I ask Dipak's older sister while Dipak searches for his warm clothes.

She screws up her face. 'Yes. I stay with my father's brother one month, but I no like, so I come back.'

Dipak has a cheaply made jacket which looks a bit warm. Also a sweater, a fur hat, gloves and cheap canvas running-shoes. I examine the running-shoes. 'You'll have to find better shoes if you want to come to Ghorepani,' I say as I poke my fingers through holes. They laugh at him, and he laughs at himself hilariously and selfconsciously.

During the night I hear the Indian snoring downstairs. Just outside the open window beside the bed, bundles of maize and peppers hang to dry from the overhanging roof; beyond, the outline of the mountains under the three-quarters moon. It is good to be here, and I feel content despite being alone. I try reading for a while by flashlight, but am far more interested in the ghostly landscape outside, the terraced fields, the forests, the twinkle of a fire in a home across the valley and my own thoughts. And memories. Even the snoring Indian seems an integral part of the good atmosphere. I leave the window open all night, despite the cold air, to let in the magic, and fall asleep dreaming of all the good times with Kirsten.

HILLE–GHOREPANI

The mules' hoofs click on the flagstones outside the open window. I am smiling though I am half-asleep, happy to still be in these mountains, savouring the elation. Last night I was not alone. Kirsten was with me as much as she was four years ago.

The Indian leaves with his trays of tomatoes and cauliflowers. The father comes in with a container full of fresh buffalo milk. The older sister has already made a small pot of hot chocolate. 'No charge,' Dipak tells me grandly.

Under relentless pressure, I agree to let Dipak come with me to Ghorepani. He asks for advice. 'These shoes, or these? Good jacket? Or no?' He adds, 'I am happy today to go with my *daai*.' He calls me his '*daai*', his older brother, and I call him my '*baai*', younger brother, although he is more like a son than a younger brother. He stands around selfconsciously, hands in trouser pockets, shrugging his shoulders forward manfully and giving me nonchalant looks every time I turn to him or ask him a question. The father churns milk from the buffalo, in a wooden pot, to make butter for breakfast, as a special treat before we leave.

After Dipak and I set out, we are soon confronted by wild-looking *bhotia* mule drivers descending from inner Mustang or Dolpo, or perhaps even Tibet. Their faces are unwashed, almost black. The men have long hair wound into topknots above their heads. The women carry children or loads of personal belongings. An old man accompanying the group fingers his prayer beads and audibly mumbles, '*Om Mani Padme Hum.*'

'*Bhotia*,' Dipak says scornfully. One speaks to Dipak, asking him where he is going. 'Ghorepani,' he replies proudly.

'Why?' they ask.

The exchange is too fast for me to understand, but there is much laughter from the *bhotia*. 'Why are they laughing?' I ask as we continue up the path.

'They asking what I am doing. I say I am guide for you. But they laughing.' He laughs at himself too. 'Me is too small, but guide.'

At Tirkhedugaa we pass villagers negotiating the price of stiff, salted goat skins. They pull out the goat hair to test the quality. A boy approaches me. 'Hashish?' he solicits. I ignore him.

Dipak has overheard the vital exchange. 'What he say?'

'He asked me if I wanted hashish.'

'What you say?' he asks.

'I say nothing.'

'Good.'

We begin a steep climb. The guidebook claims there are three-thousand seven-hundred and sixty-seven steps. Soon I am dripping in perspiration, but I am not tired. 'You tired?' Dipak asks concerned. I shake my head negative, sweat dripping off with the motion. 'You are a donkey and I am a monkey,' he sings, making fun of me as I labour under my heavy pack and he carries nothing. We both laugh at that.

Caught in the middle of a mule train, Dipak jokes and banters with the drivers. I am amazed at how he seems to know all the mule drivers we meet. Villagers in huts along the path ask him where he is going. He tells them he is my guide. They ask how much he is being paid. 'Four-hundred rupees,' he tells them untruthfully.

We pass two Americans, the man carrying his wife's pack on his front, as well as his own considerable pack on his back. Dipak asks, 'You is need help?'

The man puts down his wife's pack, then unshackles his own. 'Sure,' he says good-naturedly, breathing hard. Dipak picks up her pack and hoists it onto his back. He is so small the bottom of her pack reaches below his knees. He marches off looking like a beetle under its protective shell, borne by scurrying, spindly beetle legs. 'Is he OK carrying that?' the man asks me, concerned, watching Dipak-the-beetle bustling up the path.

'I'll watch him closely. If it gets too heavy I'll tell him to put it down.'

'I feel bad,' the American says.

'It's all right. You are not employing him as a porter. He can put it down whenever he wants.' Dipak and I take off together like a beetle and turtle, and soon I see him perspiring too. 'Not too heavy?' He shakes his head. 'Now you are a donkey too.'

That makes him laugh hysterically.

Two hours after leaving Dipak's home we reach Ulleri. Dipak points out his school. He walks up and down here every day. We enter a rhododendron forest with generically beautiful waterfalls and pools formed in the sculptured rocks. There is a constant sound of bird-song. In the forest we meet more Khampa types. '*Bhotia*' as Dipak disparagingly calls them. The men are fierce-looking, their stature enhanced by hair bound over their heads, long bulky *chupas* reaching almost down to the knees, sheepskin coats turned inside out, silver-sheathed knives hanging down at the side from belts. Children, about the same size as Dipak, but undoubtedly younger, stop and stare at him. They talk but they cannot understand Dipak, and Dipak cannot comprehend them. They have no common language. They stare at each other fixedly.

As we get higher we walk across patches of snow and wait for the Americans at Ghorepani. It is late afternoon and the soft light illuminates the Annapurnas. When the Americans show up, and after dropping our packs at a convenient lodge in Deurali, Dipak and I continue up to Poon Hill. We are the only ones on the summit. I point out the different Himalayan peaks. A three-quarters moon emerges.

The sun sets: Dhauligiri is back-lit, while the Annapurnas are a full pyrotechnic display. It is so quiet my ears ring. We are totally alone. Dipak is patient as I contemplate, savouring the stillness and the awesome view. Then together we walk down the path and soon it is dark and we must rely on the moonlight to find our way. Dipak holds my hand coming down, and I sense he is scared. Dinner is minimal, soggy and cold. There is an Annapurna Base Camp feel about the lodge. Despite the children running around, there is not a friendly family atmosphere and Dipak stays close to me, uncharacteristically aloof from the hosts. In our shared room Dipak crawls under several blankets, fully clothed. After a few minutes, he whispers to me, 'You think American can give me money for carrying bag?'

'I think so.'

'How much?'

'I don't know.'

'You tell him four-hundred rupees, OK?'

'OK.'

GHOREPANI–TATOPANI

I wake Dipak to climb Poon Hill. He jumps out of bed, pulls on his fur hat and is ready to go. It takes me longer to get dressed. 'You is go Tatopani today?' Dipak asks.

'Yes.'

'I come with you?'

To avoid negotiating so early in the morning, when Dipak is likely to get the better of me, I tell him, 'Maybe.' He lets it go at that, for the time being. It is completely dark as we start climbing Poon Hill. A satellite passes overhead, unbelievably clear. The way it moves reminds me of a recurring nightmare I have, of a billiard ball rolling steadily, consistently, inevitably, over a table of green velvet. It has that same constant movement. At the summit of Poon Hill there is a growing crowd of trekkers. Where did they all come from? We had seen hardly anyone in the village yesterday evening, and our lodge is empty.

Dipak is excited by the atmosphere, and he stands around as coolly as he possibly can, his hands stuck deep into his pockets, flapping his elbows selfconsciously every time I look at him. He has a broad smile on his face. I suppose he has never seen so many Westerners in one place at one time before. I give Dipak money to buy tea from the enterprising Nepali who has carried up thermoses, but the tea is sold out. 'Dipak, if you get four-hundred rupees from the American for carrying his wife's bag, what are you going to do with the money?'

'I must pay ninety rupees every month, school fees. If he pay me, I give to mother, so she pay school fees four months. After, forty rupees change.' He has it all worked out. I believe him. I could almost hear him calculating the figures last night before he fell asleep.

There is no 'sunrise'. At least, there is no ball of fire exploding out of the horizon, but the subtle early morning light is beautiful nonetheless. The tea man asks, 'You here before? With Michel?'

'Yes,' I reply, surprised. Michel had not climbed up Poon Hill with me. Then I remember, we had eaten with him in the kitchen of the *bhaati* Sangpo had recommended we stay at. He gives me a chocolate bar. I reach into my pocket. 'No, no charge. You is friend.' He smiles and walks away having enhanced his karma. I do the same thing and split the chocolate with Dipak. I am continuously amazed at the generosity of these people. What little they have they are willing to share, even with those obviously so much richer than themselves.

By the time the Americans arrive the mountains are already a stark white. Neil asks me, 'How much should I give Dipak for carrying Shelly's bag?'

'Would four-hundred rupees seem too much?' I say, hesitantly.

'Eight dollars. Seems a lot.'

'That's the amount he asked me to ask from you. He is going to use the money to pay for his school fees. He is a serious boy, and you can be sure the money is going to the right place. Look on it as your own charitable project, but realise that he did you a service first.'

Neil needs no convincing. He strides over to Dipak, towering over him, and counts out four-hundred rupees. Dipak puts it in his pocket, and looks surreptitiously at me. We are in collusion. On our way down from Poon Hill I tell him, 'He thought four-hundred rupees was too much, but I told him you were going to give the money to your mother for school, so he said it is OK.' He does not say anything, but I can feel we are more brothers than ever. We are looking after each other's interests.

'I come with you to Tatopani?'

'Your parents will worry about you.'

'No! I can do anything! My parents no worry.'

I am sure he is right. But I do not want to have the responsibility of his parents' potential worry. I invoke this concern again.

'No problem. I tell man with mules, he say I go Tatopani.'

'OK, but you make sure you tell the mule drivers to tell your parents.' He puts his hands in his pockets, and shrugs his shoulders and flaps his elbows and smiles happily.

The walk down from Deurali Pass towards Tatopani is on a snow-covered, north-facing slope. The mud on the path is frozen solid. The grove looks different, with a foot of snow lying on the forest floor. The winter scene reminds me of home, wherever that is, and I feel a momentary pang of homesickness.

Dipak satisfies my demands by telling several mule-train drivers to tell his parents he is going on to Tatopani. They are curious why he is coming with me. He replies he is my guide, although it is in fact I who am his guide. Sometimes a porter passes by and Dipak exchanges information with him. He is acquainted with a bewildering array of porters and mule drivers, because they either stay at his lodge, or he has tried to solicit their business on their march through Hille. They all seem to be amused at his new-found vocation. I am beginning to sense Dipak is a character unto himself. Gregarious to an extreme, he will talk to anyone.

The only mule drivers who do not seem to know him are the *bhotia*. But there is often no common language, and I can see Dipak looks down on them. He tells me, 'You see poor man. Dirty, no money. But lots of money! Gold! Hidden!' He gestures with his hands to convey that beneath their robes, they conceal money and gold. 'Too much money,' he concludes shaking his head.

We walk through a landslide area. A path has been formed out of the loose gravel. A shovel and pick lie astride the path. When we get to the other side a man approaches us. He has a book in his hand which he hands over to me, 'Please sir.' I read the covering page of the hard-cover notebook:

Project- to plant some trees- please can you give a donation to help
repair this trail and plant some trees.
Trekkers add to the erosion. Your donation will be appreciated. This
path is broken in the monsoon every year and takes a long time to
mend. A donation will help.
We villagers.

I give a donation. They are, I can see, working on repairing the path,
and I want to show my concern, and appreciation for the help, which
does after all, affect us trekkers directly. Dipak talks to me non-stop.
He also likes to hold my hand. This is uncharted territory for him, and
he is insecure. Despite his apparent maturity, Dipak is only a child, and
as a nervous child he wants the tactile contact with me for security.

I slip with my heavy back-pack a couple of times on the melting
snow and ice, and this encourages Dipak to hold on to me even tighter,
and more persistently. This is a reaction to help me, not only to give
him more security.

He asks, 'I come Norway for work?'

'Not possible,' I reply.

'No is possible?'

'No is possible. Before, maybe possible, but now too many Norway
people no have jobs, no work. If you come to Norway to work and
Norwegian people want work but cannot find work, then they are
angry. Before was easy, but now is difficult. Many problems now in
Western countries because many people want work but cannot find
work.'

I feel it is important for Dipak to realise that this easy way out is not
as feasible as it was, and it is more realistic for him to concentrate on
what he can do and achieve here in Nepal. He understands. Dipak's
older brother is studying in Pokhara but wants to go to Korea, Saudi
Arabia or Japan to get a job; if that is not possible, he will continue
with his studying.

We walk into a Brahmin and Chetri village. Half-a-dozen local
teenage boys walk towards us. This time Dipak is some distance ahead
of me. I can see the boys are aggressive; like a pack of dogs protecting
their territory, they focus on Dipak. At the last minute, they realise
Dipak is with me. He sidesteps them, and I face them down until they
move aside at the last possible instant.

It is a magnificent walk, sometimes through Magar-Poon villages, sometimes through Brahmin-Chetri villages, sometimes through forest, sometimes on the edge of a ridge. This is, was, the major trade route between Pokhara and Mustang and Tibet. We pass by several large *bhotia* mule trains.

Three Western boys ascend the path. They study us. Ever since the encounter with the belligerent local boys, Dipak has held his hand in mine. I can see them talking among themselves, and as they pass by, one smirks and says, 'Found yourself a bum-boy have you?' By the time I understand the insinuation, they are already a distance up the path.

At first I am angry at the implication of their comment and have an urge to drop my pack and run after the creeps and take them on physically. That initial reaction is overtaken by one of compassion, for the sick mentality that has contrived their conclusion. Besides, I think gleefully, it is I who should be thankful. If I can bear their offensive attitudes with patience and forgiveness, then the more I benefit, as they enhance my karma and open up the path of liberation. Easy would have been proud of me. So would Michel, come to think of it.

'Why you is laughing?' Dipak asks.

'I'm laughing at what those boys said to me.' That satisfies Dipak, and he doesn't ask me to explain further. We walk without stopping and by one-thirty we are in Tatopani and find ourselves a room at the Dhauligiri Lodge. There are fewer trekkers than there were a month ago.

In the effluent of the hot springs I wash my sweat-soaked clothes, then sit in one of the two spring-fed pools. Dipak joins for a while, but is clearly impatient to get back up to the lodge where he has caught sight of the television, the first he has ever seen. The novelty of the hot spring pools is nothing compared with that of the TV.

'Hindu.' He still cannot get my name right, 'Let's go,' he chides in Nepali. His face has lost the grey-ashen colour resulting from layers of accumulated dust and dirt. He is probably cleaner now than he has been for a long time. We walk back up to the lodge together.

'Hungry?' I ask.

'Leetle.'

We goggle the dizzying array of cakes and pies displayed in a glass cabinet. 'Which would you like?'

He hesitates, then points at a sad-looking, plain roll. I guess he is being polite. I point out a large, dark-brown chocolate cake dripping in thick white icing. 'How about that one?' He pauses, and I know. 'Two slices of that chocolate cake please.' The portions are huge, and Dipak eats ravenously, his first chocolate cake ever. Afterwards he sits next to me, idly leafing through my notebooks as I finish the cake at a more leisurely pace. I do not feel entirely comfortable.

'Dipak, this is one of the best lodges in Nepal, because the food is so good. They can cook many things in this lodge that you could also learn. How to soak the salad in iodine solution for example, so tourists do not get sick.' I have realised over the last two days I must give Dipak more credit than I think, for his ability to understand not only English, but also concepts. 'Do you understand?'

'Yes.'

I think he does. 'This is a famous lodge, and you can pick up many good ideas here. Dipak Lodge is also very good, but smaller. If you want, you can find out about things in the kitchen.'

'If I go, I am small, they no help me,' he complains. Of course, he is right, they would not pay him any attention. But I can change that.

'If I go with you, and tell the chief cook you want to learn how he makes such good food, then it is OK?'

He nods, 'Yes.' I can see he is enthusiastic about the idea. We go to the kitchen. The cook remembers me, I had complimented him on the delicious specially made *dal bhaat* I had eaten here before with Michel. 'This is Dipak, from Dipak Lodge in Hille. It is a small lodge, but a very good one. He would like to learn from you, whatever you can teach him, because I have told him you are the best cook in Nepal. Can you help?'

The cook shakes his head in agreement. 'No problem.'

'He can only watch, or he can help, as you wish.' The cook and his helpers laugh, and soon Dipak is involved in preparing dinner. The cook understands what I am trying to do, and I think he even appreciates it on Dipak's behalf.

An hour later I go back to see how Dipak is doing, and find him in the thick of things, laughing and joking with the others, already having charmed the kitchen staff. He comes out of the kitchen occasionally to make sure I am still there, then dives back into the foray.

Bhuwan, the owner, joins me. We drink beer. He is in a weird mood. He waxes philosophical but it is impossible to pin him down to answer anything. A question is answered with a question: the Western analytical method gone awry. The dialectical training taught by the Jesuit fathers at St Xavier's in Kathmandu is mixed with a blend of Oriental mysticism he has recently re-discovered in searching for his own roots.

We spend hours talking, about Nepal, identities, development. I mention the road sneaking up the Kali Gandaki. 'Andrew,' he says. 'The road is not your problem. We will handle the road.'

He may be right. But his objectivity is suspect. If the road gets closer to Tatopani, it will mean massively increased business for him. He will be sitting on a gold mine. 'My brother,' he tells me candidly, confirming my suspicions, 'works for the Ministry responsible for road construction.'

It is twelve-thirty by the time we stop talking. Dipak is still in the kitchen, at ease with the staff, and ready for bed. In our room Dipak crawls under a cover, I crawl into my sleeping-bag. Too stimulated by the conversation with Bhuwan to sleep straight away, I read for an hour before turning the light off. I think Dipak is asleep when he says, 'Clothes outside. Tips?'

My washed laundry has been left hanging on the clothes line outside. I had forgotten them. My *baai* is keeping an eye out for me. 'Don't worry. No thieves.'

TATOPANI–GHOREPANI

'Peace. Peace.'

At first I think Dipak is having nightmares about the warring between Indian Hindus and Muslims witnessed on the televised news last night. Then I realise what he is getting at.

'Sure. Go ahead. Peace.' I turn the light on for him.

He runs to piss in the garden.

When we get up Dipak sings happily as I pack.

He says as I re-stuff our belongings, 'I carry my coat.'

'It is easier if I carry it.' He curls the jacket up protectively and I shove it into the pack. Crumbs fall out of the pockets. 'What have you got in there?' I ask.

'From kitchen.' He shows his jacket pockets which are full of discarded, crushed tea-biscuit crumbs. 'I take to Hille. Good for buffalo. Good for milk.'

For breakfast Dipak has two slices of triple-layered chocolate cake dripping in white icing, and I have a more conventional *dal bhaat*. I give Dipak one-thousand rupees to pay for our food and lodging. When he comes back he counts out the change telling me how the bill added up to so much. He has meticulously checked each item against the prices on the menu.

At the suspension bridge crossing the Kali Gandaki, we wait for a mule train to cross first. The mules move lackadaisically, as if sleepwalking. They are decorated with colourful harnesses, from which bells hang. Some mules sport red woollen mats on their foreheads with an image of the Dalai Lama embedded in the centre. Garlands of marigolds are strung across the river; Buddhist prayer flags hang from the bridge over a shimmering mercurial river. Sun glimmers from cascading waters bouncing over boulders, a spectacular light show of bulging waves and splashing droplets, eddying pools and glistening rocks.

At the police checkpoint I sign myself, 'Andrew Bahadur Gurung'. The police ask to see my trekking permit. They do not seem to be concerned when they see the discrepancy in names.

Dipak tells me, 'Next time we eat at lodge, you give me money for me, OK?'

'Sure, why?'

'In lodges, asking, "Who is paying? You or tourist?" If I say tourist, then price for me is same price you pay. Lodge keeper give me half. If I say I am paying, then cheeep price for me.'

No wonder porters eat so much, when their trekker employers pay directly for the food cost at *bhaatis*. The porter not only gets his food free, but he actually makes a little money on each dish he can stuff into himself.

Another mule caravan comes down the path. The lead mule has a headress comprised of four layers of yak tails, white, red, white, orange. The drivers' cries and whistles chivvy the sleepy animals onwards. The muleteers are not the only ones who depend on this traditional mode of traffic. *Bhaatis* like Dipak's, which may not get that much Western tourist traffic now, rely heavily on the traditional mule trains and porters, for survival. But that traffic too will be replaced if the road ascends much further up the Kali Gandaki.

We pass an old man carrying a *doko* full of tins of oil. He recognises Dipak. Dipak tells me, 'He is Brahmin, but poor. He stay at Dipak Lodge many times.'

'How much does he pay?'

'Because he is Brahmin, he cooking own meal. He buying rice eight rupees, vegetables three rupees, then sleeping free. Three rupees for buffalo milk. Other porters, sometimes paying twenty-five rupees for *dal bhaat*, but sleeping is free.'

The porters paying twenty-five rupees for a meal are obviously sponsored by their clients. Still, at fifty rupees to the dollar, the rates are 'cheeep'.

Dipak has explained the porter is poor, although he is Brahmin. I try to get an idea of Dipak's sense of caste. 'Brahmin is better than Gurung?'

He nods. This Brahmin, who must work as a menial porter carrying cooking oil up to the mountains on his back to earn a living, is still 'better' than Dipak as a Gurung and a land owner.

'What about other castes?'

'Gurung better than Poon, better than Magar, better than Tamang, better than Rai, better than Thakali, better than *bhotia*, then Kami and Saki.'

Elements of Hinduism go back to the Indo-Aryans who invaded the Indian subcontinent two-thousand years BC. The Indo-Aryans brought with them religious texts, the Vedas, and the sacred languages of Hindi and Sanskrit, which have commingled with indigenous beliefs. The Indo-Aryans also brought with them ideas about social stratification, the caste system. Theoretically the Brahmins and the Chetris were the dominant groups. Outside this group were the outcasts. Dipak has developed his own social stratification including mountain tribes based loosely on the Hindu caste system.

'What work you do when you is home?'

'I have my two businesses. One is for rafting, the other for trekking. Tourists come from outside Norway, and my companies take them either rafting or mountain climbing. It is very similar to the same kind of businesses here in Nepal.'

'How much money you paid in Norway?' Dipak asks, mentally

trying to figure out where I fit into a different class scheme, measured by material wealth.

I take an arbitrarily low figure, of one-hundred dollars a day, and convert it into rupees. 'Five-thousand rupees.'

'Pibe-thousand rupees! Eberyday?' he asks incredulously.

I realise I have made a mistake.

'You are reeech.'

'No, I am not rich. I will tell you why. Also I must pay taxes. In Norway half of what I earn is taken by the government.'

Dipak calculates. 'You not paid pibe-thousand dollars eberyday?' he asks, clearly disappointed.

'I am paid five-thousand rupees every day yes, but the government takes half before I get it, so only two-and-a-half-thousand rupees for me.' He calculates. 'Also, I do not have Dipak Lodge. I must rent my apartment from someone and it costs fifty-thousand rupees per month. I do not have a buffalo for milk, or fields to grow food, so I must buy all my food. That costs more than fifty-thousand rupees per month. I have to go to work by car, because my work is too far to walk. The car costs me more than fifty-thousand rupees per month.'

He is still calculating. Finally. 'How you pay eberything if only getting pibe-thousand rupees ebery day?' He has hit the nail on the head. 'Not so reeech.'

'That's right.'

A boy overtakes us carrying a satchel and a book. I suspect he is going to ask us for a donation for the landslide rehabilitation project. He stands at a strategic vantage point overlooking the landslide and, sure enough, asks for a donation. Dipak protectively says I paid yesterday. I take the book to show the boy and am surprised to see there is just the covering page asking for a donation, and that the list of names and donations from yesterday has been torn out. How often have they done this? The landslide is not new. Looking carefully, I can see bushes growing which are at least a year-and-half old. How much money have they collected, and who keeps the money? Crossing the landslide area, we see the symbolic pick and shovel exactly where they were yesterday, lying on the path as if they had just been put down temporarily.

We climb through patches of snow into Deurali, and cross through Deurali down the other side into Ghorepani proper, staying at a lodge of Dipak's choice. There are no other guests. It is late afternoon, and as I strip off my clothes, clouds of steam rise from my sopping shirt and back-pack, filling the room with mist. Before dinner, I take advantage of the fading light to walk through the village of Ghorepani, consisting almost entirely of lodges. There are very few trekkers, yet all the lodges have wood-consuming fires burning, evidenced by blue smoke curling from their chimneys.

Dipak likes this *bhaati*. He helps in the kitchen then brings two glasses of *rakshi*, one for him, one for me. 'I tell them two *rakshi* for me,' he whispers conspiratorially. 'Half-price. Cheeep.' He sits by the space-heater to keep warm. He is exhausted, hardly able to keep his eyes open.

A young Poon girl, her brother and a pretty girl helper, run the lodge. The atmosphere is friendly and relaxed. *Dal bhaat* is ready, and we stuff ourselves, replacing calories burnt all day climbing six hours, non-stop, from the bottom of the Kali Gandaki, carrying what must be some twenty-four kilos in my back-pack. I am impressed by my level of fitness after these weeks of daily exercise. Despite the fact that I have eaten no meat during this time, or perhaps because of it, I feel healthier than ever before, although my body weight is way down and I am thin by Western aesthetic standards. When I pinch the skin over my hips, there is no body fat contained in the skin between my fingers.

We both have second helpings of everything. Dipak smiles as he eats, despite his fatigue. Already I feel melancholic that tomorrow I shall leave this little friend who has accompanied and looked after me. 'I am sad tomorrow you go to Hille, and I go to Ghandrung.'

'I sad too.' But his face is lit up with happiness. He radiates well-being, for right now he is happy. And tomorrow? Well, tomorrow is tomorrow.

We eat fresh, hot, apple pie he helped make. He eats it with a knife and fork, as I do, but has the utensils reversed. He uses the knife to put the pie in his mouth. Dipak brings two more glasses of *rakshi*. 'I pay', he tells me. I write by candlelight, and he talks and plays with the two girls and boy in the kitchen.

When the candles burn out, Dipak replaces them. He informs me, 'I sleep in kitchen, no cost.'

I go outside for 'peace'. It is a full moon and cold. Ghorepani is so still that only the trickle of water flowing down the path can be heard.

I too am exhausted; it feels wonderful to be physically drained and spiritually fulfilled. Drums and Nepali folk songs in the distance send me off to a deep sleep, dreaming of Nepal and the Annapurnas.

GHOREPANI–TADAPANI

The kitchen fire is already burning, Dipak is still asleep. When he wakens I ask for some porridge, and he has *dal bhaat*. We leave the lodge together, and a short distance down the path we stop. Dipak will descend back to Hille. I will climb up for some time onto a ridge, then descend through a narrow gorge back to Tadapani. I ask the girl from the lodge who has accompanied us down the path to wish us farewell, to take a photo of the two of us together. This time the camera works.

I give Dipak some rupees for 'guiding' me and then show him one of the Muktinath bracelets on my wrist, the one I did not make a wish on. 'Do you like this?'

I am surprised when he says, 'Yes.'

'Would you like it?'

'Yes.'

'It is a friendship bracelet.' I take it off my wrist, and tie it onto his tiny wrist. 'When I tie the knot now, you must make a wish. When the bracelet comes off, you must make the same wish, and it will come true.' All through this, Dipak is fighting back tears. His lower jaw juts out manfully, but his chin trembles with emotion.

He reaches his hand out to shake mine. I take the proffered hand, tiny in mine. Then he pulls his fur hat down over his head, turns and walks down the enormous flagstones, his oversized jacket and pockets bulging with crushed biscuits for his buffalo, because it is good for its milk. As I see his little figure, dwarfed by the surrounding forests, disappear down the stone steps, I feel like running after him, to tell him that he can come with me to Ghandrung. I could only hope to have as fine a son as him one day. I watch as he descends the path. When he is almost out of sight, he turns around and waves. He is smiling happily.

Ascending into the forest, I am soon walking through deep snow. I stop occasionally to absorb its peaceful silence, the snow absorbing every vestige of sound, which is not much anyway in these high mountains. Patches of sunlight reflect off the hard ice crystals on the white pillowy surface, like billions of glittering diamonds.

The wood has a magnetic pull of its own. I had looked forward to returning to this secluded area, but the experience is better than expected, alone in the grove, so much at peace. I perspire as the snow becomes deeper, and I climb higher, walking once again in – not beside – my shoes.

A barely distinguishable smaller path leads off, and I follow it, curious, climbing steeply. Despite the assistance from the ski pole, I fall a number of times in the snow-drifts. Sometimes I am reduced to crawling on hands and knees to get myself and my back-pack under toppled tree-trunks, but reach, eventually, another ridge, dense with tall pines. Reaching the top of this ridge, there is not a puff of wind, not a wisp of cloud. The intense sunlight has melted the exposed snow revealing blue flowers, gentian, poking out of the ground. The smell of the sun-warmed ground reminds me confusingly of spring.

Inexplicably, a four-storey wooden tower, built like an ambitious child's tree-fort, reaches into the uppermost branches of the pines. Why has the tower been constructed here? The crudely made structure is unstable, and sways as I climb, but at the top I am rewarded with a spectacular view of the Annapurnas. From this vantage point, I have a view of three-hundred-and-sixty degrees.

To the west is Poon Hill, and behind that, snow-covered Himals as far as the eye can see. Looking at my map I recognise most of the peaks. Further to the east more unidentifiable Himals and snow-dusted Just Hills, as far as the horizon stretches. I recognise where I entered into the Himals from Dumre, and where I have come out from Kagbeni. The sight is impressive, as are the distances.

Terraced yellow mustard-seed and green paddy fields are bathed in sunlight far, far down below. Further south, layer upon layer of Just Hills recede, first dark green, then fading with decreasing intensities of blue into the whiteness of the Indian subcontinent. In the stillness, I strip to the waist, taking off my shirt and thermal undershirt to hang out to dry, and to let the sun evaporate the perspiration off my body. I feel omnipotent in this four-storey tree-fort, commanding a view over thousands of kilometres. In a way, this is the apex of the trip, for I have the best overview of the Circuit.

I am reluctant to leave this place of perfect solitude. When I do, I repeatedly look around to cram in one last glimpse. Descending the narrow and snow-filled gorge, I am terrified of slipping. The path is partly covered in ice and a fall would often mean a headlong plunge some considerable distance. Judging from the lack of footprints in the snow, I would not be found by anyone for a long period. A couple of times I do slip, landing harmlessly on my sleeping-bag tucked under the pack; insignificant, but enough to scare me.

Snow is piled high everywhere. On the forest floor, on the rocks in the middle of the stream, in clearings. It is so much like spring, with the sun warming the air and the melting snow. Fantastic ice sculptures form around boulders in partly frozen streams. The smell of firewood burning wakens my appetite. Hungry, I fantasise about a heaping pile of steaming rice and lentils and spinach-like greens.

Emerging from the forest Sita recognises me as I walk into Tadapani. She has been basking in the warmth of the evening sunlight, combing her long hair. 'You have come back!' she says with an enthusiasm that makes me feel as if I am coming home.

'I said I might.' She binds her tresses and gets up to make tea and prepare dinner. There are no other trekkers in Tadapani.

The sky is an iridescent Cibrachrome print, the clouds luminescent. Machapuchare becomes silhouetted by a full moon against a one-dimensional sky. A shooting star streaks the sky over Annapurna South and I expect it to hit the mountain and burst into flames. A kid-goat cries in the mists of the forest below, like a human child being strangled. I eat in the kitchen and laugh familiarly with Sita and Siley and the little girl Sunita until late in the night.

Even later, I write, on the flagstone terrace, by candlelight. When the two candles burn down to the damp, frost-whitened table, I scribble by the light of the moon, directly overhead.

TADAPANI–GHANDRUNG

In the kitchen Sunita, the little girl, asks, 'Bruce Lee?'

'Yes please.' She hands me my muesli. It could be from the smoke in the kitchen, although the oven does not emit much, but Siley has tears in her eyes when we say goodbye.

Almost immediately I am swallowed up by the forest again. As I descend there is no longer snow on the ground, the forest floor a pot-pourri of brown, red, yellow and orange leaves and multicoloured flowers. Strands of pale Spanish moss drip spookily from the branches; deep carpets of dark green moss grow on the trunks so thick it is hard to identify the trees. Vines hang in tangled knots from upper branches.

I take off my back-pack and sit on the dank earth for a while and listen, see and smell and touch all I can, so that the memory might be indelible. These personal minutes are intense, peaceful, joyful, inter-nal. How could I describe them to others? A walk in the Himalayas, I have discovered, is more easily measured in physical terms of summits climbed, of passes crossed, of villages reached. The solitary rhythmic pad of my boots over the leaf-strewn path is a now familiar, hypnotic, constant refrain, soothing, echoing the beat of my heart.

A leaf falls. This time, however, I recognise the sound for what it is. The temperature drops, and I descend a narrow defile. A thick bank of mist moves rapidly up the gorge, swirling around the trees, blotting out the sunlight. Before I enter Ghandrung, the mist hugging the gorge dis-appears. At the Sangri La Lodge Drubar is playing cards on the terrace with friends. He is surprised to see me again, and jumps up to give me my old room. 'No other tourists,' he says gleefully. It is the end of the season for him, and time to relax. He rejoins the waiting card players.

Far to the south, a tropical sky looms. As it gets darker, firelight flickers in homesteads as far up the valley as Chomrong and far down into the valley. Now, in Ghandrung itself, electric lights illuminate the village, powered by a new mini hydroelectric generator. Above, clouds patterned like sand ripples on a mud flat after the tide has gone out, become crimson in a final bloodbath of light. I wait for the moon to rise over Machapuchare before going inside.

A lonely trekker has arrived. 'Where are you from?' she asks.

'Canada. Where are you from?'

That is all she needs. 'America. I've been travelling around the world for eighteen months. Got another eighteen months to go. Started with my boyfriend, but we didn't get along after some months. Couldn't agree on how to travel. I gave up everything to come on this trip. Sold my house, car, gave up my job. So I figured I wasn't going to head back, even if he did. So . . . here I am.' She goes on at some length describing her family, her loneliness travelling, how her family are begging her to come back. 'Haven't been sick 'til I got to Kathmandu. Then I got giardia.' She plucks the skin off boiled potatoes. 'Had a luxury hotel in Kathmandu. Big rooms, big comfortable bed, hot shower, clean toilets, you know, the flushing kind you sit on. Even had an electric heater and hot water bottle . . . Got here about three today . . .'

'Seen much of the village?' I ask.

'Too tired when I got here so we have to save energy for tomorrow. We are going to Tatopani. So how far is it to get to Tatopani?' she asks her porter wearing the bottom half of her matching track-suit top. A strange variant of the Get There People, the three-week time limit stretched to three years.

The American says, 'So I've got to move. Want to be home by Christmas next year, so I'm going to have to do the remaining countries a lot faster. Got the Eastern Bloc countries to do in two months, do Japan in a month, China in a month. I didn't do Papua New Guinea, or Philippines, so I'm missing those countries so . . .' Her sentences often begin or trail off with 'so'.

Back out in the solitude of the terrace, I hear something below. Didi, Drubar's wife, has scolded me gently several times for not locking my bedroom door. Is she safeguarding us against a thief, I wonder? I peer over the edge of the terrace. A mule eats the grass growing out of the chinks in the stone wall. The mule's head is so close to my feet that I can scratch it behind the ear. I sit and caress it at length and I am not sure who has the most pleasure, for this is the first intimate contact I have had in over two months.

GHANDRUNG

At the entrance to the ACAP Headquarters is an award:

15th J. Paul Getty Wildlife Prize of World Wildlife
Fund
awarded to

Ghandrung Forest Management Committee
'The committee, a dynamic model of grassroots
conservation organisation, in collaboration with the
Annapurna Conservation Area Project and the
Government of Nepal, employs community-based designs
which enable local residents to play a leading
role in managing and conserving the rich natural
resources of the Annapurna region.

February 21, 1992, Caracas, Venezuela.

I am amazed at the improvements ACAP has achieved in the four years
since I was here last. It expounds development rhetoric one finds else-
where, but here the philosophy has begun to work. Utilising funds collected from the entrance fees to the Annapurnas, ACAP has been able
to fund itself and the projects it supports.

Villagers understand that the Annapurna Conservation Area does
not preclude them: they will not be thrown out, as has been the case in
other protected areas of Nepal; not only are they not being forcibly
removed, but increasing powers are being vested in them. Previously, a
villager was required to travel to Pokhara to obtain a licence to cut a
tree down. If one harvested a tree illegally, there was no community
outrage, the tree 'belonged' to the government.

Now permission to harvest a tree comes from the relevant Village
Forest Committee. It is once again the community forest; people know
that without protection the forests will be cleared, and fewer tourists
will come. They are able to regulate relatively easily the cutting of
trees, legal or otherwise. Forest control, and in effect ownership,
reverts back to the traditional forest management existing two generations ago, before the government nationalised all forests.

It is easy to become jaded about development work, yet here is a
project showing promise, based on its heady success. But the question of The Road, and what it will do to the environment, culture
and economic structure of the whole area is ignored. It seems silly
to take the environment and culture of the Annapurnas and its
people so seriously when a road going up the Kali Gandaki will
make a mockery of all the environmentally and culturally sensitive
issues raised. Within years, ACAP's success will be wiped out by

infrastructure costing in dollar terms far more than any foreseen economic benefit.

Returning to Drubar's lodge, I stop at the Excellent View Lodge to talk with Nirmila, a good friend of Siley's. Like Siley, Nirmila is single. I had heard she had travelled to Long Island, New York, as the guest of an American she had nursed back to health when he became sick during his trek. 'Did you like it there?'

'Good question,' she replies non-committally.

'How long did you stay?'

'Six months.' A *bhotia* girl, much like Krisna, and also an orphan, fetches a photo album and together the three of us sit leafing through it. There is a picture of Nirmila in an apartment in Manhattan. 'I worked four days a week with a family in Long Island, and two or three days a week I visited friends in Manhattan.'

There are many photos of her at the Long Island house: standing tiny next to an enormous double-doored refrigerator/freezer; sitting in a chair watching television; talking on a cordless telephone in the backyard beside a swimming-pool; and a picture of five apparently naked Americans in a jacuzzi. She looks out of place in these photos of America. Now, she is far removed from that world, in this primitive *bhaati* with a fire stove, dirt floor and mud walls, black soot-stained roof with smoked meat hanging down from the rafters, firewood piled on the floor, blackened pots, buckets of water for plumbing, rough-hewn wood for table, stool and shelves.

'You did what so many young Nepalese men want to do. You went to America to live and work. Yet you do not seem very impressed.'

'I like it better here.'

'Why?'

She hesitates before telling me. 'America is not what I thought. There are many rich, but there are many poor, with no place to live. There are old people begging. People are always rushing, working so hard to make money. They have many things, cars, big houses, televisions. They have everything. But that is all they have got. They do not have time to enjoy. Everything is rush. Always doing. They do not have time to think. They do not live with their families. Their friends are far away.' She shakes her head again at the memories. She was disillusioned and disappointed. 'I am happy here,' she says simply.

I am happy here too. But unlike Nirmila I must go back in some days, for this is not my home.

GHANDRUNG–DHAMPUS

Drubar and his wife say goodbye. They had been so kind and generous to me, caring, as if they were siblings. I walk through the narrow passageways of Ghandrung for the last time. Shafts of sunlight illuminate the narrow smoke-filled pathways between dwellings: a painter's canvas of light and shadow. A buffalo stands in my path, his thick bristly hairs and black shiny horns reflecting sunlight. He smells me and retreats through the narrow passageways barely wide enough to accommodate his bulky galloping form. At the prayer wall I spin the wheels and wish again. Or is it a prayer after all?

Leaving the snake path wriggling along the ridge, I descend the precipitous steps to the Modi Khola. A Kami boy half-heartedly asks me for my pen, *mitaai* sweets, rupees, and rather strangely, my shoes, which reminds me that if the Chinese-built road does go through these mountains, the occupational castes all the way up the valley will be displaced by the proliferation of shoes, metalwork and other handicraft made in China or India.

Entering a severely depleted forest area, I am approached by aggressive little children who run out from Sinde Lodge. They ask for sweets, pens, money. They yell at me, '*NAMESTE!*' I ignore their belligerence and continue walking. A rock is thrown at me, just missing my head.

At a steep incline, an agricultural extension worker from the British Lumle Agricultural Project is helpful and friendly. 'You should not walk through this area by yourself sir. There have been many problems in the past.' He does not explain the reason for his advice, but I can guess. Before we part he asks, 'Do you have some dollars you would like to change?' I change twenty dollars, enough local currency, which I have almost run out of, to make sure I get back to Pokhara. I wonder if I am changing his money, or the British taxpayers'.

The mist is insidious, and swills about the forest. If I were to have problems with thugs, it would be here. I admit to feeling uneasy. There are not many people, and no other trekkers on the path, yet I feel as if I am being watched.

A sense of sadness hangs over me, with the realisation that I am already out of the mountains and on the extended outskirts of Pokhara. Gone are the pristine villages and forests. Water trickles down glossy, marble-like steps descending a steep gully. I am lost in my thoughts when I slip backwards on the wet stone slabs and then trip forward as I try to regain my balance. As I fall head first, the heavy back-pack propels me over an abrupt drop. The external-frame back-pack's roll-over bar, which protrudes over my head, absorbs most of the impact when I hit the ground. I lie still for some seconds, partly stunned, partly in shock, before I realise I am not seriously hurt. But I am pinned by the weight of the pack among the rocks, with my head uncomfortably downhill. I cannot get up. Water flowing between the boulders soaks me. I lie like a helpless inverted turtle: the protective shell, having served me well, immobilises me just as effectively.

Unstrapping the shoulder and waist straps, I slide head first out of the pack's embrace. I have sustained cuts and abrasions on my hands, shins and knees, but nothing else. If I had not rolled onto my back, my face and ribs would have been crushed against the rocks.

The metal frame looping over the top of the pack has been crushed. I check inside the pack. The lens of the Nikon is visibly skewed. My tape-recorder is mangled and no longer works. I strap the pack on again, and gingerly pick my way over the rocks and descend the gorge. I have been lucky. Or perhaps it was not my time to die. Not now.

A boy asks me, 'Where are you?'

'I am here,' I reply thankfully, 'Where are you?'

He looks at me wanly, then asks, 'One rupee?'

When I say 'No', he silently hands me a note:

Students Club
Subject
About buy football
Please Nameste
Please in our village want to buy football

Have not got football, net or any sports equipment
So how much can you help for this group?
Thanks. Nameste.

The Students Club member is incredulous when I refuse to donate. Burst coloured balloons litter the path.

Another boy hands me a similar note, this one asking only for a soccer ball. It is from the 'New Students Club', an improved version no doubt. With my beard, filthy pink clothes, overstuffed back-pack, and menacing ski pole, I must be somewhat intimidating to would-be Pen Brigade members, yet I am still harassed.

Thirty villagers in an organised lumbering expedition carry chopped wood in *dokos* down the path to the road, to be taken to Pokhara. As I follow them, six large birds, *kalij* pheasants with long crests and tails, fly noisily from tree to tree, protesting against the destruction of their habitat.

DHAMPUS–POKHARA

The path cuts off earlier than the one Kirsten and I used four years ago. Then the path followed the ridge-line to Suiket. We had hiked the full length of the ridge, then walked all the way into Pokhara. The memory of that walk is all the more intense for the realisation that the new road has destroyed the hiking route for ever.

Soon after leaving Dhampus I see and hear the traffic on the Chinese road. Great thundering mechanical beasts belch their way up the switch-backs to Naudanda, leaving behind a spoor of diesel fumes. It occurs to me that never in my life have I been away from vehicles for such an extended period. From a venerable Himalayan trekker I have been transformed within seconds of my feet hitting tarmac into a humble hitchhiker. It was easier to adjust to the culture shock of entering the isolation of the mountains than it is to return to civilisation.

Half-a-dozen taxis lie in wait at Phedi. 'How much to Lakeside?' I ask.

'Three-hundred-and-fifty rupees.'

I start walking. One of the taxis follows me. There are two men in the front, the one riding shotgun hassles me. 'How much?' I ignore him. 'How much?' He yells at me, reeking of alcohol.

At the gravel pits, where buses are allowed to come from Pokhara, but no further on the road still under construction, I am accosted by scores of hustlers. 'Where you from?' a young man in a black leather jacket asks me.

'Mars.'

'Oh, I like Marsh too much. You take me Marsh, OK? Get job.'

'Sure.'

A boy leads his horribly deformed father to me to beg. Protruding growths erupt from his face, so massive they have closed his eyes; his nose is not recognisable, his nostrils have disappeared in the mound of exploding flesh: even his mouth is barely visible. Someone's shoulder bumps into the sensitive protuberant, and he recoils in pain. I place a note in the man's outstretched hand.

Jostling taxi drivers accost me. 'How much?'

'One-hundred-and-fifty rupees,' I reply.

'OK.'

We wrestle the back-pack into the trunk of a Toyota Corolla, and I slip through the throng into the car's back seat and close the door. Someone opens it. I close it. Someone opens it and bangs on the window. The driver, wearing black leather jacket and dark sunglasses, careens us along the new Chinese road at breakneck speed; he pushes a switch on the gear-stick lever which elicits rattling, machine-gun sounds. Another toggle on the dashboard emits a pitch like the siren wail of a police car. He alternates the sound effects according to his schizophrenic disposition.

Nepal's own version of Tom Cruise straight out of *Top Gun* looks paranoiacally through the cockpit windows for enemy fighters. With his foot pushing the accelerator flat to the floorboards, we swerve from one side of the road to the other, avoiding enemy cows, chickens and pedestrains which scatter under the withering machine-gunfire.

Having walked around the Himalayas for over two months, I am now primarily concerned to survive the thirty-minute taxi ride into Pokhara, Nepal's second largest town and popular tourist attraction. We pull up in front of Lakeside Hotel in a cloud of dust, to the accompaniment of screeching brakes, wailing sirens and chattering machine-guns. I am exhausted. 'One-hundred-and-seventy rupees.'

'You said one-hundred-and-fifty rupees,' I respond, my patience wearing thin. The moment one steps close to civilisation, one is subjected to constant hassle over money.

'Twenty I give boy at taxi stand.'

There is a shower in my room and outside it there are two big flip-flops thoughtfully laid out for the guests' use. They are size nine, one left foot, one right foot. Perfect. I wonder if anyone would notice if I left my two left-footed size five flip-flops in their place?

In the local *Rising Nepal*, I read in the tranquil gardens of a lakeside restaurant that the small stretch of road under repair from Malekhu to Mugling, between Kathmandu and Pokhara, 'will cost eight-hundred and sixty-seven million rupees to rehabilitate. The money will be donated by the British Government. Rehabilitation is calculated to cost twenty-one million rupees per kilometre. The road will not require any repairing for ten years.'

Late afternoon, I rent a bicycle, and cycle out to the grass-strip airfield to meet Dr Gurung, the director of the Annapurna Conservation Area Project. In Kathmandu we had made a tentative appointment to meet today, before he proceeds to Ghandrung. A DC-3 lands on the strip, and a few passengers bail out. Dr Gurung agrees to meet me at the Pumpernickel at seven o'clock before leaving in the protective custody of his staff and an ACAP vehicle.

Dr Gurung is easy to talk to, although his colleagues are silent throughout the meal. It is an enjoyable evening and he inspires confidence. But there is one question on the tip of my tongue. 'The Chinese road going up the Kali Gandaki; does ACAP have . . .?'

He responds 'No!' before I have formulated the question. He does not want to answer it. But it seems to me that this is the most important issue facing ACAP and the Annapurnas, with the devastating cultural and environmental effects the road would have on the region.

'You have no jurisdiction over the road?' I interpret his apparent denial.

'No. We do. I thought you were going to ask if ACAP can prevent the road. That, we cannot do.' For political reasons he is not in a position even to hint at lobbying against the road.

'It depends on the will of the people, right?'

'That is correct. They must decide.' An elusive answer. 'Only seven- or eight-thousand reside there permanently although officially there are fifteen-thousand people living in the area affected by the potential road. If your abode is in a remote area, you are entitled to certain Government benefits. Many actually live in Pokhara, unofficially, and commute to their remote area villages as the need arises. Those inhabitants would clearly like to see a road built.'

Without question, the road will destroy the natural beauty of the region. The balance of the delicate ecosystem of the Kali Gandaki, and the vulnerable culture of its diverse people, will be radically changed. Do the Kali Gandaki inhabitants know this? If they knew what we knew, what Nirmila knows having spent six months in America, would they accept the prospect of a road and all its ultimate development implications, so unquestioningly?

Michel would remind me that change is part of life, and we have to accept it. Who am I, after all, to come here from the comforts of my developed world and insist that this corner of the world be kept untouched to satisfy my need for access to an unsullied environment?

Tomorrow Dr Gurung leaves for Ghandrung, to prepare for next month's visit by the Prime Minister, who will inaugurate the new mini hydroelectric project there. Dr Gurung and his entourage leave.

Although it is late, I am too agitated to go to bed. I head for the Billy Bunter restaurant for a late calorie bomb, and order a rich chocolate cake. When the restaurant closes, I wander down Lakeside back to my hotel. I am on a sugar high from the cake, and my mind is raving. The electric lights in the hillside village of Sarankot float discombobulated above Lake Phewa. Security guards stroll by with truncheons. Shops close. Hands reach out of the corrugated sheds to fasten the hinged shutters. One after another, the shop lights are turned off. It is the same with my senses. I can feel them shutting down too. It is time to go home. This extraordinary trip in the Himalayan mountains and its people has come to an end.

But I am unable to sleep. I think back over the trip. The second night, with Easy and Shay, exhausted, with everyone in the hamlet staring at us as we changed into dry clothes. Of Tal with the three silver-beaded yak and the waterfall. Of Saishama in Upper Pisang, the incredible view on the north side of the Himalayas and the beautiful voices in the underground room of the *gompa*. Of the realisation that Buddhism would not after all be a convenient panacea to all my spiritual searchings. Of being sick in Manang, of climbing Thorong La, of Muktinath and the peace it inspired. Of that magical day with Trea in the caves near Kagbeni. Of Michel and Sangpo. Of more magical days riding into inner Mustang with Kharma. Of the little 'souf' girl at the lodge in Jharkot. Of Dipak and his family. Of Krisna and her little brother in the Sanctuary. Of the affections of Siley, Sita and Sunita. Of the peace at Sangri La, and the care of Drubar and his wife Didi. Of Nirmila's comparison of life in America with what she has now. Of thousands of laughing Pen Brigade members, rushing on tiny legs to intercept trekkers to ask for pens. Of the Chinese-built road. Of the Himalayas.

Nothing happened, but so much happened. What has happened has been within. I have changed. When asked if he was a god or a man, the Buddha replied simply, 'I am awake.'

After these months of stumbling through the Himalayas I may not be fully awake, but in the process of awakening, I have faced and become better acquainted with an old friend, re-discovered an inner peace and an intimate awareness of who I am. Life has slowed down and I have had the luxury of time and harmony of mind to nurture that essence of being, the netherland between understanding and unconsciousness, the soul; but there is still a long way to go.

And now I must face the reality of coming home. Is what seemed so perfectly possible and simple up in the rarefied air and solitude of the mountains still possible within the realities of everyday life back home? I think so. It is mostly a matter of choice. As Henry Ford said, 'If you think you can, or you think you can't, you are probably right.'

Tramping around the Himalayas with a heavy back-pack on my back, spending something like two or three dollars a day, I have been as happy as I could ever be. I have enjoyed life with an intensity I have not experienced in the last couple of years. I lived for the moment. I have learnt much from the materially poor but spiritually affluent people living very simply in the Himalayas. But as Bhuwan pointed out, I do not belong here. I must go home.

Poverty is not fun. In the West, however, we have a superfluity of wealth and belongings; we are too easily caught up in our short-term attachment to these tangible things, and do not focus enough on the longer-term spiritual aspects of life. And yet more of the world is becoming increasingly Westernised with all its material ambitions and concomitant complications.

Over and over again I have discovered, and had to re-discover: the simpler life is, the better. The most elementary pleasures give the greatest rewards. Too often in our consumer-oriented societies we are drawn into gross materialism. We get greedily caught up in the small details of life, frittering our lives away and forgetting the bigger picture. Money corrupts. As Easy said, quoting the Buddha, attachment to material things is not the way to happiness . . . Give or take an exception the Buddha did not know about.

Still, I cannot sleep, no longer in harmony with my environment or with myself. The cement walls of the hotel room make me feel claustrophobic. I slip out of the bed sheets, unpack my sleeping-bag, snuggle into it on the floor, close my eyes and pretend I am still in the mountains. But my mind is in overdrive, demanding a thoughtful and rational conclusion to the investment of time and energy spent on this trip; a formal resolving of the dichotomies within my soul, preparation for my return home.

At five it is still dark, the tourist buses are already cruising up and down Lakeside, their horns blaring, 'Hi-low, hi-low'. I stagger to the lake, mentally and physically exhausted, and prop my monumental pack against a wall. It has been loaded with another dozen books. I can barely lift it. My stomach turns.

It is a clear sky above. The snow-capped peaks of the Annapurnas reflect the orange morning light, as clear and postcard perfect as can be. I feel a tightening in my chest. I have become a part of something larger than myself. The infinite beauty of the mountains and its people and their lives flows within. For months I have become one with the nature around me, and myself. I wish to be transported once again into their midst, but I have wished something different every night.

Mist rises off the mirror-smooth waters of Lake Phewa. Like vapour from hot ice on a theatre stage, the effect is melodramatic. The vapour rises thickly, and begins to form a solid bank of cloud in the middle of the lake. Shreds of mist hug the surrounding Just Hills. A plume of black smoke rises from behind the hotel. Is it a factory, or urchins setting alight a rubber tyre for warmth? The column of thick black smoke rises, then hits a layer of dense air, and spreads out horizontally.

Within minutes a layer of noxious black smog has obscured the mountains. The black cloud mixing with the white mist over the lake is accompanied by the smell of burning rubber. A dark kite sits motionless and silent in the leafless branches of a nearby tree. Under the tree, beside the road, in a pile of growing rubbish, a domestic hen aggressively chases away a crow, to scratch alone at the surface of the garbage heap. Across the open field, the sun plops over the horizon, a spherical orange ball. For an instant, I think there has been a mistake: it should only be a half-circle, a half-moon. But of course, it is the sun, not the moon, and I am confused and tired.

Buses cruise by, horns blaring. The first flight bound for Jomosom flies low overhead. My bus arrives. A boy clad in black leather jacket and matching driving-gloves and dark sunglasses hangs from the doorway and jumps off the bus before it has stopped. Together we manoeuvre the ponderous pack onto the roof. I climb into the bus. Through the tinted glass windows and the thickening black pall of smoke outside, I can no longer see the mountains.

The boy hangs out the doorway and thumps twice on the metal sides of the bus. In a spume of diesel, we lurch forward. Between repeated blares of the bus horn, I hear the tinny refrain from Bob Marley's song *Three Little Birds*:

> Don't worry, 'bout a thing,
> cos every little thing
> s'gonna be all right.

Miserable, I wish I had enough sense and faith to sit back and follow his advice. My stomach has been twisting and turning. Is it psychological? Is it my re-entry to civilisation? Or is it giardia?

The drive to Kathmandu is an agony of gut-wrenching cramps and sulphurous burps and farts, confirmation of giardia. The Japanese girl seated in front pukes regularly out of the window as we veer our way through the switch-backs of the mountains. Vomit splatters the protective glass pane, blocking the view. I dare not open the window to let in fresh air, for fear of having her breakfast and dinner garnish my face. Between her retching sessions instigated by the lurching vehicle, and my sulphurous rotten-egg burps and farts released by jolting potholes, our share of the bus is particularly odorous.

The boy sitting next to me does not say a word. His head is tilted at an unnatural angle as if his neck is broken. He is either asleep, or has passed out from the noxious combination of fumes enveloping him. He at least, seems to be following Bob Marley's constantly replayed advice.

KATHMANDU

❖

After a day recuperating from the bus trip and giardia, I meet Pat, an ex-colleague, who is in Nepal for a short evaluation trip of a Canadian aid programme. Over dinner at KC's restaurant in Thamel we gossip about our lives and changes since we were last together in Canada.

'But Andrew,' she says, 'I'm shocked at the change in Nepal since the elections, especially Kathmandu. Look at all the shops on Durbar Marg and Thamel. They are all run by Indians now. And they are so aggressive. You can't walk through Thamel without being badgered to buy something. The Nepalese were never like that. Nepal is being swallowed up by India. You wait, within our lifetimes, Nepal will become a part of India.' No wonder the Chinese are trying to build a road from Nepal into Tibet.

Pat's memories of Kathmandu go back twenty years. I am shocked enough at the changes in the last four years. I walk her back to the exclusive Yak and Yeti Hotel where the Canadian Government insists she stay. We pass street children in the chilly night air, beside burning mounds of garbage, their palms outstretched, facing the flames.

In her hotel room, a complimentary copy of the *International Herald Tribune* has been slipped under the door of her room. A chocolate mint lies on the clean white pillow-case. A CNN feature story on satellite colour television focuses on the illegal immigrant problem in the European Economic Community. This is followed by images of Africans arriving on Spanish shores in boats, seeking the economic opportunities their own countries cannot provide.

It is late enough that the narrow streets of Thamel are almost deserted. A Nepalese sidles up to me and whispers, 'Hash?' A drunk Westerner, momentarily perfectly balanced, hands and legs akimbo, is barely able to stand upright. A drugged Nepalese lies curled up beside the street-curb, a baseball hat inscribed 'Friend' perched precariously on his head.

In the morning smog, street children search through mounds of rubbish, looking for something to eat. A child gnaws at an orange peel. Small urchins have managed to set a mound of garbage alight, and sit close to it, trying to keep warm in the chill morning air. Smoke from the fire mixes with the mist. Traffic weaving its way through narrow passages adds petrol and diesel exhaust to the noxious mix.

A horribly disfigured boy, burnt over most of his head and body, tests my compassion. The skin has been pulled tight over his face, one eye is white and blind with no protective eyelid. He holds out a taut arm. 'One rupee?'

I ignore him, walk to the counter of a restaurant and negotiate the price of a chocolate bar. He watches, accepting the fact I will not donate, even if he does not understand why not. But he has nothing better to do than observe me. Perhaps he is imagining he is me, just as I am beginning to wonder what it must be like to be him.

In the street I give him the bar of chocolate and the equivalent value in rupees. He accepts without saying anything, putting both in his ragged breast pocket. He slips away; in semi-privacy, he pulls the paper money out of his pocket, examines it carefully with his good eye, then looks up at me and smiles gruesomely.

Durbar Square: I feel restless. Sitting on the steps of the Maju Deval, I am waiting for something to happen, but the charms of this ancient city are lost on me. More than anything, I am waiting to sort out impressions formed from the trip. The penny has not dropped. Like the proverbial traveller in the arrival lounge of the airport, waiting for his soul to catch up with his body, I too wait for my re-cultivated soul to come down from the mountains.

Young Nepalese men in black leather jackets and sunglasses try to make conversation. I pretend I cannot speak English.

'Nepal is beautiful, huh?'

It is hard not to be positive, there is a reservoir of good feeling I have for Nepal, and the Nepalese, but Kathmandu is not enforcing it. The cold mist and smog, the recently depleted tourist population, have created a forlorn atmosphere about the place, and the excitement I felt when I first arrived has gone. I do not know what to do with the time until my fixed Aeroflot flight back home. I alternate between reading in Thamel restaurants and lying in the cemented walls of my hotel room, thinking.

Two Dutch girls I meet on one of my sorties to Helena's Restaurant ask, 'When did you arrive in Kathmandu?'

'About four days ago,' I reply truthfully but misleadingly. I put on my best smile and make an effort to appear friendly.

'What have you been doing?'

'Reading, eating, walking around.'

They regale me with how it is important to discover the real Nepal, and not just sit in Kathmandu every day. One, a nurse, says, 'So many tourists come to Nepal and just sit around in Kathmandu restaurants and eat. We take a bus or walk to the suburbs of Kathmandu everyday, and meet the real people. Find out about their lives, their living standards, health problems and facilities.' She sucks hard on her cigarette, lifting her pursed lips high in modest deference to the non-smokers, and exhales with self-satisfied, half-closed eyes.

The other, a dental assistant, says, 'It is so easy to make friends with the people. They invite you into their homes, give you tea. Maybe we give the children some presents in exchange, some balloons or sweets.'

Sitting at one of the tables of a fast-food restaurant in the popular, Westernised section of Patan, I look through the menu. Hamburgers, fried chicken, pizza. The prices are relatively high. The restaurant fills with mostly international aid-agency employees.

Two Japanese expatriates pick at their food with knife and fork held in one hand like chopsticks. If I close my eyes almost completely and peer through small gaps between fingers held up against my face, they look as if they are in fact using chopsticks.

'Mind if we share your table?' Three office-garbed Westerners approach me as I practise my optical illusion, interrupting me in mid-squint. They sit down. One has a CARE pin stuck in his jacket lapel.

A Dutchman, apparently the resident CARE Director, talks about his most pressing concerns. 'My children will be coming back from boarding-school for the Christmas holidays soon and we still have not got our car yet. It takes forever.' The other two, from Denmark, express sympathies. The two visiting Danes describe their field-trip to Mustang in terms of reference to which the average trekker would easily relate. 'The food and lodging was best in Marpha,' the woman concludes.

'I saw your CARE water fountains in Kagbeni,' I intrude.

The three of them look at me, at first as if I were indeed a Martian who had just spoken some unintelligible language, then with distaste, as if I had leprosy. Perhaps it's because I'm eating my vegetarian lasagne with my fingers, feeling its consistency, playing with it, as if it were *dal bhaat* and I was still in the mountains.

At the Aeroflot offices I am told once again there is no hope of getting an earlier flight. I resign myself to my prolonged stay in Kathmandu.

The day has no possibilities. I am surprised how quickly my buoyant spirits have sunk to new lows. The cement walls of the hotel room seem like a cell, Kathmandu the prison. Am I experiencing withdrawal symptoms from the adrenaline and endorphins that coursed in increasing amounts through my body as I lugged my back-pack up and down mountains? I feel deflated, a shadow of myself. My eyes are itchy from the pollution, and I have a chronic headache.

At the office of an ex-colleague, from my previous days as a development worker, I collect my mail and try to telephone home to Norway, but I have forgotten Kirsten's office phone number. I make three expensive calls to wrong numbers before discovering the pen I am using has her number written on it.

Letters confirm that my postcards, even the one I sent from Tasi's rusty old mailbox in Manang, reached their destinations. So did the telegram from Jomosom.

There is also a greetings card from Shay and Easy from their next stop after Nepal, New Zealand: 'We were married in a civilian ceremony here, and are tempted to settle. You'd like New Zealand.' In small writing at the bottom, they have added, 'We figured out what you've been wishing for every night. Let us know when it is finished.'

A simple card from Trea, without postmark, gives an update on their walk down the Kali Gandaki. Sybreen had been sick and they had spent a week at Marpha until he recovered. I must have just missed them.

There is another written message waiting for me. I recognise the almost illegible doctor's handwriting: 'You know you are welcome to come and stay with us. Call me at my office. Michel.' I need to get out of Thamel's consumerist environment and the fog of my aimless thought processes. I call Michel and he insists on picking me up immediately.

Waiting at the entrance of the Potala Guest House, I am greeted by a joyful cripple, eyes sparkling, full of happiness, despite his infirmities. My sour countenance can hardly portray someone who has no real problems in life. I give him fifty rupees, and some of his joy comes back to me.

'Ça va?' Michel rolls up on a small motorcycle. He leans over and gives me a hug.

'Ça va.' Seeing Michel again, I am transported back to the mountains, a warmth fills me, as if I am meeting the mutual friend of a not-yet forgotten lover.

'You are invited to a Newari wedding tonight,' he tells me as I straddle the rear of the motorbike with the back-pack on my back. The front wheels of the bike lift off the ground as we wobble off.

At the wedding reception I am introduced to a Newar, an engineer, smartly dressed in suit and tie. He tells me proudly that the Newars of Tibeto-Burmese origin moved into the Nepal valley several centuries ago and continue to be the backbone of Nepalese intellectual and cultural life. Conversation soon turns to money. 'There is too much money now in Kathmandu,' he says. 'Most of it comes from international development aid organisations. There is so much money pouring in we do not even know what to do with it. So we raise salaries, pay more consultants, create departments, buy more vehicles. Now Indians come to make money on the development money coming here. Since the revolution and the Nepali Congress Party, there are no restrictions what Indians can do or buy in Nepal.'

'I am a qualified engineer with a degree from India. My salary is three-thousand rupees per month as a senior engineer. I have two properties in Thamel which I inherited from my family. My family is not rich. My father bought these properties a long time ago for almost nothing. I can sell them now, to Indians, for ten-million rupees each.'

He does not have to do the equation. That is a total of over four-hundred-thousand dollars for someone earning sixty dollars a month. 'We rent out the ground floor to shopkeepers for the same amount as my salary. We need both this rent, my salary and my wife's to live, yet we own twenty-million rupees in property.' Going to the office is meaningless, except for the fact that he needs the salary to live on.

'Now we are renting some rooms in one house to tourists, and developing more floors. I shall keep my job so long as I need this income.' He is unhappy.

'What about the building regulations?' I ask. 'In the old days, Patan and Bhatgaon and Kathmandu seemed to have had better town planning than they have now.' The early Malla kingdoms from the fifteenth century onwards centred around the three ancient cities of Bhatgaon (Bhaktapur), which was mostly Hindu, Patan (Lalitpur), which was mostly Buddhist, and Kathmandu, the most recent of the three cities, which was and continues to be both Buddhist and Hindu. The three cities are almost indistinguishable now in the suburban sprawl called Kathmandu.

'This is quite correct,' he tells me, primly. 'We are working on building restrictions, but . . . money and corruption . . .,' and he sighs, worn out by the whole thing. 'Now there is a plan to build a tunnel out of the Kathmandu valley to the Terai on the border with India. And plans to build an airport in the Terai for jumbo jets. And two-hundred-and-seventy-million dollars is being allocated to clean up the air in the Kathmandu valley so the development aid population can breathe better air in a valley they helped to pollute. But building a tunnel through the mountains to the Terai will mean even more heavy traffic and more development money and more experts and more cars.' He has the look of someone whose fate is out of control.

Automobiles had to be carried into the isolated and roadless Kathmandu Valley as recently as 1955. This relatively young Newar can remember days when Kathmandu was virtually untouched by direct Western influence, its borders effectively shut to the outside world.

Rap music plays and Michel, as happy as his hosts, gyrates. As the evening wears on and the guests become more inebriated, the atmosphere becomes more relaxed. A bonfire is lit; as there is no firewood, the wooden posts delineating the new addition to the reinforced concrete house are thrown on the fire. A Nepalese servant, a peasant from the mountains, is as drunk as the guests, and he adds a note of authenticity by dancing Nepalese folk dances to the strains of Western disco music. A Newar videotapes everything, the camera an appendage to his face as much as his nose.

Michel is the life of the party, as is Agnes. They are in their element, fluent Newari dialect tripping off their tongues. They remind me, rather misleadingly in this guise, of an exotic Zelda and Scott Fitzgerald. At one-thirty in the morning we leave the party and stagger down the alley. The streets are deserted. A car pulls up beside us, crammed full of inebriated Nepalese.

'Where are you going?' one asks, gratingly imitating an American accent.

Michel totters to their car and leans through the door window. He has his peculiar all-encompassing smile on his face. 'Where are you going?' he asks back, slurring his words.

The Nepalese think he is making fun of them, and tempers flare. 'Where are you coming from?' the driver asks. There is definitely an aggressive edge to his question, and Michel is totally oblivious to it. Agnes sticks her head in the window too. The two of them are more in than out of the car.

'France,' Michel mumbles.

'Franche?' one of the Nepalese repeats unsuccessfully.

'Fraaanse,' Michel clarifies.

'England?'

'No. I am French.'

'French?'

'*Oui*, I mean yes.'

'Where are you going?'

'Nowhere, we are living here,' Michel replies, pulling his hand out of the car and pointing at his feet.

The Nepalese retorts, 'You don't live here. You can't live here. You are not Nepalese!'

'I am living here!' Michel leans further into the car, then he starts speaking Nepali and is joined by Agnes. The half-dozen Nepalese in the car are astounded, and whatever tension there was dissipates.

Everyone laughs, the Nepalese not sure what to make of the two Westerners as inebriated and as fluent in Nepali as they are. The buttocks of Agnes and Michel gyrate gently back and forth, as a torrent of Nepali spills out of the car. 'Too good. Too much good,' Michel concludes as the Nepalese take off happily in their Corolla.

It is not often Michel and Agnes party like this, but both are clearly in the mood to continue. At their home Michel pours champagne into glasses. Agnes sits on floor cushions, the only furniture in their bohemian abode, and sips delicately, before slowly keeling over, her long, lithe body elegantly pillowed in an otherwise Spartan room. Michel sits on the floor, lotus position, in front of a sophisticated stereo, with massive speakers on either side. Beside him is a shallow box full of compact discs. He selects one. 'Andrew, this is for you.'

Edith Piaf sings *La vie en rose*. He cranks the volume up high, and we both sing at the top of our lungs with Edith, the stereo volume so loud that our voices, fortunately, are overwhelmed. I am transported back to a mountainside, together with Sangpo, descending into a valley, covered in sepia rhododendron forest, the sounds of our voices reverberating with the celebration of life.

Michel sits, an emaciated Ghandi-like figure, his worn silk scarf wrapped incongruously over his suit. His body has folded into itself, his head, his mouth, lungs and shoulders moving in time to the words and the rhythm. He could be handicapped, his body has become so tiny, his dominant head perched tenuously on a scrawny neck. He changes discs with the frequency and dexterity of a professional disc jockey. Maria Callas sings arias from Alfredo Catalani's *La Wally*. Michel sings, mimes, clenches his closed fist to his heart, and soon he is crying.

Around the room are dozens of photographs of his children and other reminders of family life: wooden blocks, books and toys lie between cushions on the floor, dropped here and there. A veritable 'bordelle' full of love. Each piece dropped seems a fragile and necessary component of the scene.

We move to the Dollar Brand Duo, Abdullah Ibrahim, *Good News from Africa*. The music is turned louder to fight back the everyday assaults on one's senses.

Michel is now running on high-grade octane, after-burners glowing, heading into orbit, at the cockpit controls, master of his own destiny.

Michel also has an appointment with the Minister of Health at ten o'clock in the morning.

Next we put on Gabriel Fauré's *Requiem* opus 48, performed by the Montreal Orchestra. Michel told me, in the mountains, that he was passionate about playing music. 'Once,' he told me, 'When Agnes was away, I woke up at five in the morning and played Pink Floyd's *Wish you were here* at full volume. My Italian neighbours came over to ask me to play the music after eight in the morning in the future.' On another occasion, the French neighbours on the other side came over to complain that their children could not sleep. 'Mine are asleep,' Michel replied, 'I don't see why yours aren't.'

Michel's father was a musician and a free spirit who left his son at a young age in the care of his mother. If Michel were not a doctor, he would undoubtedly be a musician.

Vapour forms in front of my face as I breathe. Through the windows I can see the dawn. Michel comes back to earth, the music stops, he lies down next to Agnes. I put a blanket over them and crawl under a sleeping-bag on the cushions to find myself face to face with a fat pink hippo wearing sunglasses. I pull the hippo towards me for company. Amid the debris of wooden trucks, badminton racquets, stuffed giraffe, balls of assorted sizes and shapes, Lego pieces, I too curl up and try to go to sleep. But Michel's re-entry has projected me into orbit, and now I float around, with memories of the past, reflections on the present and decisions to be made fuelling my mind.

Giggles. Agnes, resurrected, stands over Michel. Like actors backstage, they compare performances of what they can remember. There are no recriminations, of themselves or each other; just an afterglow of happiness from an enjoyable evening. 'Shall I play some music?' Agnes asks.

'*Oui, mais doucement. Doucement.*' She turns on the stereo, with the same disc already in the player, at a reasonable level. '*Mais non,*' says Michel, 'We listened to that last night.' Agnes cannot remember.

'*Et alors?*' she says, unconcerned.

Michel is not the sort of person who can possibly listen to the same music as the night before. '*Et alors,* we must play something different.' Still wearing his tie and jacket, he crawls over on all fours back to the cockpit and sifts through the CDs looking for something special, ripe for the occasion, something he did not play during his three-hour orbit earlier this morning.

Neither Agnes nor Michel shows signs of suffering this morning. Amazed at their apparent resilience with no signs of a hangover, I ask, '*Tu n'as pas un guele de bois ce matin?*'

'*Si, si,*' he replies, holding his hand to his head. He looks about the room, '*Putain. Quelle bordelle!*' and laughs.

Weaving through the bustle of vehicles on Michel's borrowed bike on my daily vain visit to the Aeroflot office, I see Sangpo in the back of a tricycle scooter bus. I signal to him with one hand as I intermingle with the traffic, that I will meet him at Bodhnath.

We stroll clockwise around the huge Buddhist stupa the mandatory three times. He invites me to have tea with him in his apartment. At the top of the five-storey staircase of a nearby reinforced-concrete apartment building, we enter the tiny drab cement unit he shares with his mother. There is barely space enough to move. The mother sleeps on the floor, Sangpo on the bed. The only furniture is a rough-hewn cabinet with pictures of the Dalai Lama optimistically illuminated by a naked light bulb painted red. Instead of shelves, plastic bags hung from nails on the wall hold their meagre belongings. Hunched over the edge of the bed in the windowless room, Sangpo seems just a shadow of the man who accompanied Michel and me into Mustang.

They offer Tibetan tea. I am overwhelmed with sadness as I try to converse with the mother and son, while recalling a different Sangpo, laughing carefree and happy in the freedom of the high mountains. I think, too, of their family in Tibet, the way they must have been before their lives were snatched away from them.

Cycling to Patan to visit the ACAP Headquarters, I am tempted instead by the Empire Circus, its big top squatting on an island in the middle of the Bagmati River. Together with an assortment of Nepalese, we press our faces to the bars, trying to catch a glimpse of the show in progress. Scratchy music bellows loudly from enormous speakers. Awful painted billboards with hand-painted images of semi-clad female circus performers advertise the titillating show within. None of the painted images of girls could be described as remotely erotic by Western standards. Girls riding on lions, hanging from the trunks of elephants, juggling, performing contortions.

Zoos and circuses have never appealed to me. But this is a medieval show I cannot resist. I buy a ticket from someone sitting in what could be a lion cage. I take a careful look at him through the bars to see if he is part of the show, but he is not.

Like spotlights, the sun's rays shine through gaps in the dust-mote filled tent. We are all excited. There are civil servants 'out of the office', families, Tibetans who look as if they have just come down from the Tibetan Plateau, and fat Indian businessmen with leers already creasing their lecherous faces. All the children, whatever their racial features, have looks of utter awe and innocent wonder on their faces.

The show of lion and tiger tamers, acrobats, leaping jeeps, motorbikes and elephants is predictable and monotonous. The ringmaster has a look of perpetual boredom on his face. The woman lion tamer is barely awake as she sticks her head into tigers' mouths. There is indeed a profusion of young girls of all shades, from Indo-Aryan to Mongolian, to suit all tastes. They wear old-fashioned swimsuit-like outfits with the line at the leg cut horizontally, giving them a stumpy look. The young girls attempt to adopt bored looks on their faces, but it is clear they are thrilled by their own stage performances.

Even the weight-lifter is a woman, grotesquely ugly and overweight. She lifts massive concrete barbells and other assorted weights, all of which look suspiciously hollow and relatively weightless. But when she lies down on giant cushions, with a door placed over her like a see-saw, and a real elephant walks on top of the door, there are gasps of admiration from the audience; an instant weight-loss programme. The woman gets up, nursing the small of her back, and staggers out of the ring to the cheers of the ecstatic crowd.

The biggest hit of the show is a tiny baby elephant who follows his elders in spastic, jerky movements, his trunk totally out of control. Like a clown, he has a tendency to step on and trip over his rubbery proboscis. He is not part of the routine programme and does what he pleases. The spontaneity of the miniature Ganesh captivates the audience.

For a couple of hours I am transported away from Kathmandu into a different world. The animals, it is clear, are not maltreated and are well fed. The story circulating around Kathmandu of new motorcycles being paid by the circus in exchange for two-hundred dogs brought in dead or alive must be a publicity ploy. Two-hundred dogs would keep the half-dozen lions and tigers fed for a long time – unless the girls are helping themselves. They, for the most part, look suspiciously plump too.

A ragamuffin slips under the canvas walls of the tent. Two guards crawl after him. The diminutive gate-crasher eludes his pursuers by running straight across the arena where he abruptly sits bolt upright, alone in a front row 'VIP' chair, absolutely captivated by the show, oblivious to his pursuers. The circus dwarf performs routines, directly in front of the little boy. For a few minutes there is magic, and the audience laughs at the extemporaneous exchange between the ragged miscreant solitary in the Dress Circle, and the hideous dwarf who has been shaken out of the monotony of his automatically performed daily programme.

The mechanics of the circus are low tech. Six overweight girls, spinning around by their teeth and dangling under an X-shaped cross, are pulled to the roof by two dozen scrawny men hauling on ropes. At least that is the idea. Collectively, the undernourished male circus attendants are unable to hoist the well-fed girls, and there is much shouting as more skinny assistants are press-ganged in the effort. Even the guards are waylaid from their continued pursuit of the ticketless little guttersnipe to help lug the plump girls to the top. Yet still they have problems.

I climb over the rows of chairs and grab onto the tug-of-war rope. With renewed energy and cheers from both the crowd and ourselves, we drag the rope and the girls rise to the top, faster and higher than ever before. The ringmaster laughs for the first time. I always wanted to be in a circus.

That evening, at a tiny Tibetan restaurant off Freak Street, I bump into Yanzeh, the American from Hawaii. He looks at the menu. '"Buffalow". The closest we get to buffalo now are seeing their feet outside the butchers shops, or on our plates. I miss them. I like their grunts.' He blows his nose loudly and effectively and examines the detritus. 'Sick on the trip?' he asks.

'Not really. You?'

'All the time. Diarrhoea, giardia, colds, headaches going up Thorong La. Never been so sick in all my life.'

We had the same health problems, yet our perceptions, our realities, are so different. I ask him about his porter.

'I kind'a hoped to have a porter who would sort'a be my lama. You know, a guru. Like, we'd sit down and meditate together, that kind'a thing. He was pretty basic. Materialistic. Westernised. When we walked into Sarankot he developed a leg problem, on our last day. At his own expense, he hired a porter in Sarankot to carry my load down into Pokhara the next morning. We met lots of his friends in Pokhara, and I realised he wanted to pass himself off to his friends as my guide, not just a porter. Anyway, he's got that job in Saudi Arabia he was waitin' for and is leavin' as soon as he gets his visa.' Yanzeh blows his nose again, then brightens. 'Sold all my camping gear in Pokhara, and had fifty pairs of shorts and one-hundred pairs of pants made by a tailor. I'll sell them in Hawaii. Should make a hundred per cent profit.' Our food arrives, interrupting the narrative of capitalistic exploits. 'Boy,' he continues. 'Did you get asked for donations?' I nod. 'Where do all those kids come from? I mean, they must import them. Nepal could set up a thriving business exporting pens and soccer balls.'

As he talks, I watch a young Nepalese man on the other side of the restaurant, apparently deaf and dumb. A Western boy sitting at the table with him knows some basic sign-language and laboriously spells out individual words. The Nepalese boy returns the communications in an esoteric semaphore of his own making. He becomes increasingly excited as his hands flash a myriad of messages the Westerner opposite clearly cannot understand. Despite the Westerner's obvious difficulty comprehending, the Nepalese gets carried away with incessant and complicated hand signals. Yanzeh continues to talk, but I no longer hear him. I concentrate.

There is something about the gesticulating digits; they are not so much conventional hand signals as impromptu descriptions of a story. There is something about them I intuitively understand . . . some thought processes that they trigger . . . Yes! The secrecy of these esoteric semaphore transmissions is easy to crack, once you know the code. The circus.

The mute Nepalese has eyes constantly roving the room in a restless quest for communication, even as his hands execute contortions; his eyes catch mine. I signal to him and point two fingers at my eyes, then curve my index finger in front of my nose and move it spastically. Yes! His eyes flash understanding. The baby elephant.

We have both been to the circus. We have the same realities. He is ecstatic. He gives me a thumbs up, then describes the instant weight-loss programme. He undulates vertically descending hand motions delineating a curvaceous woman, then crosses her out and describes the outline of the globular weight-lifter, lifts a couple of imaginary weights, indicates her lying on the ground while the elephant walks over her, then holding the small of her back as she walks out of the ring. He laughs silently but hysterically at the memory, and describes the dwarf bouncing on all fours on the trampoline like a spider, the acrobats, the bear on a motorbike, the parrot riding a bicycle on a tight rope, the human cannonball, the ramp-jumping jeep, the motorcycles circulating around the spherical cage, the six spinning girls being hoisted to the roof. Without having seen the circus it is impossible to understand his sign-language. For those who have been to the circus, it is easy.

Manage spends the rest of the evening with me re-enacting every single act of the show. He has been six times, and has not forgotten a single detail.

The early morning sun poking over the hill lights the temple of Pashupatinath. A woman's corpse, shrouded in white, lies on a sloping stone slab in front of the temple, the exposed feet wet in the waters of the Bagmati River where golden marigold heads eddy past.

The corpse is removed from the stone slab and carried by the priest, the husband and two sons to the *ghats* lower down the river where the body is laid on top of a pile of thick logs. The husband walks around the body three times. When he becomes overwhelmed by emotion he is helped by the priest. He lights the funeral pyre. The flames burn fiercely. The priest offers the husband, whose head is wrapped in a white bandage as if he had a toothache, a cigarette, and the two of them sit and smoke on the *ghat* steps, watching the fire.

Tourists by the busload arrive, some as if dressed for the beach. Cameras click, videos record the action as they pass nonchalantly by.

Yellow liquid spurts out of the midsection of the blackened corpse, projecting a neat arch into the air with such force it reaches the river. The priest gets up and covers the leak with damp straw. A bull tries to steal some of the priest's stored straw and is chased away by the Brahmin.

The fingers, hand and arm of the woman rise above the charred body, stretching up as if waving farewell. The husband stares at this macabre departing, sobs uncontrollably, then unable to watch any longer, slumps his head, exhausted, and falls asleep.

A colourfully dressed wedding party, accompanied by a local drum band with bagpipes, plays Nepalese folk music and traverses the bridge beside the burning ghettos. The old widower awakes, and over the funeral pyre of his gesticulating wife, gazes at the procession of a happy young couple celebrating their betrothal.

The priest stirs the body about. The legs have separated from the pelvis, and he doubles the body back on itself, stirring the crumpled mixture of logs and body parts. There is a crack, as the skull explodes.

It is early afternoon. The husband has faced the day with the detailed aspects of his wife's passing from this earthly realm: undressing and washing her, the intricate and intimate rituals, lifting her body onto the funeral pyre, lighting the flames, watching the body burn to nothing. He has participated actively in the passing form of his wife, from the body that was hers, perhaps to the spirit, and the memory.

The intruding wedding party is a reminder that life continues its endless cycle. He has been forced to come to terms with the reality of her death, so easily avoided in our modern world where antiseptic funeral homes and hospital rooms remove the unsightliness and reality of death, and high-technology television, videos and computer games remove the reality of life.

Then I remember the occasion when I had decided to make this pilgrimage to the Himalayas: at the funeral of Thomas's mother in Oslo almost ten months ago. So much has happened within me during these last two-and-a-half months. The timing of the two funerals only reinforces the realisation that I have changed.

Women lay clothes on the steps beside the burning *ghat* to dry; men gamble nearby; two dogs fight; children play; pigeons flap noisily overhead; tourists stroll by; hawkers sell souvenirs to tourists, or to the devout Hindus going to the temples; monkeys scratch their bums; the sun shines and is reflected off the river; sadhus pose for photographs;

[223]

the sacred bull rests his head on the parapets of the bridge, dozing; flowers from the wedding party float down the river.

The priest pushes the remains of ashes and embers of the pyre into the flowing river. The coals and burning logs hiss, then steam and smoke as they float downstream, past the hundreds of people washing in the river. Someone salvages the partly burnt logs and pulls them out to dry. The priest sluices the *ghat* with buckets of water which spill into the river or evaporate in steaming clouds.

Three young boys diligently sift the riverbed for the woman's gold ornaments. The bull climbs onto the *ghat* and drinks dry the still-steaming water collecting in a slight depression in the centre of the pyre. After the bull leaves, a dog curls up on the warm stones and sleeps.

Nothing is wasted, not even the warmth from the funeral pyre.